Religion at Bowdoin College: A History

Ernst Christian Helmreich

*Thomas Brackett Reed Professor of
History and Political Science Emeritus*

Bowdoin College
Brunswick, Maine
1981

Cover photograph by Stephen E. Merrill
Bowdoin College Archives, Special Collections
Printed by J. S. McCarthy Co., Inc., Augusta, Maine

ISBN: 0-916606-03-1
Library of Congress Catalog Card Number: 81-71331
Copyright 1982, the President and Trustees of Bowdoin College
All rights reserved

To Bowdoin Students
Past and Present

"The history of man is inseparable from the history of religion."
Justice Black in *Engel* v. *Vitale*

Contents

Foreword	vii
Preface	ix
Chapter I	
The Founding of the College	1
Chapter II	
The College Under Way	9
Chapter III	
The College and the First Parish	19
Chapter IV	
College Regulations and Their Enforcement	35
Chapter V	
Religious Societies	49
Chapter VI	
The Building of the New Chapel	63
Chapter VII	
Endowments and the Issue of Denominationalism	89
Chapter VIII	
Religious Life at the College, 1867-1917	107
Chapter IX	
The Sills Era	131
Chapter X	
The Recent Decades	153
Illustrations	following page 88
Notes	169
Bibliography	201
Index	207

Foreword

AFTER A DISTINGUISHED CAREER of over forty years as a Bowdoin teacher and scholar, Professor Helmreich has made yet another important contribution to history with this study of religion at Bowdoin College. In it, he teaches us much that we did not know about the lives and concerns of the men and, recently, the women who, for nearly 200 years, have assumed the responsibility for guiding this college. From the founding of the institution to the present, religion has been a concern of Bowdoin presidents and of many members of the student body, faculty, and the Governing Boards. More difficult to trace, but clearly discernible here, is the story of how these people perceived religion, how they felt religion should or should not be realized at the College, and how their views changed over the years.

This would not be a true account of men and women as we know them if, in confronting religious issues, they were not serious, compelling, and dedicated — and even, at times, puzzled and perhaps absurd. So are they revealed in the events chronicled here. This is, I believe, as much a portrait of human nature as it is a history of a college addressing itself to religion in the chapel program, in the curriculum, and in the daily lives of its members.

At this time when there is a renewed interest in religion on the campus and in the nation, it is well to be reminded of our past, of how we have fared in our efforts to give expression to religious values in our public and private lives. We are, therefore, in debt to Professor Helmreich for devoting a part of his retirement to playing once more the teacher and the historian and for playing those important roles with such distinction.

A. LeRoy Greason
President of Bowdoin College

November 1981

Preface

HAVING COMPLETED MY VOLUME on *The German Churches Under Hitler: Background, Struggle, and Epilogue* (Detroit, 1979), I wanted a problem to work on where all the primary sources were at hand. It occurred to me that a study of religion at Bowdoin was such a topic. The subject had the fascination of being an aspect of the history of the College where major changes had taken place, where one epoch had ended and another had begun. I knew much about what had happened in respect to religion at the College since I came to Bowdoin in 1931; I knew very little about what had gone on before. While the various histories of the College and of its leaders touched on religion at Bowdoin, I soon discovered that there was much more to be learned about it. What was the status of religion at Bowdoin when the College opened its doors in 1802, and how, why, and when were changes made that have led to its present status on campus? It took pages to deal with religious matters in the first printed by-laws of the College; today there is one sentence forbidding the imposition of any creedal tests in the choice of officers and faculty or the admission of students.

Practically all historical writing about Bowdoin has been done without footnotes, and I early decided to follow a different practice. Readers have a right to know where the material was found and how complete it is. Such references will also be of help to others in carrying on research on subjects not directly connected with Bowdoin. What happened at the College occurred at other institutions as well; Bowdoin did not stand apart but was in the mainstream of collegiate education in the United States.

After completing a book an author always has many people to thank. The staffs of the Hawthorne-Longfellow Library, of the Business Office, and of the Registrar's Office invariably have been helpful. It is not out of ingratitude that I do not name them personally. I must, however, single out Mrs. Mary H. Hughes and Dianne M. Gutscher of Special Collections at the library for particular thanks. They have been tireless in helping me find my way through the rich source material which is available. I also wish to thank President Enteman for his interest during the early stages of this project, and especially President Greason, who read the manuscript and arranged for the necessary funds for its publication. I trust these funds will be repaid, probably very gradually, as the book is sold. At the College Editor's Office, Peter H. Vaughn and Susan L. Ransom have been most cooperative in seeing the volume through the press. As always, most thanks are due to my wife, Louise, who has helped with all the work and editing which goes into preparing a manuscript and getting it into print.

Ernst C. Helmreich

Bowdoin College
Brunswick, Maine
August 1981

I.

The Founding of the College

BOWDOIN COLLEGE WAS FOUNDED in an age of religious indifference. The religious excitement of the mid-eighteenth century, aroused by the revivalistic preaching of the Great Awakening, had been dissipated by the disruptions of the Revolutionary War. The deism heralded by the leaders of the Enlightenment had challenged old religious orthodox views. Skepticism was rife and church attendance at a low ebb.[1]

The settlements on the frontier brought new problems for the churches, and the District of Maine was part of the frontier of that day. It was sparsely settled, the number of organized churches small. In 1784 there were only thirty-one settled Congregational and Presbyterian ministers in the district. There was a well-established German Lutheran church at Waldoboro, but no Catholic churches, although there were a few Catholic mission stations with their small number of Indian converts. Six Quaker societies existed with probably around a thousand members. Baptists had made their appearance at Kittery in 1681, yet it was not until 1767 that they founded their first church. By 1784 there were six Calvinistic Baptist societies in the district, as well as a number of Free Will Baptist churches. This split among the Baptists, like the growing movement towards Unitarianism in the Congregational societies, added to the religious diversity in Maine, a diversity enhanced in the last decade of the century by the preaching of Methodist circuit riders.[2] In spite of the encroachments of these other religious groups, Congregationalism remained dominant. The "establishment," to borrow a modern term, was Congregationalist, and it was these leaders who initiated and carried out the founding of Bowdoin College.

The first evidence we have of an interest in establishing a college in the District of Maine is an act submitted to the General Court of the Commonwealth of Massachusetts by a representative from Lincoln County in 1787. The preamble stated:

> Whereas the surest and most durable foundation of true and rational liberty is best promoted and secured by a cultivation of the means of virtue and knowledge, and a general diffusion of them among the

great body of the people; and by making these means easily attainable, especially by the poorer classes in the community. And whereas these important purposes are best answered, by seminaries for literature being erected, and adequately endowed and supported in various parts of the state, upon the broadest basis of liberal principles and equally open to people of every class and denomination for the purposes of education.

To this end a college, holding the name of Winthrop, honoring a family long prominent in the affairs of the commonwealth, was to be established. The act was in line with the prevailing rational philosophy of the period. Little is said about religion in the whole document, except that the college should be non-denominational and that the ministers of the seven next adjoining towns—wherever the college should be located—should be members of the Board of Overseers in a college government modelled on that of Harvard College. It called upon "the liberal man, the lovers of science, the friends of religion and the equal liberty of the whole human race with patriots of every class and description" to make donations to supplement the land grants anticipated from the state to get the college underway.[3]

Nothing came of this act, but the next year steps were undertaken which led directly to the founding of Bowdoin. On May 20, 1788, the Cumberland Association of Ministers, consisting of eight Congregational ministers, was established.[4] In their third meeting, held on November fourth of that year, they voted: "To petition the General Court (Mass.) for the establishment of a college and endowment of the same in the County of Cumberland."[5] The petition was immediately drafted and signed by Tho. Browne, moderator, and Samuel Deane, clerk, "in the name and by the desire of the association," and dated Falmouth, Nov. 5, 1788. At about the same time the justices of the Court of General Sessions of the Peace for the County of Cumberland drew up a like petition. This was not dated, and so it is impossible to determine which petition was drawn up first or if there was any negotiation between the two groups of petitioners. The petitions were taken in charge by Judge Josiah Thacher of Gorham, then a senator from Cumberland, and both petitions were received in the Senate and House on November twenty-second.[6]

The two petitions are similar in form and brevity, but in content there are some interesting differences. The petition of the Cumberland Association of Ministers speaks of the members being mostly sons of Harvard and naturally interested in having a similar institution in the eastern half of the state, so that their sons might not be excluded from "obtaining a liberal education" because of the great expense of sending them to Cambridge. Nothing is said about religion or its furtherance; they petition simply for the establishment of a college "to promote the interests of learning" and that it be endowed with considerable portions of the unlocated lands of the commonwealth. The petition of the justices of the Court of General Sessions, on the other hand, starts out by quoting from the constitution of the commonwealth:

> That the encouragement of Arts and Sciences and all good Literature tend to the Honor of God, the advantages of the Christian Religion, and the great Benefit of this and the other United States of America — That Wisdom and Knowledge as well as Virtue diffused generally among the People is necessary for the presentation of their Rights and Liberties — That these depend on spreading the opportunities and advantages of education in the various parts of the Country and among the different orders of the People — And that it shall be the Duty of the Legislators and Magistrates in all future Periods of this Commonwealth to cherish the Interests of Literature and the Sciences.

The justices considered it impossible to make a stronger statement on the subject of education and the importance of wisdom, knowledge, and virtue, than these words contained in the state constitution itself, so they confined themselves simply to petitioning for the incorporation of a college in some convenient place in Cumberland County and that it be endowed with unlocated land.[7]

The General Court in Boston moved slowly, and it was not until February 1790 that the petitioners were granted leave to bring in a bill. This was done the following January, and it was promptly passed in the Senate, but failed in the House, largely because Gorham had been designated as the site of the college. Citizens of Freeport, Yarmouth, Portland, and Brunswick now undertook to raise subscriptions to get the college located in their respective towns. This did not facilitate matters. Agreement between the two houses of the legislature could not be reached in 1791 or in the summer session of 1792, mainly because they could not concur on the location of the college.[8]

During the winter session of 1792-1793, it occurred to some interested individuals, among them Alfred Johnson of Freeport, to make an effort to obtain a patron for the college. He obtained an introduction to James Bowdoin, the son of the famed Revolutionary Governor of Massachusetts, and discussed with him the possibility of naming the sought-for college in Maine after his father. James Bowdoin took to the suggestion and expressed his willingness to help the college as much as he was able. He cautioned that his father's name not be given to the college in the act but left to the Boards for later decision, "as he thought such was Gov. Hancock's antipathy to his father, that he would never approve of an act for a college with his father's name given to it, and related some curious anecdotes to confirm his suspicions."[9] Mr. Johnson, however, thought that Governor

Hancock would not be influenced by such considerations, "and thinking it best to make sure of the patronage and not subject the name to future dispute, caused the name of Bowdoin to be inserted in the Bill." The bill was passed by both houses in 1793, but Governor Hancock, for what reasons is not certain, refused to sign it. There was still controversy over where the college was to be located, and this was not definitely stated in the measure. In February and June of 1794 the bill was again up for consideration, and the committee in charge sought the opinion of each member of the General Court from the District of Maine. They found that a large majority favored Brunswick. Most of the representatives were from east of the Androscoggin River and naturally wished to get the college as near to their constituents as possible. On the other hand, they did not feel it right to move it out of Cumberland County, as the petitions that had initiated the movement for a college had originated there. The charter of the college was finally passed on June 24, 1794, and received the signature of Governor Samuel Adams. It definitely settled two matters which had caused much controversy and delay—the name was to be Bowdoin, and the location was to be Brunswick.

Three days later, on June 27, 1794, James Bowdoin wrote a letter to the Overseers on the purpose of the new college:

> The General Court having established a public Seminary of Learning, in the District of Maine, for the purpose of diffusing literature and knowledge, that the seeds of Science, deeply sown in the natural Genius of its Inhabitants, will soon be seen to blossom, to fructify and contribute to the general stock of scientific information, in the United States.[10]

It is an interesting statement in respect to the nature and character of the college to be established. It is to be a public institution, and there is no reference to religion. He went on to say "that the honourable Testimonial of respect paid in the Establishment of the Name, the Character, the Talents, and Virtues of my late Father, must attach me in a peculiar Degree to an Institution, in the success of which I feel myself deeply interested." He promised that "Bowdoin College shall receive the public aid of my Endeavors, to promote its Usefulness, Interest and Welfare" and as a first step to that design he offered to the college one thousand dollars in specie and a thousand acres of land in the town of Bowdoin. The college now had not only a charter, but also a generous patron.

The charter as passed has no customary flowery preamble indicating purposes of the act, but simply states, in Section 1, that a college will be established "for the purpose of educating youth" and that it will be under the "government and regulation of two certain bodies, politic and corporate...."[11] These were to be the Trustees, who were given primary responsibility in directing the institution. Their actions—in line with the then dominant theory of checks and balances—had to be approved by a Board of Overseers. To get the college started, the charter specifically named the first Board of Trustees, consisting of six clergy and five laymen, and a Board of Overseers, consisting of fourteen clergy and twenty-eight laymen. Many of the latter were named because of their official station, and approximately a third of the members never attended a meeting.[12] There is no mention in the charter of a desire to provide for an educated ministry, to christianize the Indians, or to spread the gospel, matters which were mentioned in the founding documents of so many early colleges.[13] The closest the Bowdoin charter comes to such a statement is in Section 6, where in regard to appropriations it provides:

> That the clear rents, issues and profits of all the estate, real and personal, of which the said corporation shall be seized or possessed, shall be appropriated to the endowment of the said College, in such manner as shall most effectually promote virtue and piety and the knowledge of such of the languages and of the useful and liberal arts and sciences, as shall hereafter be directed, from time to time, by the said corporation.

In respect to the five townships of land of six square miles each which were granted by the commonwealth as an endowment to the college, the Trustees were obligated to reserve "in each township three lots of three hundred and twenty acres each, for the following uses, viz. one lot for the first settled Minister—one lot for the use of the Ministry—and one lot for the use of schools in each of said townships" (Section 17). This was a customary restriction whenever grants were made of public lands. The Boards were also restricted to granting only bachelor and master of arts degrees until January 1, 1810. Why this provision was inserted in the charter is uncertain, but it is generally thought to have been designed to prevent the immediate creation of numerous doctors of divinity.[14]

On establishment, the College was clearly not directly concerned with religion, let alone being connected with any denomination. It was not Puritan or Church of England, not Congregational or Baptist. As Bowdoin's President Sills was to observe many years later: "It is interesting to note that Bowdoin began, not as a school or seminary or theological institution, but it began as a college, a college devoted to the study of the languages, then Latin and Greek, and of the useful arts and sciences."[15] But if the College was non-sectarian in origin, it was never meant that it should be cut off from religion or its influences. As pointed out above, it was among other things to "promote virtue and piety." It is impossible to define exactly what is covered by these words. Both are general terms and at times have had various meanings and connotations. Virtue certainly did not exclude religion, for in the eighteenth century religion was generally considered to be the very foundation of this quality and an integral part of it. Jonathan Edwards, the great American preacher and philosopher, held in his *Dissertation on the Nature of True Virtue* that "the principle of virtue...is identical with the principle of religion."[16] No philosopher was better known or held in more esteem in colonial America than John Locke. In his essay "Some Thoughts Concerning Education," Locke wrote that a gentleman in desiring an education for his son should consider "Virtue, Wisdom, Breeding, and Learning." And of these four he noted:

> I place Vertue as the first and most necessary of those Endowments, that belong to Man or a Gentleman as absolutely requisite to make him valued or beloved by others, acceptable or tolerable to himself. Without that I think, he will be happy neither in this, nor the other World.
>
> As to the Foundation of this, [i.e. virtue] there ought very early to be imprinted on his mind a true notion of God as of the independent Supreme Being, Author and Maker of All things, from whom we receive all our Good, who loves us, and gives us all Things. And consequent to this, instill into him a love and Reverence of this Supreme Being. This is enough to begin with, without going to explain this matter any further....And I am apt to think, the keeping Children constantly Morning and Evening to acts of Devotion to God as to their Maker, Preserver and Benefactor, in some plain and short Form of Prayer, suitable to their Age and Capacity will be of much more use to them in Religion, Knowledge and Vertue, than to distract their Thoughts with curious Enquiries into this unscrutable Essence and Being.[17]

In the regime that later was to be established at the College, it is as if the Bowdoin authorities had made this last precept of Locke the very cornerstone of their educational philosophy.

If virtue might be taken to cover many moral qualities and precepts, including religion and a belief in God, the word piety is more definite and constant in meaning. Piety centers in religious devotion and reverence to God, and it would be nigh impossible to promote piety without encouraging religion and religious values. And if promotion of virtue and piety were not enough to give religion a place in the development of Bowdoin, the very fact of its being a college would have assured religion a prominent position in its day-by-day existence. Religion was closely associated with all colleges at that time, as in fact it had been with universities ever since they were founded in the late Middle Ages. Bowdoin was not meant to be an exception, but was founded and patterned after existing colleges, especially Harvard. What Professor Morison has written about the founders of Harvard would no doubt apply equally to the founders of Bowdoin:

> We should miss the spirit of early Harvard if we supposed the founders' purpose to be secular. *In Christi Gloriam*, inscribed on the

College Seal of 1650, expressed the fundamental object of their foundation. The English mind had barely conceived a lay system of higher education, and any such plan would have been abhorred by puritans. Like the medieval schoolmen, they believed that all knowledge without Christ was vain. *Veritas* to them, as to Dante, meant the divine truth, although, more humble than he, they never hoped to attain it. The first college laws declared that every student was to be plainly instructed that the 'maine end of his life and studies' was *'to know God and Jesus Christ*... and therefore to lay *Christ* in the bottome, as the only foundation of all sound knowledge and Learning.'[18]

Indeed changing concepts of how to promote virtue and piety and further the ends of a liberal education — always influenced in greater or lesser degree by the development of higher education in general — for many years made religion an integral but constantly shifting part of Bowdoin's life and being.

II.

The College Under Way

THE CHARTER OBTAINED, it was now up to the Trustees and Overseers to get the College into operation. Things moved slowly, and it was not until February 1796 that the College was in possession of the five townships granted by the commonwealth. The market for the land was poor, and funds were not available. Although the College was to be in Brunswick, just where it was to be located had not been decided, and there were several small settlements in the town. Finally, in July 1796, the Boards of the College held a joint meeting in Brunswick and decided on its present location contingent on receiving the land as a gift. The land was forthcoming, and two years later the Boards began to erect a "House" for the use of the College. The walls and temporary roof were finished in 1799, and then for two years the windows were boarded up and construction was at a standstill. When various efforts to raise funds failed, the Boards, in 1801, sold two of the college townships, Dixmont and Foxcroft. With these funds at hand, the construction of the "House" was immediately resumed, and by the spring of 1802 the first two floors were completed. It was deemed that these were sufficient to accommodate the College.[1] The eastern portion, with kitchen, parlor, and pantry on the first floor and bed chambers on the second, was designed as living quarters for the president. The two rooms on the first floor of the western side of the building were thrown into one for use as a chapel and hall, while the two rooms on the second floor were for the occupation of students. Recitations were to be held in the student rooms.[2]

With the construction of the College House again under way, the Boards proceeded to the selection of a president. Various men were suggested for the office, but there was no electoral controversy. In an apparently harmonious meeting on July 9, 1801, the Boards elected the Reverend Joseph McKeen, pastor of the Congregational church in Lower Beverly, Massachusetts, as the first president of Bowdoin College.[3]

President McKeen, who was born in Londonderry, New Hampshire, on October 15, 1757, was of Scotch-Irish ancestry and had been brought up as a Presbyterian. After graduating from Dartmouth at the age of seventeen, he taught school for eight years in Londonderry. In 1782 he studied mathematics and astronomy with Professor Samuel Williams in Cambridge, Massachusetts, and shortly thereafter undertook the study of theology with the Reverend Dr. Simon Williams of Windham, New Hampshire, with whom he had earlier fitted for college. While assisting at Phillips (Andover) Academy he began to preach, principally in Presbyterian congregations. In 1781 Dr. Joseph Willard, pastor of the large and wealthy Congregational church in Lower Beverly, Massachusetts, had been called to be president of Harvard. The church at Beverly had been four years with no settled minister when in 1785 it extended a call to Mr. McKeen. Having accepted the call, Mr. McKeen in May of that year severed his connection with the Presbytery and was ordained in the Congregational ministry. Shortly thereafter he married Alice Anderson of Londonderry.[4]

Although Rev. McKeen accepted the election to the presidency of Bowdoin, there were still some matters to be negotiated. There were some differences over the proposed salary, and McKeen requested a grant of a thousand acres of the College's wild lands as a provision for his family after his death. He also asked that the College build a separate dwelling for him, certainly a wise and moderate request as the McKeens had two daughters and three sons and needed larger quarters than those provided in the College House. While these negotiations were being carried on, McKeen took the precaution to consult with James Bowdoin and received his support. Mr. Bowdoin even promised to give him one hundred dollars to help defray the cost of moving to Brunswick.[5] The Trustees agreed to McKeen's wishes, being unwilling to affront their greatest benefactor and also run the risk of losing their president-elect.[6]

The choice of McKeen was a wise and fortunate one. As pastor of the Lower Beverly church he had gained wide experience and renown as a preacher. Professor Cleaveland states:

> The society [Beverly church] was not without its divisions, political and religious. McKeen was not quite orthodox in the opinion of some of his parishioners, nor so liberal in his theological views as others would have liked. But he was candid, upright, prudent, and conciliatory. He soon showed himself to be a man of great ability and learning, and of excellent judgment. Under his faithful and peaceful ministry the discordant elements subsided and for the most part seemed to coalesce.[7]

Professor Cleaveland, who spoke to many men who knew McKeen well as president of the College, writes further:

> He was tall, of robust frame, and of athletic vigor. He had a countenance that was both winning and commanding.... In manners he was gentlemanly, easy, affable, — a man whom everybody liked

and respected too, for he could not have been more correct in his deportment or more upright in conduct had he been ever so stiffly starched. He was mild and yet firm. He was dignified yet perfectly accessible. He was serious and yet habitually cheerful.... On all those great questions which involve man's responsibility and duty to his neighbor, his country, and his Maker, Dr. McKeen was earnest and decided in opinion and feeling, but at the same time perfectly tolerant. In theology he belonged to the milder school of the moderate Calvinists. No one who knew him could doubt the sincerity of his Christian profession, or the genuineness of his piety.[8]

Such was the man to whom Professor Alpheus Spring Packard paid high tribute in his address to the Bowdoin Alumni Association in 1858, saying: "Succeeding generations will have occasion to remember with gratitude that the choice of the first President fell on one who, of a true catholic spirit, with firmness and wisdom gave the right direction to the religious character of the College...."[9]

McKeen was not only to fulfill the duties of president, but he was to teach as well. No one thought otherwise, and thus there began the tradition of the president of Bowdoin being a teaching member of the faculty, a tradition which has been followed throughout the history of the College. To aid him in teaching, Mr. John Abbot, a member of a prominent Massachusetts family, was elected professor of languages. He was a graduate of Harvard and had been a tutor there from 1787 to 1792. He studied for the ministry but never was ordained and at the time of his election to the professorship was acting as a cashier in a Portland bank. He was not exactly a fortunate choice, for he did not distinguish himself as a teacher, and in 1816 resigned to become treasurer of the College and a member of the Board of Trustees.

By the end of the summer of 1802, all was set for the opening of the College. The new president's dwelling was not yet completed, and the family was temporarily ensconced in the apartments in the College House. At noon on September 2, 1802, the first academic procession in Maine took place when the assembled dignitaries marched from the College House to a large platform which had been erected on a clearing in the surrounding pines. Here as the first official act of the day, the president of the Board of Overseers called upon the vice president of the Trustees to give a name to College House. It was to be "Massachusetts Hall," and the vice president "gave a short address pertinent to the occasion."[10] Then President McKeen was formally installed, and he in turn, with leave from the Boards, declared Mr. Abbot professor of languages. Numerous speeches in Latin and English were made. In his inaugural address President McKeen set forth his views of what the College was and the policies to be followed. Few college presidents in their inaugurals have done so with as much clarity and brevity. In a passage often quoted in subsequent years, he said:

> It ought always to be remembered, that literary institutions are founded and endowed for the common good, and not for the private advantage of those who resort to them for education. It is not that they may be able to pass through life in an easy or reputable manner, but that their mental powers may be cultivated and improved for the benefit of society. If it be true no man should live for himself alone, we may safely assert that every man who has been aided by a public institution to acquire an education and to qualify himself for usefulness, is under peculiar obligations to exert his talents for the public good.[11]

At that time the issue of whether Bowdoin was a private or public institution was not acute, but it is nevertheless interesting that the new president chose to stress its public character. There was, however, much more in the address than this famous passage. He pointed out how pleasing it was "to observe a growing disposition in the inhabitants to promote education, without which, the prospect of the future state of society must be painful to the reflecting mind." Sound training was necessary lest people "easily fall a prey to the delusive arts of any new pretender to superior knowledge especially in medicine and theology." He made a plea for an educated clergy, for too often man was "contented with such instructions on the subject of his eternal interests as he can obtain from the most illiterate vagrants, who understand neither what they say, nor whereof they affirm."[12] He went on to say:

> I would not be understood to assert, nor even intimate, that human learning is alone sufficient to make a man a good teacher of religion. I believe that he must have so felt the power of the divine truth upon his heart, as to be brought under its governing influence. But since the days of inspiration are over, an acquaintance with the force of language, with the rules of legitimate reasoning, and especially with the sacred scriptures, which can be acquired only by reading, study, and meditation, is necessary to qualify one for the office of a teacher in the church. That the inhabitants of this district may have their own sons to fill the liberal professions among them, and particularly to instruct them in the principles and practice of our holy religion, is doubtless the object of this institution....[13]

He cautioned, moreover, that it should never be imagined "that the sole object of education is to make youth acquainted with languages, sciences and arts. It is of incalculable importance, that, as education increases their mental energies, these energies should be rightly directed." "It is doubtless a desirable thing to facilitate the acquisition of knowledge; but, in aiming at this, there is a serious danger to be avoided, that of inducing an impatience of application, and an aversion to every thing that requires labor.... In this connection, it may not be improper to suggest an advantage arising from the study of what are called the learned languages; it inures a youthful mind to application, and is, in this respect, useful; even if no advantage arose from the knowledge of them. The mind acquires strength and vigor from exercise, as well as the body." The "early formation of habits of industry and investigation" he considered were "of more importance than mere knowledge."

McKeen not only expressed his ideas in respect to what may be considered the more strictly academic aspects of the college; he also advanced views which were to set the tone of life at Bowdoin for many years to come.

> The governors and instructors of a literary institution owe to God and society the sacred duty of guarding the morals of the youth committed to their care. A young man of talents, who gains an acquaintance with literature and science, but at the same time imbibes irreligious and immoral principles, and contracts vicious habits at college, is likely to become a dangerous member of society. It had been better for him, and for the community, that he had lived in ignorance; in which case, he would have had less guilt, and possessed fewer mischievous accomplishments. He is more dangerous than a madman, armed with instruments of death, and let loose among the defenseless inhabitants of a village.[14]

The new president no doubt summarized his hopes for the College in his closing words when he called upon all those present "to unite in fervent supplications to the great Father of light, knowledge, and all good, that his blessing may descend upon this seminary; that it may eminently contribute to the advancement of useful knowledge, the religion of Jesus Christ, the best interests of man, and the glory of God."[15] Clearly Bowdoin was not to be a purely secular institution; there was to be no separation between the College and religion.

Between the time of his election to the presidency and his assumption of the office, President McKeen had taken steps to prepare himself for his new office. In May of 1802 he and Professor John Abbot had been added by the Boards to a committee of three appointed exactly a year earlier "to form laws and rules for governing and regulating the college."[16] It was customary at all colleges to have such laws.[17] In order to acquaint themselves at first hand with these matters, President McKeen and Professor Abbot, in the summer of 1802, visited Harvard, Brown, Yale, and Williams.[18] How much of the information they gathered was incorporated into the Bowdoin laws it is impossible to say. At any rate, the laws were drawn up and ready for approval by the Boards at their meeting before the inauguration ceremony. But while the Trustees approved them, the Overseers failed to concur. A joint committee was then formed to revise the college laws, and these were adopted on November 3, 1802.[19]

These laws no doubt laid down the qualifications for admission, stated the curriculum, and regulated many other matters. Unfortunately, no copy of these early laws has come down to us, and so it is impossible to be exact about admissions, curriculum, and conduct in these early years of the College. The Trustee records show there were some minor revisions of the laws, and in 1808 the Trustees voted to have 400 copies of the laws printed, but the Overseers did not concur. In 1812 the Trustees tried again to have the laws printed, and again the Overseers refused. This time, however, a joint committee was appointed to consider "the expediency of revising and printing the Laws of the College."[20] A year later the Trustees voted and the Overseers concurred "that the afternoon of Wednesday be appropriated to study and that the 6th section of the 3rd chapter of college laws be altered accordingly by erasing the word "Wednesdays" from this section.[21] Certainly this was not a momentous change. Then on June 6, 1814, another committee was appointed "to consider what further literary qualifications shall be required of candidates for admission," and the report of this committee was accepted on May 16, 1815.[22] The nature of this report, or what the committee on revision of the laws came up with, is not revealed in the records. Finally, on May 20, 1817, the Trustees voted and the Overseers concurred that 400 copies of the *Laws of Bowdoin* be printed. We have copies of this publication, and there have been numerous revisions since, for there were hardly any meetings of the Boards when some law was not changed.[23] Through these laws, and with the help of modern catalogues, which in 1822 replaced the early catalogues consisting of single broadsides that simply listed the officers of instruction and the names of the students, we can trace quite accurately academic changes at Bowdoin.

That there were changes between the laws of 1802 and those of 1817 is certain, but in all probability they were not fundamental. College procedures, college life, do not change rapidly, at least they did not in these early days. The Reverend William Jenks, in his eulogy of President McKeen, states that one of the valuable results of the visits paid by McKeen and Abbot to the other colleges in the summer of 1802 was:

> the requirement of such qualifications for entrance to this institution [Bowdoin], as immediately ranked the infant College in this respect, second in the Eastern States.... It may not be amiss to observe that the laws require for admission, an ability in the candidate to sustain a strict examination in the principles of the Latin and Greek languages, the select orations of Cicero, the *Aeneid* of Virgil, Arithmetic as far as the rule of three and also to translate English into Latin; being the same qualifications as were required at Cambridge before the regulations of 1805.[24]

These were the requirements; how strictly they were enforced is not recorded. Anyway, the next day after the installation eight men varying in age from thirteen to twenty-three, with only two over sixteen, were examined and admitted as Bowdoin's first class. There is no mention of anyone having failed to pass the entrance examinations.

Classes were held in the students' rooms, with recitations three times a day, which were started at the rapping of the president's cane on the stairs. For these classes the two student rooms were rotated on successive weeks, the occupants being obliged to borrow chairs from the other while their turn lasted. No record is available of exactly what was taught in the opening years, or how the curriculum was shaped as the college developed into a four-year institution.[25] The *Laws of Bowdoin College* as published in 1817 state, in regard to the curriculum:

> The course of studies shall be the following, as nearly, as may be convenient.
>
> In the first year, the English, Latin, and Greek languages, and Arithmetic; in the second, the several languages continued, together with Geography, Algebra, Geometry, plane Trigonometry, Mensuration of Superficies, and Solids, Rhetoric, and Logic; — in the third, the several languages continued, together with Heights and Distances, Gauging, Surveying, Navigation, Conic Sections, Natural Philosophy, Chemistry, Metaphysics, History, and Theology; — in the fourth, Chemistry, Metaphysics, and Theology continued, together with Astronomy, Dialling, Spherical Geometry and Trigonometry, with their application to astronomical problems; Ethics, Natural Law, and Civil Policy. With these studies shall be intermixed frequent essays in Elocution, English Composition and Forensic Disputation.
>
> The Sophomores and Juniors shall frequently read specimens of their compositions in English, before their respective Instructers and Classes: and the Junior and Senior Sophisters shall, when directed, dispute forensically.
>
> And the several Classes shall recite such books and in such manner, as the Executive Government shall appoint and direct.[26]

Curriculums are not evolved or changed overnight, and it may be assumed that the above was not too unlike what was taught in the very earliest years of the College, although the appointment of Parker Cleaveland to the faculty in 1805 as professor of mathematics and natural and experimental philosophy brought an expansion in the scientific fields. It is interesting to note that "Theology" is not listed as a subject of study until the junior and senior years. President McKeen had given a course in intellectual and moral philosophy and no doubt included in it many references to religious principles.[27] Just what "Theology" as listed in the 1817 curriculum covered is uncertain. Yet the patterns for instructing in religion at Bowdoin were early set. Theology was to be a limited but required part of the curriculum, and much of the religious life at the College was left to be nurtured on an extracurricular basis.

Chapel services attended by faculty and students were a regular feature of college life at this time. It took some days to inaugurate this program at Bowdoin, and it was not until the end of September 1802, about four weeks after the inauguration of President McKeen, that the policy of holding daily chapel services was started. The students were summoned to attend by the same signal as at the beginning of their classes, the rapping of the president's cane on the stairs, only in this case "a little louder and more prolonged than for the recitations."[28] Well might that be, for morning prayers were held at daybreak, and it must have taken some urging to get the students out of bed and down the stairs to the chapel on the first floor. This was a sparsely furnished room with no pulpit and only a table and chair at the south end.

After this first chapel service conducted by President McKeen and attended by Tutor Abbot and the eight students, they gathered around the steps of the building exchanging remarks. One of the students, George Thorndike, happened to notice an acorn on the ground. It aroused his attention, for there were no oak trees nearby, and on the spur of the moment he took a chip, made a hole in the ground near the steps, and planted the acorn. The acorn, no doubt, had been brought there with the oak leaves which had been used to decorate for the dinner following the inauguration of the president. The next spring President McKeen invited the students to help lay out a garden to the rear of his new house. Young Thorndike remembered planting the acorn and, discovering that it had begun to sprout, transplanted it to the president's garden. Here it grew and flourished. Young Thorndike was to die in St. Petersburg, Russia, five years after his graduation, but the tree he planted after the first chapel service was to become a living memorial to him on the campus as the Thorndike Oak.[29]

Immediately after the morning chapel service, the first recitation of the day was held, and only then were students permitted to have breakfast. There were also evening prayers at the close of the last recitation, but the laws of 1817 mercifully state that the time of recitations might be subject "to such variations, as the Instructors may find expedient."[30] Not only were students required to attend daily prayers but also regular church services. The 1817 laws so well depict religion at Bowdoin in the early years that they will be quoted directly:

Chapter II.

of Devotional Exercises, and the Observance of the Lord's Day.

I. All resident Graduates and Undergraduates, whether dwelling in the College buildings or not, shall attend morning and evening prayers in the chapel. If any Undergraduate arrive after the exercises are begun, he may be fined three cents, and if he be absent, six cents. If any one be frequently tardy or absent, the President or some Instructor shall enquire into the reasons of such neglect, and, if they appear insufficient, shall give him a private admonition; if he persist in his neglect, he shall be publicly admonished, and, if he do not reform, he shall then be suspended or rusticated, according to the aggravation of the offence.

II. If at prayers, or immediately before or after, in the chapel, any Undergraduate shall be guilty of indecent, irreverent, or disorderly conduct, he shall be fined, not exceeding one dollar, or be admonished, suspended, or rusticated, according to the aggravation of the offence.

III. Whereas some Christians consider the evening of Saturday, and others the evening of Sunday, as part of the Sabbath, every Student shall, on both those evenings, abstain from such diversions and business, as tend to disturb those, who religiously observe the time. And it is enjoined on all the Students carefully to apply themselves to the duties of religion on the Lord's day. Whoever shall profane the same by unnecessary business, visiting, walking abroad, diversion, or any thing inconsistent with the duties of Holy Time, he may be fined not exceeding one dollar, or be admonished, or suspended, according to the nature and aggravation of the offence.

IV. If any Student shall be absent from publick worship on the Lord's day, or on a day of fasting, or thanksgiving, or from any theological lecture, without previously offering a sufficient reason to some one of the Executive Government, [i.e. faculty] he may be fined not exceeding twenty cents, and for tardiness, not exceeding two cents; and any one, guilty of irreverent or indecent behaviour, while attending, may be fined not exceeding one dollar, or be admonished, suspended, or rusticated, according to the aggravation of the offence.

V. All Undergraduates are required to attend publick worship at the usual and appointed place. Provided, however, that, if any one shall desire to attend statedly on the service of any other regular Christian society, in the town of Brunswick, he may, if of the age of twenty one years, signify his desire to the Executive Government; and if a minor, may produce a written request from his Parent or Guardian for that purpose, and such application shall entitle the applicant to attend on such particular society, but not on any other. And in this case, such evidence of a punctual attendance shall be given, as the Executive Government shall direct.[31]

Such was the legalistic regime under which religion at Bowdoin started. Over the years it was to undergo many changes, which will be recounted in the following chapters.

III.

The College and the First Parish

THE REQUIREMENT OF BEING PRESENT at public worship on the Lord's day and on other special occasions calls for an explanation of the religious situation in Brunswick at that time. Early Brunswick had two main settlements: one along the New Meadows River, mostly people of English background who had migrated from Massachusetts and were by tradition Puritans and Congregationalists; the other near Maquoit Bay and along the road to the falls of the Androscoggin. These latter settlers were largely Scotch-Irish and Presbyterians.[1]

The building of the first meeting house in Brunswick was authorized on January 9, 1719, but it was not completed until 1735.[2] Even then the interior was not completely finished, and although repairs were often made, it remained unfinished until it was destroyed by fire on October 20, 1834. This building was located about two miles south of the falls on the road to Maquoit Bay, where today a burial ground still marks its location. The church was supported by town taxes, and church affairs were decided in Town Meeting. To the people living to the east along the New Meadows River not only was the long distance a hardship, but even more, the Presbyterian cast of the service and preaching was distasteful. By private subscription, the settlers at New Meadows built their own meeting house in 1756. The same minister was to serve both the east and west congregations, but this division of the parish was a cause for religious controversy and financial difficulties and was one of the reasons why the town was so often for long periods without a minister.

It was difficult in this early period to obtain a qualified pastor, for there were not many available. At times ministers who happened to be in the neighborhood preached for short periods. It was also customary for a man who was invited to take the position as "pastor and teacher" to serve a probationary period of varying length before he became the permanent or "settled minister." This involved reaching an agreement as to salary and providing him with a "settlement" which might consist of an additional sum of money, a dwelling, and the use of certain lands. He also had to be formally installed by an "Ecclesiastical Council" with invited ministers and lay delegates from neighboring churches participating. The early

Pejepscot Proprietors had set aside in their original plans for Brunswick a lot of land for a meeting house, another lot for the first settled minister, and a third for the use of all subsequent settled ministers in the town.[3] The first three men to preach for short periods in Brunswick were Presbyterians and were known as resident ministers. Rev. Robert Dunlap, also a Presbyterian, was the first settled minister, and he served at both the west and east ends of the town from July 8, 1747, to October 29, 1760. For two years the town was "destitute of preaching," and then Rev. John Miller became the settled minister (1762-1789). He was to preach at New Meadows only eight Sabbaths during the year. There had long been differences in the Brunswick church between those leaning towards Presbyterianism and those leaning to Congregationalism. This now was at least formally ended when in 1769 the church adopted a covenant and Rev. Miller declared he was "Pastor of this Church on the Congregational plan...."[4] This was important not only for the church but also later for Bowdoin. With the covenant, a step was also taken towards regularizing church membership, for only by signing it did one become a member of the church, as distinct from being a citizen of the town and thereby a member of the parish.

Mr. Miller served as minister through the difficult Revolutionary War years. His ministry, however, was not without controversies, and in Town Meeting numerous attempts were made to reduce his salary and dismiss him. In 1788 the town voted to pay him no salary, but it is pleasant to record that after his death on January 25, 1789, the town voted at its next meeting to pay to his estate all arrears due him, amounting to £123 6s 8d.[5] After an interim of five years, the Reverend Ebenezer Coffin was settled as minister. His pastorate began in the year Bowdoin received its charter and for two years (1794-1796) he served as an Overseer; his pastorate ended in 1802 just as the College opened its doors.

It was not a strong, united church that Rev. Coffin presided over. Differences which had plagued the Brunswick parish for years continued, and the general religious indifference of the times did not pass the town by. Baptist missionaries, the first one of whom we have record in Brunswick appeared in 1783, also added to the problems.[6] Soon members of the established church began to absent themselves from the Table of the Lord. A committee was appointed to ascertain the reasons and found these persons had become Baptists and denied infant baptism. Others openly refused to pay their ministerial tax, and so great had the opposition to the payment of the town ministerial tax become that at Town Meeting in April 1792 it was voted "that all persons who can produce a certificate from any Society that they pay a ministerial tax to that Society the Assessors shall forbear taxing such for the future."[7] Later votes definitely mentioned members of the Baptist Society as being exempt from paying the regular ministerial tax. By 1794 the Baptists were strong enough to organize a

Baptist Society of Brunswick, Harpswell, and Bath. They continued to increase in numbers and on petition to the General Court of the Commonwealth they were granted on February 22, 1802, a charter incorporating the Baptist Society of Brunswick. This brought a new relationship between the First Religious Society in Brunswick (that is, the Congregational church) and the Town of Brunswick. In June 1803 the first parish meeting as distinct from Town Meeting was held. The parish now undertook those religious functions formerly exercised by the town. All citizens of the town who supported the parish by their activity and financial support were automatically members of the parish; those who signed the covenant and made a confession of faith were members of the church as well. Ever since, parish and church have remained separate, but in polity both are congregational and united in their association with other denominational Congregational churches.

The existence of these two entities — parish and church — side by side, but constituting one organic whole, has been favorable to establishing good relations between the College and the parish and thus with the church as well. The College could be closely related to the parish without as such adhering to any creedal statements, subscribing to any covenant, or having any overt connection with the church. Always faculty and students could be members of the parish and join in its activities and governance without necessarily joining the church. The only qualification was that to vote in parish meeting they must be entitled to vote in town affairs. Well into the nineteenth century, becoming a church member involved not only accepting the covenant, but also publicly recounting conversion or other religious experiences. This, along with the possibility of being subject to church discipline, again a very public matter, largely accounts for the small church membership which existed at times in the parish.

After the departure of Rev. Coffin in the fall of 1802, the parish had no settled minister for the next nine years. It was only natural that the parish turned to the new president of the College for aid. President McKeen was the only ordained Congregational minister in the community, and he regularly preached in the meeting house. This building, however, was inconveniently located both for members of the College and for an increasing number of inhabitants of the town who were settling in the area between the College and the river.

In 1804 a minor crisis occurred. The Reverend Clark Brown appeared in Brunswick. He had been minister in Machias, Maine, but his heretical teaching split the church, and he was dismissed in 1795. From here he went to Brimfield, Massachusetts, where in November 1803 he was again dismissed. He was a smooth talker, and now some parishioners wanted to call him to the church at Brunswick. Yet those who knew about him realized that he was a troublemaker and in many ways a charlatan. President McKeen strongly opposed the calling of Rev. Brown, and he with the members of the College along with some members of the church began to meet for services in the college chapel.[8] Fortunately the parish did not settle Rev. Brown, but the incident may well account for a provision in regard to future pastors of the parish which was inserted in an important vote of the Boards in September 1805, discussed below.

With the College about to admit its fourth class, it was obvious to all that additional quarters were needed. The year 1805 was to be a year of expansion. On May fifteenth the Boards voted:

> Whereas the library and philosophical apparatus are exposed to hazard by fire in their present situation, and additional apartments will probably be soon necessary for the accommodation of students:
> Ordered, that a building forty feet long, twenty five feet wide, and two stories high, the lower story to be twelve feet, and the upper story nine feet in the clear, for the purposes of a Chapel and place of deposit for the library and philosophical apparatus, be erected of wood by an agent to be appointed for that purpose and that the sum of twelve hundred dollars be appropriated to that purpose.[9]

At this same meeting Parker Cleaveland was elected professor of mathematics and philosophy.

On July 13, 1805, President McKeen as agent of the College reached an agreement with Samuel Melcher, a Brunswick master builder, to erect the chapel for a contract price of $1,200 and to be finished in October.[10] The chapel was placed to face the west about four hundred feet south of Massachusetts Hall. It was a plain, unpainted structure of wood with white trimmings, and no adequate heating was ever provided.[11] The lower floor, which was to serve as the chapel, had a chair and reading desk at the rear end with a window looking out on the pines to the east. On each side of the desk there was an enclosed bench, one for the faculty, the other for guests.[12] Seniors were to occupy the front seats and the other classes in order. The building progressed rapidly, and on October 23, 1805, the new chapel was the scene of Parker Cleaveland's inauguration as professor of mathematics and natural philosophy.[13] The service was replete with prayers, music, and orations. Perhaps it served as a dedicatory service, for there is no record of a special dedication of the chapel ever being held. That same day the Trustees voted: "That the President be authorized to cause a plank way to be made from the college to the chapel, and also from his house to the chapel."[14] These walks were the early forerunners of the "duck boards" which in later years were to be placed on the main paths in the autumn and removed in the spring. The chapel, however, was not completely finished at this time, and the president was authorized "to procure such additional accommodations in the library room, as shall in his judgment be necessary for the preservation of the books and for the use and convenience of the Professor of Mathematics."[15] There is an entry in

Mr. Melcher's day book on November first stating that his men were painting inside the chapel.[16] His ledger closes the chapel account with the notation: "Complete January 20 to the satisfaction of the Agent and Corporation."[17] Construction had cost $975.69, and the College had made Mr. Melcher three payments of $600.00, $200.00, and $400.00 for a total of $1,200.00, the contract price and the sum originally voted by the Boards. As his careful accounts show, there was a "neat profit" of $224.31. Whether this was in line with the motto he inscribed on the opening page of his day book: "Better is A Little with righteousness, Then Great revenues without right," is a matter of judgment.

In the summer of 1818 the chapel was enlarged, moved a short distance to higher ground, and turned to face north towards Massachusetts Hall.[18] A belfry was added and the bell transferred from Massachusetts Hall. At last the building received a coat of light yellow paint. The building was always meant to be only a temporary structure, but it served the College until the present chapel was built.

Along with the new chapel, two projects were considered in 1805 which would give the College more necessary space. In a meeting on September 3, 1805, the Overseers refused to concur with a vote of the Trustees to build a new dormitory but were willing to agree to plan for one. The accepted vote stated:

> That the President and Treasurer be a committee to take in consideration the expediency of erecting a building for the accommodation of the students, the proper dimensions of the same; and that they prepare a plan for the inspection of the two boards at the next meeting. And said Committee is further authorized to contract for such quantity of bricks as they may judge necessary for a building according to the plan they shall report.

This vote eventually led to the erection of Maine Hall.

The other project was the erection of a new meeting house for the First Parish. Although the evidence is scanty it was probably President McKeen and Professor John Abbot who started the move to build a new meeting house nearer the campus.[19] At least the first definite mention we have of the project is in the records of the Governing Boards of the College, where on September 3, 1805, it was recorded:

> That the President and Treasurer be authorized to subscribe eight shares in the Meeting House proposed to be built by subscription near the College, in pursuance of the proposals of a committee of subscribers. Provided that the Meeting House shall be located within one hundred rods from Massachusetts Hall, and such accommodations in said Meeting House be secured to the College as the President and Treasurer shall deem necessary. Provided also, that

whenever the Proprietors of said Meeting House shall settle or employ any other than a Congregational Minister, the said Proprietors shall refund to the President and Trustees the amount of money subscribed and paid for their shares in said House.[20]

There are some important things to be pointed out in regard to this vote. The College subscribed eight shares in the meeting house, but the sum of money involved is not stated. From a later vote of the Boards we know this amounted to $800.[21] Just what rights the College should have in the new house are not spelled out in the vote but were left to further agreement except for one proviso. If the proprietors should ever settle or employ anyone but a Congregational minister they were bound to refund the money paid by the College. In a measure this provision gave the College a voice in who was to become a settled minister in the parish. It was no doubt inserted in the vote as a result of the recent differences between President McKeen and some members of the parish over the proposed settlement of the Reverend Clark Brown. It was also meant to insure that the parish would remain "Orthodox and Trinitarian" and not go over to Unitarianism. It is early evidence of the close ties that existed for many years between the College and denominational Congregationalism.

A term in the vote also needs explanation. The meeting house was not to be erected by the parish but by a group of private individuals known as the proprietors. This was a common practice of the time, and in this instance there were forty proprietors who subscribed funds to erect the building. Benjamin J. Porter, treasurer of the College, signed for himself and also for the College.[22] Just where the building was to be located, aside from the fact that it was to be within a hundred rods of Massachusetts Hall, was uncertain. On October 23, 1805, the day the Trustees met to share in the inauguration of Professor Cleaveland in the new college chapel, they voted to convey to the subscribers of the meeting house — the terms and considerations to be fixed by a committee to be appointed — land for the erection of the building.[23] In the end, however, the proprietors did not avail themselves of this offer but purchased lands from owners just north of the college properties. In 1806, on the land where the First Parish Church now stands, the second meeting house in the history of the parish was erected. Samuel Melcher, who had just finished the college chapel, was the builder.

By September of 1806 the building was far enough along to hold the first commencement exercises of the College. Many notables and guests were in Brunswick for the occasion. Unfortunately there was a terrific storm on the date set for the exercises, and the Boards voted to postpone the exercises until the next day. The next day, September 4, 1806, was not much better, but the exercises were held. The roof was not completely finished, and President McKeen sat on the platform with an umbrella over his head while awarding degrees to seven members of the first graduating class. One of the men who had entered with them in 1802 had been lost at sea.[24]

On completion of the meeting house the proprietors, as always planned, transferred the building to the First Parish on August 8, 1808, the parish voting "to accept the new Meeting House upon the conditions offered by the Proprietors."[25] The parish undertook "never, in that house, to employ or settle a minister other than one of the Congregational order." Thus was honored one of the conditions originally set by the College. The proprietors and the College had apparently reached an understanding on some other matters. The parish agreed that the north gallery in the new building "was reserved exclusively for the sole use of Bowdoin College, perpetually. The College was to have free use of the building on Commencement days, and was to repair all damages done to the building at such times."[26] This last provision was no doubt inserted because it was recognized that a special platform would have to be erected annually for commencement, and this might involve damages to the building.[27] The proprietors had all along expected to sell pews in the new meeting house and thus be reimbursed for the money they had expended. They were now given the right to sell the pews at auction to the highest bidder under certain restrictions. Settlement with Bowdoin College was postponed because dispute had arisen over the exact rights the College had in the property, other than the use of the north gallery and the right to hold commencement in the building. This dispute was to be submitted to a referee, and the settlement of the College's rights to the proceeds from the sale of the pews was deferred until an agreement was reached.[28]

On November 5, 1808, the assessors of the First Parish "in consideration of the sum of one hundred and seventy-eight dollars to us paid by the President and Trustees of Bowdoin College, the receipt whereof we hereby acknowledge, do hereby give, grant, bargain, sell and convey unto the said President and Trustees of Bowdoin College, their successors and assigns a certain pew on the lower floor in said meeting house, numbered 28. To have and to hold the aforesaid granted pew to the said President and Trustees, their successors and assigns, to their use and behoof forever."[29] The College now had a pew, the north gallery, and the right to hold commencement in the meeting house. However, there were other matters still to be settled. Was the College to be reimbursed in any way from the proceeds from the sale of pews? Did the College have the right to hold other meetings in the meeting house other than those of the commencement week? On May 19, 1818, and August 31, 1819, almost identical votes were passed by the Boards authorizing an agent of the College to meet with agents of the First Parish to agree upon the appointment "of referees to decide what privileges the college shall enjoy in the meeting house of said parish, in addition to those it already enjoys in consideration of the sum of eight hundred dollars paid by the college towards the building of said house, or to settle the same upon such terms and conditions as to the said committee may seem just and legal...."[30]

A settlement was finally reached on an indenture on August 15, 1821, and duly registered in the Cumberland County Registry of Deeds on July 23, 1829.[31] It is important and merits direct quotation:

> That the Members of the said Parish in consideration of the sum of five Dollars to them paid by the said President and Trustees, do hereby grant, sell, release and convey to the said President and Trustees, one undivided ninth part of all the right, title and interest, which the said Parish have in and to the Lot of Land upon which the Meeting House now used as a place of publick worship by the said Parish is situated, purchased of William Stanwood and Robert D. Dunning, together with the right to the several use of the North Gallery in said house, as now occupied by the officers and students of said College, with a right to pass into and out of the same, together with the use of said house upon the Days of annual commencement, to have and to hold the same to them the said President and Trustees, their Successors and Assigns forever. Reserving to the Members of the said Parish at all times except in Commencement Days, as aforesaid, the use in severalty of all the residue of said meeting house excepting the said North Gallery, and the Pew No. 28 heretofore sold to the said President and Trustees.
>
> And that the said President and Trustees on their part in consideration of the promises, do hereby release and discharge to the Members of the said Parish, their Successors or assigns, all right and claims on account of any sum or sums of money advanced and paid by the said President and Trustees towards the erecting and finishing of the house aforesaid, or on account of the proceeds of pews sold in said house by virtue of the agreement between the said Parish and the original proprietors of the said house or otherwise; and the said President and Trustees do further convenant and agree, that all damages occasioned to the said house on Commencement Days, shall from time to time and without delay be repaired by and at the expense of the said President and Trustees.

Thus by this agreement the College received one-ninth of the land on which the meeting house stood, the right to the use of the north balcony and pew 28, and the right to the use of the whole building during commencement week. In return, the College surrendered all claims for compensation for the sum advanced for the construction of the meeting house,[32] and undertook to make all repairs of damages resulting from the use of the house during commencement week. Nothing was said in the agreement about holding college exercises in the meeting house aside from those of commencement week. The opportunity to nail down these rights came in connection with the purchase of a bell for the meeting house.

The first reference we have to a bell in the community dates to 1811, and it hung in the belfry atop Massachusetts Hall.[33] After the new meeting house was built, the parish used this college bell, even after it was moved to the new belfry erected on the chapel in 1818.[34] This arrangement, however, was not satisfactory to the parish, and in 1824 a subscription paper was circulated to buy a bell for the meeting house. It was a popular move, and soon $510.75 was at hand. Of this sum, fifty dollars had been subscribed by the Standing Committee of the College on November 16, 1824, on "condition that, by vote of the Parish, the President and Trustees of Bowdoin College have the right to the use of the Bell and the Meeting House for all Public Literary meetings in commencement week, and for other Public Literary meetings, during other parts of the year such as exhibitions, inaugurations etc."[35] These conditions necessitated a meeting of the parish, and on December 3, 1824, the following vote was passed:

> Voted, in consideration of the sum of fifty dollars paid by the President and Trustees of Bowdoin College for the purchase of a bell for the Meeting House, that the President and Trustees of Bowdoin College have the right to the use of the bell and the Meeting House for all public and literary meetings in Commencement week (excepting the right formerly voted to the Peucinian Society) and for other public literary meetings during other parts of the year, such as exhibitions, inaugurations, etc., they giving the chairman of the Parish assessors at least ten days' notice, except at Commencement week; provided that if the Parish shall hereafter pay said President and Trustees the sum of fifty dollars, they may withdraw the grant now made.[36]

The agreement no doubt only regulated what had become customary practice, except for the ten-day notice to the chairman of the Board of Assessors of the parish. This was a reasonable requirement so that a schedule for the use of the building could be arranged. Attempts were made in 1826 and again in 1835 by some members of the parish to repay the fifty dollars and cancel the agreement, but in each case the articles in the parish warrant were dismissed.[37]

These several agreements show that there was early established a close connection between the College and the First Parish of Brunswick. However, it is not so clear what the exact proprietory rights and obligations of the College in this relationship were. In general it necessitated further consultation and negotiation as occasion arose. For example, on August 31, 1830, the Boards voted that "thirty-three dollars and fifty-one cents be paid to the Treasurer of the First Parish in Brunswick towards the expenses of painting and repairing the meeting house owned by the said Parish and Bowdoin College."[38] On December 15, 1834, the faculty, apparently from funds at its disposal, voted "to pay thirty dollars to the parish for improvement in that part of the gallery of the Meeting House, which is owned by the College, and for the expense of a permanent stage for exhibitions."[39] Again, on September 2, 1835, the Boards appropriated "the sum of $60.93 for the payment of expenses in altering the Meeting House as stated in a letter of C. Packard."[40] How they ever arrived at these precise amounts in dollars and cents is not stated. Perhaps this was the result of a pew tax, for that was a favorite way of raising revenue in the parish, or it may have been a ninth of the total cost.[41]

In 1840 the parish voted to establish a committee "to inquire into the expediency of enlarging the Meeting House...."[42] Not much is known about this committee's work, but on October 27, 1843, the Boards voted:

> That the Treasurer of the college be authorized to pay the sum of $200 to the First Parish in Brunswick to aid them in repairing their meeting house, on the condition that the Parish shall rebuild or repair the north or College Gallery so as to render it more convenient for the students, and shall fit it up with good pews, corresponding, with the exception of doors in them, with the pews which shall be made in the opposite gallery, and on the condition also when it shall be found necessary by the College, that the College exhibitions may be held in said Meeting house, in the daytime and its other rights in the house be continued.[43]

The last condition indicates that there must have been some differences over the use of the meeting house by the College.

The parish in the end decided not to repair the meeting house, but to build a new one. There are no records of consultation between the parish and the College on this important decision. Members of the faculty were also members of the parish and so were in on the decision. President Woods was also instrumental in putting the parish officers in touch with Richard Upjohn, the architect of the new college chapel. The decision, once made (February 15, 1845), was rapidly carried out. On April 6, 1845, the last service was held in the second meeting house, and for the next months the services were held in the vestry owned by the church on School Street.[44] The old meeting house was immediately "taken, but not torn" down, a careful distinction in terminology made at that time.[45] By April seventeenth this had advanced to the stage where the tower was pulled down. The dove which had served as a weathercock was appropriated by a student as a relic for the Caluvian Society.[46] The first service held in the second meeting house was the Bowdoin Commencement of 1806, and likewise the new third meeting house was far enough along for the Commencement exercises of September 3, 1845, to be held there. The building was rapidly finished and was ready for dedication on March 18, 1846. In his dedicatory sermon, Dr. Adams touched on the relations of the parish to the College when he stated:

> A church should not be for ordinary, worldly purposes. We have or ought to have, other buildings for worldly purposes. We should build our churches for religion. We should not give them to God today and take them back for Mammon tomorrow. Let us also avail ourselves of the laws of association! Let us have one place where no sounds but those of prayer and praise, and the teaching of holiness shall break the silence; — one place where every association shall remind us of God and the Gospel and of Heaven! Some might suppose that these principles would exclude the Commencement exercises from this Church. But these annual exercises appear eminently appropriate to a House of worship. I would that all our young men and maidens, when about to enter upon the duties of life, might be gathered in the Church, in the presence of fathers and mothers and be sent forth with a 'God be with you'![47]

His wish carried over into practice, and all graduates of Bowdoin received their degrees in the third meeting house until the small midwinter commencements during World War II.[48]

When the new parish church was being built the College was in grave financial straits, being occupied with the erection of a new dormitory (Appleton Hall) and a new chapel. There is no record of any appropriations being made to help pay for the third meeting house aside from the appropriation made in 1843 for repairs to the old house. At Commencement in September 1846 the Boards received a communication from the First Parish relating to the new meeting house, which it referred to the Visiting Committee to report back "at this meeting." The communication of the parish apparently raised no problems for the Visiting Committee, which reported:

> That considering that the meeting house is so much more beautiful and so much more convenient for college purposes than was contemplated when the Boards voted $200 towards the repairs of the old building, they therefore cordially recommend that the terms proposed by the Parish be complied with and that Charles S. Daveis Esq. be a committee to see that the votes of the Parish and Church confirming such agreement have been duly passed, and then further recommend that said votes when duly certified be entered on the college records.[49]

This report was accepted by the Boards. No documentation has been found that Mr. Daveis, Class of 1807, performed his duties, but from the parish records we know what the parish proposals were. The new meeting house was "not to be used for any secular purpose whatever or for any purpose other than those that are strictly religious" with the exceptions made in favor of Bowdoin College. These were:

> For the accommodation of Bowdoin College, and in view of certain contributions made by the President and Trustees of the College, the Parish grants to the President and Trustees the use of their new House, in the daytime, for all literary exercises held during the week of Commencement in addition to the ordinary Commencement exercises, as may be appointed or approved by said President and Trustees; also on other days during the year for the inauguration of College officers; and also for any extraordinary services for which the Assessors of the Parish, for the time being may give their consent, provided however, that the said President and Trustees shall be held bound to repair all damages that may occur in said House the use of it as specified by this vote, and provided also that, with the exception of Commencement week, ten days notice shall be given to the Assessors of the Parish of the intended use of the House.[50]

These terms were largely a reaffirmation of the rights the College had to the use of the old meeting house. For exercises now excluded from the new meeting house (exhibitions and class and society programs at other times than commencement) the parish offered the use of the vestry on School Street. An advantage of this arrangement was that this building could be used in the evening, whereas the parish had voted "that all services in the New House without exceptions should be held in the daytime "and that no apparatus for lighting the House shall be provided or admitted into it."[51] Furthermore "in lieu of the North Gallery owned by the President and Trustees in the Old House" the parish designated the south transept gallery for the use of the students. There was an outside entry to this gallery, and it was far more convenient for the students than the old north gallery had been. No mention was made of a college pew, but the plan of sittings in the meeting house indicates that the College was assigned No. 26.[52] The College, with little or no cost, had indeed benefited greatly by the erection of the commodious new meeting house. In subsequent years there were to be further agreements between the parish and the College about the building.

The erection of the second and third meeting houses of the First Parish in Brunswick and the regulation of the rights of the College to their use are only two aspects of the relationship which developed between the College and the parish. From 1802 until 1811, the parish had no settled minister. President McKeen and later President Appleton occupied the pulpit regularly and literally kept the church services going. That they received regular supply fees is doubtful, although these would no doubt have been a welcome addition to their modest salaries. In 1811 the parish elected Winthrop Bailey, a tutor at Bowdoin, to serve as its settled minister. Times were hard, and the parish, still beset by internal dissension, was unable to raise the promised salary, and it is not surprising that Rev. Bailey found it necessary to tender his resignation in the spring of 1814.[53] Again President Appleton stepped into the breach and took over the services. This was not viewed favorably by the Boards, and in September 1814 they expressed their concern "that the health of the Rev. President is endangered by his preaching in the meeting house. That he be requested to give his ministerial labors, in future, in the chapel."[54] President Appleton was not one to be deterred by such a vote, nor was he one to spare himself. He continued to supply the First Parish pulpit either directly or through exchanges with nearby ministers.[55] President Allen also preached often in the meeting house,[56] and it was probably at his instigation that the parish finally began to make serious efforts to get a settled minister. The parish in 1821 proposed to the College that they cooperate in settling a minister who would also teach moral philosophy and religion to the senior class four days a week. The parish felt $700 would be a reasonable salary but that it could raise no more than $400 and requested that the College pay $300 a year. The Boards met the request by appropriating an annual sum of $200 to be at the disposal of the faculty for the instruction of the students in moral philosophy and religion. The faculty agreed to the proposal and voted "that the Treasurer pay to the Rev. John Keep the sum of two hundred dollars annually, provided he preached stately in the Meeting House near the College, and instruct the senior class on moral philosophy, if the Executive Government require it, having not exceeding four recitations in each week — and in such manner as they may direct."[57] The Reverend John Keep, who had been proposed as a candidate for the dual position, refused the invitation because of the lack of unanimity in the parish. The parish, thinking that the agreement with the College still held, went ahead and late in 1822 called the Reverend Asa Mead to be its settled minister. The faculty also apparently felt the agreement held, for on November 18, 1822, they passed the same vote in respect to Rev. Mead that they had passed in respect to Rev. Keep a year before.[58] Rev. Mead, however, never taught at the College, and there is some ambiguity about the appropriations made by the College. In 1823 it was voted that the money be appropriated for religious instruction exclusively for the ensuing year under the direction of the faculty; in 1824 it was appropriated "for preaching the year to come"; and in 1825, "that the Rev. Mr. Mead be paid for his services up to the day in December next [Dec. 22] on which he was settled and no longer, at the rate of two hundred dollars per annum."[59] These votes are of interest as they are the only instances when the College contributed directly to the salary of the minister at the First Parish. As if to deny responsibility for these events of the past few years in their relationship to the parish, the Trustees in September 1826 passed this cryptic vote: "To disavow all connection with the settlement of Mr. Mead and not send the vote to the Overseers."[60] Without concurrence on the part of the Overseers it was, of course, no official vote of the Boards, but merely an expression of opinion by the Trustees. Why it was passed can only be surmised. It was probably brought about by a letter of September 5, 1826, from a committee of First Parish protesting "the vote at last commencement [1825] to discontinue payment of $200 as part of the salary of Mr. Mead."[61] The Committee wrote that they understood that it was "the usage of most other Colleges and seminaries of learning in the country to contribute a portion of the salary of the minister, upon whom their pupils regularly attend in the publick worship of God." No record of the reply by the Boards to this letter is at hand, but the vote by the Trustees in 1826 is an indication that they were determined to sever connections with Rev. Mead. Their attitude might well have been influenced by the appointment of Professor Thomas C. Upham to a newly established chair of metaphysics and moral philosophy in September 1824, since there was no longer need for Mr. Mead as a teacher. The Reverend Mead was not popular with the students, and this may also have been a factor. The students were required to attend church services twice on Sundays and were not always too attentive or orderly in their sanctum of the north gallery. The Reverend Mead was not above stopping in his sermon and rebuking them. One Sunday a student entered the gallery in what Mr. Mead thought to be an intoxicated condition. The minister was an ardent temperance advocate—a fact which had aroused the misgivings of some of his parishioners. He now took time to berate the student soundly and in turn was answered by the students with noise and a loud scraping of feet. Later in the day the students marched to the north end of the mall and there hanged Mr. Mead in effigy in the hay scales, meanwhile singing an improvised tune, the first verse being:

My name is Asa Mead
And I preached and I preached
I insulted William Browne
And the scholars scraped me down.[62]

It should be added that on April 7, 1823, the faculty found Browne guilty of being drunk at the morning service at the meeting house and suspended him from college until the first of August.[63]

To judge Rev. Mead by this episode would do him injustice. He was a hard worker, and under his direction the church grew in membership and new activities were undertaken. After he resigned in 1829, under pressure from a minority of the members, the parish called the Reverend George Eliashib Adams of Bangor to be the settled minister. The latter was an exceptionally able man, and during his long pastorate, which lasted until 1870, very close ties were established between the parish and the College.[64]

Aside from the connections between the College and the parish, centering in the meeting house, the service of the presidents of the College in filling the pulpit and the willingness in turn of the ministers of the parish to minister to the College and its students, there is one other group which did much to tie college and parish together. This was the faculty. They helped make the "Church on the Hill" what it was often called, "The College Church," although it never was this officially. In the early days the faculty were all members of the parish, and they took a leading part in its affairs.[65] They served college, parish, and church, and what they did for one could not well be distinguished from what they did for the other. Students saw the faculty not only in the classroom but also in chapel, at Sunday services, and at prayer meetings. The faculty did not shun but were active participants in the religious life of the College and of the community. Whether they were successful or not is not to be judged, but they and the administrators of the College strove to give the students what President Hyde later called the opportunity "to form character under professors who were Christians."[66]

IV.

College Regulations and Their Enforcement

As has been pointed out, the first Board of Trustees named in the original charter was made up of six clergymen and five laymen; the Board of Overseers of fourteen clergymen and twenty-eight laymen. In the following years the balance gradually shifted in favor of the laity. During the first hundred years of the history of the College there were 250 Trustees appointed, of whom 91 or 28.57 percent were clergymen; of the 344 Overseers there were 96 or 27.91 percent clergymen.[1] Bowdoin was not a clerically run college, although the Boards were always friendly towards religion and upheld its cause. As Chief Justice Fuller stated in his 1894 Centennial Anniversary address: "Those were the days...when all alike regarded virtue and piety as essential elements of education, and religion as the chief corner-stone of an educational institution."[2]

From the very beginning lay candidates for the presidency of the College had been proposed. In 1807 the Honorable Isaac Parker had even been elected as president by the Trustees, but the Overseers refused to concur—for what reasons we do not know.[3] All the presidents the Boards elected in the first century of the College's existence were ordained Congregational ministers except for President Joshua L. Chamberlain, and he had graduated from the Bangor Theological Seminary.

Students at Bowdoin have never been fitted to enter the ministry directly on graduation. But the College has always offered a training which prepared them well to become members of that profession. This involved, particularly in the early days, a strong emphasis on Latin and Greek, and from 1827 to 1866 Hebrew was a voluntary subject.[4] At the time of the founding of the College it was still customary for a man who wanted to become a minister to associate himself with an established member of the profession. He "read theology" as a man desiring to become a lawyer "read law." This practice gradually declined, thanks to the establishment of specialized theological seminaries. Because of the spread of the Unitarian movement at Harvard, the Orthodox Congregationalists founded the Andover Theological Seminary in 1807, to be followed by a second seminary at Bangor in 1816. A close relationship between Bowdoin and these institutions was soon established. Bowdoin men went primarily there to complete their theological studies but there were also some who went to other divinity schools which were being founded: Princeton, 1812; Harvard, 1816; Yale, 1822; and Union, 1824, to name only a few.[5] Of the 448 graduates of Bowdoin's first twenty-five classes (1806-1831) 83, or approximately 18.5 percent, became clergymen, and of these 32 "read" theology, 36 went on to study at Andover, 7 to Harvard Divinity, 2 to Yale, and 6 elsewhere. The percentage of men going into the ministry was to increase notably in the decade of the thirties, when in the five years 1831-1835, 36.23 percent and in the years 1836-1840, 30.51 percent became ministers.[6] The numbers gradually declined, and when President Hyde in his inaugural address in 1885 surveyed the history of the College, he stated that of the "2145 Bowdoin graduates 429, or exactly 20% had given themselves to the ministry of the gospel in our own and foreign lands."[7]

Students, whether they expected to go into the ministry or not, all studied the same subjects, for there were for many years practically no electives. From the *College Laws* of 1817 we know that theology was a subject for the junior and senior years. Of what was covered in these courses, or in natural philosophy and metaphysics, we have no sure knowledge. With the catalogue of 1822, the first in the series which comes down to the present, we are on firmer ground. It stated that candidates for admission had to be versed in the Greek testament, and four years later this was changed to being versed in the Gospels of the Greek testament and Jacob's *Greek Reader*. This requirement remained until 1856, when knowledge of the Gospels in Greek was no longer required, but could still be offered as an equivalent to two books of Homer's *Iliad*. Four years later this was cut to the knowledge of only the first two Gospels. All mention of the Gospels in respect to admission finally disappears in the catalogue of 1867-1868, in favor of the general statement: "Real equivalents for any of the foregoing requirements will be accepted." The end of Greek as a requirement for admission came in 1879 when the faculty voted that students could be admitted to college without Greek and were to be given bachelor of science degrees.[8]

The catalogue of 1822 confirms that it was not until the junior year that students came in contact with religion as an academic subject, when they were required to study William Paley's *Evidences of Christianity* throughout the year.[9] This was a broadly conceived and able study of the origin of the Bible and the development of Christianity. It even contained a chapter on Islam and dealt with a variety of religious problems. As a basis for a survey course, it served well indeed and was used for many years. "Evidences of Christianity" as a subject for senior study was last listed in the catalogue of 1887-1888. The next year it gave way to "Bible Study— Introduction to the Gospels and Pauline Epistles; Life of Christ," one of the innovations introduced by President Hyde.

According to the 1822 catalogue the seniors were to study Paley's

Natural Theology for one term. It was more or less a companion volume to the author's *Evidences of Christianity*, and as its subtitle stated, it dealt with "Evidences of the Existence and Attributes of the Deity, Collected from the Appearances of Nature." It contained much about botany and physiology with the purpose of gathering "materials from the knowledge communicated by science where with to construct an argument for the existence and attributes of God."[10] By 1826 the juniors no longer studied Paley's *Evidences* but Enfield's *Natural Philosophy*, while the seniors studied for a term Paley's *Evidences* and also Paley's *Natural Theology*. By 1833 Upham's *Mental Philosophy* had taken over for the junior year. Thus the pattern was early set, and courses in religion came to be postponed till the senior year. In 1847 the Visiting Committee was struck by the "vices and lack of morals on the part of the students." This harsh judgment was perhaps induced by the burning of the woodshed the previous fall. The pilfering of wood by the students was a perennial problem, but the burning of the shed and wood supply was something to take note of. The committee reported:

> The want of moral instruction to a greater extent and at an earlier period, is believed to be a prominent cause of the existing irregularities and vices among the students. The first two or three years of his college life is devoted to classical and mathematical studies exclusively. Neither by recitation nor by lectures, is any instruction upon moral or religious subjects given. No opportunity therefore exists, in the way of public teaching to impress upon the student, first sentiments and principles of action, or to inculcate moral precepts in his heart. In the senior year when instruction upon these subjects is given, it is quite too late to repair the mischief which has resulted to the college by the irregularities of the previous years....They are deeply impressed, however, with the conviction that a separate Department devoted to Ethical and Moral subjects, cannot longer be delayed.[11]

The report led directly to the establishment of the Collins Professorship of Natural and Revealed Religion. Judge Shepley, who wrote the above visiting committee report, backed up his convictions by subscribing $1,000 to the subscription list establishing the professorship.[12]

The freshmen and sophomores, however, were not so religiously neglected as the above report might lead one to believe. Up until 1833, when this requirement was ended, all classes had "Recitations in the Bible every Sunday evening." What these recitations involved is not detailed, but they apparently were sessions devoted to Bible study and conducted by the president. President Appleton also regularly gave theological lectures on Thursday afternoons which all students were supposed to attend. He prepared these lectures carefully, and they constitute the greater part of the two volumes of his *Works*, which were published posthumously.[13] A glance over the topics of these lectures: The Existence of God, The Intelligence of God, The Power of God, Heathen Morals, Evidences of Christianity, Faith, Justification, Election, Atonement, to name only a few of them, indicates that he dealt with difficult and fundamental problems. The students indeed were given a solid course in theology; perhaps too advanced for many, for President Appleton certainly did not insult their intelligence by talking down to them. In this way the president carried out in practice the view expressed in his inaugural address where he questioned whether "the outlines of Christian theology, might not, with advantage, be considered as a necessary part of collegiate studies; and whether his education should not be considered as deficient, who has no particular knowledge of the facts and doctrines described in the sacred volume."[14]

Although not as systematically as President Appleton had done, later presidents carried on his tradition of theological instruction. President Allen in 1836 reported to the Visiting Committee that he had delivered in the chapel "a course of Lectures on the proof of the wisdom and goodness of God furnished by the work of Nature."[15] In 1850 President Woods reported "giving instruction as in previous years on Sunday eve to a Bible Class for Seniors who want to attend. I am happy to report that the punctuality with which these have been attended and proficiency made in these several studies has been in a high degree satisfactory."[16] With the appointment of the Collins Professor of Natural and Revealed Religion in 1850, the president came to play a lesser role in direct religious instruction, although he continued to exert great influence on the religious life of the College through his conduct of the chapel services and the courses he taught. This was also true of President Woods's successors Presidents Harris, Chamberlain, Hyde, and Sills.

President Appleton was deeply concerned with student conduct, for he stated "that the morals of students ought to be a matter of primary attention does not admit of a moment's debate."[17] To him, as to the administrators of most colleges at that time, the College had definite parietal obligations to carry out in respect to the students. To this end their life and conduct was regulated by numerous college "laws" and practices. It was during President Appleton's presidency that Bowdoin's laws, which had existed from the very beginning of the College, were revised and published for the first time in 1817.[18] By vote of the faculty, each student was given a copy of the laws along with his certificate of admission signed by the president of the College. These laws, frequently amended, remained the basis for student conduct for many years to come. Gradually and piecemeal they were relaxed and finally completely abandoned. This did not mean that Bowdoin no longer had standards of conduct, for as President Hyde and later President Sills were wont to admonish the students: Bowdoin has no rules, until they are broken, and then the College will take action.[19] The breaking of these unwritten rules has become more difficult to assess in the present more permissive day, but this guideline for conduct first enunciated by President Hyde still holds.

Students in President Appleton's day were often as young as fourteen, and this no doubt led to a need for more parietal guidance on the part of the College. Study hours were carefully regulated. From the beginning of the fall term to the first of April these were from nine to twelve in the forenoon; from the first of April to commencement, from half an hour after eight to twelve in the forenoon, and at all seasons from two to evening prayers in the afternoon. In the winter session the faculty at its discretion could assign a part of the evening to study. If a student was absent from his room without reason during these study hours or after nine o'clock in the evening he was liable to a fine not exceeding ten cents. If a student was a chronic offender and disturbed other students he might be "publicly or privately admonished, suspended or rusticated according to the degree and circumstances of the offense." If a student caused a disturbance during study hours by singing, playing an instrument, or making any noise or tumult he might be fined not exceeding twenty cents, admonished, or suspended. If the student failed to attend his recitations or was remiss in performing his assignments he was to "be fined not exceeding twenty cents; or, if his neglect became frequent and obstinate, he shall be admonished, suspended, or rusticated, as the degree of the offence shall require."[20]

The rules in regard to study were brief compared to those regarding "Misdemeanors and Criminal Offences."[21] These required five pages of the laws. Students were not permitted to leave Brunswick or Topsham without consent; if one went after permission was denied he might be fined not exceeding two dollars.[22] If he were absent for a night the fine might be increased. If a student should "in Brunswick or Topsham associate with any person of known dissolute morals or with anyone, who within three years had been dismissed from college and not restored to good standing" he was to be subject to a fine not exceeding fifty cents, or to further punishment as the case might be. He was not permitted to eat or drink in any tavern in Brunswick or Topsham except in the presence of his parents or guardian or on invitation of a family with whom he was befriended. No student was to play cards, billiards, or any game of chance, nor should, if he was under age, buy, sell, or barter with other students, books, apparel, or any other property. He was not permitted to keep a gun or pistol in his room without permission of the president, nor could he go "a gunning or fishing" without permission of some member of the faculty. He was not to fire a gun or pistol within or near a college building, make any bonfire or illumination, or set off fireworks. Playing ball within or near a college building, or engaging in any other sport which might injure the building was banned. There was a revision and a general reorganization of the laws when they were republished in 1824. The laws were still grouped in chapters but were numbered consecutively. Law 33 dealing with "Immoralities" shows that offenses had if anything increased, or at least were formulated more exactly.

> If any student shall be guilty of profaneness, intoxication, or dissoluteness; of lying or purloining; of challenging, assaulting, or fighting with any person; or shall sing indecent songs, or be indecent in conversation; or shall lead a dissipated life; or shall associate with any person of known dissolute morals; or shall violate in any other way the moral law of God; he shall be admonished, suspended, rusticated, or expelled.[23]

In addition to the many specific things which were forbidden there were more general catchalls. For example: "If any student shall disobey the lawful command, or treat with contempt the person or authority of anyone of the Executive Government [i.e. the faculty] or shall lead a life of dissipation or intemperance or shall be guilty of any gross violation of the moral law of God, he shall be admonished, suspended, rusticated, or expelled, according to the nature and aggravation of the offence."[24] Or again, "Where students may be guilty of disorders or misdemeanors, against which no express provision is made in the foregoing laws; in all such cases, the Executive Government may punish them by fine, admonition, or suspension, according to the aggravation of the offence."[25]

While the laws pretty well covered every possible dereliction on the part of the students, the authorities still were mindful of Christian charity. Repentance and a contrite heart went a long way towards alleviating the letter of the law. As the concluding paragraph of this chapter stated:

> The object of these laws, being the improvement and reputation, not the punishment and infamy of the student, if any offender, whose offence shall not require exemplary punishment, shall speedily and voluntarily evince his penitence for his fault, and by a private or publick confession thereof give satisfaction to the Executive Government, they may, at their discretion, pass over the offence, and refrain from entering the case on their records."[26]

Forgiveness and the practice of a second chance has a long history at Bowdoin.

The enforcement of such a strict code of conduct was not an easy task. It is clear that there were minor and major sins, and the faculty were not unaware of the fact that "boys will be boys" at times. In order to strengthen discipline and avoid the plea of being ignorant of regulations, the Boards in 1841 voted: "That each student at the beginning of the second term after his admission to college be required to give his pledge of honor, to be prepared by the executive government in a book for that purpose, that he will faithfully obey the laws of the College while he shall continue a member thereof."[27] It was an age when making pledges was a happy practice. Drinking was always a problem at the College, perhaps exaggerated by a rather puritanical view in respect to it. In the 1824 edition of the laws, students were forbidden to purchase or bring into the College spirituous liquors.[28] But it was easier to make a rule than to enforce it. In 1847 the Boards by formal vote "recommended to the Executive Government in the execution of the laws against intemperance to withhold matriculation from any freshman, who will not subscribe a written pledge to the effect, that he will not during his connection with the College, while under the government of college laws — use any intoxicating drinks."[29] What the faculty did about the recommendation is not clear. The Visiting Committee reported that there had been no general violation of the pledge of abstinence; there had been one bad case, and the student had been punished. Taking a pledge of abstinence, however, never found its way into the requirements for admission as stated in the college catalogues.

Smoking too was outlawed for a time. On August 8, 1822, the faculty voted "that every student who is seen smoking a cigar in the street be fined 50 cents."[30] But the Boards went even further, and in the 1825 edition of the laws students were flatly forbidden to "smoke tobacco."[31] There were soon second thoughts, but with reservations. On August 31, 1830, the Boards voted:

> That the amendment of Law 34 by striking out the words "nor shall smoke tobacco" is not to be construed into an approbation on the part of the Boards of the practice of smoking by young gentlemen. On the contrary the Boards regard the practice of using tobacco as injurious to the health, as holding out temptations to other excesses, and as a practice calculated to degrade the character of young gentlemen in College, and the amendment of the law is made with the hope, that the young gentlemen will themselves examine this subject with the attention it deserves and come to the conclusion of themselves to abandon a practice, already fixing a stigma upon the character of the students of Bowdoin College.[32]

Students, of course, did not confine their use of tobacco to smoking, but in line with the customs of the time chewed tobacco. A story, although it applies to a later time, may well be inserted here. Professor Charles Henry Smith (Cosine Smith) who taught at the College from 1874 to 1890 did not like to have his students chew tobacco in class. Students tended to think they would not get "pulled" to recite, having recited the day before. But if Smith noticed someone chewing he would call upon him and keep him on his feet for fifteen minutes or so. There was nothing for the student to do but swallow tobacco or choke, and it is said that Smith's way of dealing with the problem was very effective.[33]

Attendance and conduct at chapel and church services were constant concerns to the faculty. In January 1808 the faculty voted that every tardiness both at prayers and public worship should be noticed by the monitor. During that part of the year when because of darkness prayers could not be attended at six o'clock in the morning, the first bell was to be rung fifteen minutes before service and then tolled after an interval of ten minutes. The tolling was to stop "when the President leaves his house; and every student be noticed as tardy, who arrives at his seat after the exercises of the chapel commence; which will be immediately after the President enters the desk."[34] The bell for evening prayers was to be rung at five o'clock for two minutes and then tolled after an interval of a minute.

The 1825 edition of the college laws in the first section under Misdemeanors and Criminal Offences sharpened the regulations on conduct in chapel and church services. It stated:

> If any student shall profane the Lord's day by unnecessary business, visiting, receiving visits, or walking abroad, or by using any diversion, or in any other manner, or shall be disorderly, irreverent, or indecent in his behavior in the chapel or place of assembling for religious exercise; or shall be absent therefrom without permission, or be unseasonable in his attendance; or shall unnecessarily leave the place of worship during the services, he shall be admonished, suspended, or rusticated according to the aggravation of the offence.[35]

Such strict rules coupled with compulsory attendance resulted in numerous violations; it is surprising that there were not more trespasses. The records of the Executive Government note the punishments meted out, usually the imposition of fines, admonitions, or in extreme instances, suspension. To cite a few examples. On August 26, 1807, it was voted "that Davis, Means, Storer, Stanwood, Boyd, and Mac Arthur be fined twenty cents each for absence from public worship; that Wilde be fined sixty cents and Wise forty cents...."[36] On December 18 of that same year, Samuel D. Ellis, Class of 1809, was found "guilty of disorderly conduct in wantonly throwing a hat across chapel, thereby disturbing his fellow students, insulting the authority of College, discovering an undevotional spirit and treating with irreverence the worship of the Creator." He was suspended until June 10, 1808.[37] That some students were habitual offenders is indicated by a vote of the faculty that Stanwood, who had been absent thirty-six times from prayers during the present term; Wood, who had been absent thirty-one times; Clark, forty-two times; and Southgate, twenty-five times; be admonished before the government.[38] Repeated offenders were assigned to various professors who were to counsel with them.[39] On November 18, 1822, Bridge was fined fifty cents for reading at public worship; on August 4, 1823, Millet received a similar fine for improper position at prayers.[40]

On September 1, 1823, Cilley, Snell, and Stone were fined fifty cents for sleeping at public worship.[41] Franklin Pierce, Class of 1824, along with others was fined twenty-five cents for improper position at public worship.[42] Nathaniel Hawthorne, Class of 1825, received repeated fines for being absent from public worship and chapel prayers, and his parents were written to.[43] Henry Wadsworth Longfellow, Class of 1825, had a good record; but his brother Stephen, who was in college at the same time, made up for him in delinquencies.[44]

Such supervision of the students was an arduous task and required much monitoring on the part of the faculty. A tutor regularly sat in the student gallery at the First Parish Church; and when students, with the permission of the president, began to attend public services at other churches, such attendance was checked upon by appointing monitors.[45] Checking on attendance was not always carefully done. Thus Charles P. Roberts, Class of 1845, notes that he had received permission from the president to attend Sunday services in Topsham, "which is equivalent generally, to leave to stay at home," and so he remained in his room all day.[46] In the College's report to Roberts's parents in December 1843, it was stated that he was absent from prayers nineteen times, while his own estimate was forty times; that he was charged with no absences from church and he estimated twenty-one absences.[47] A number of absences were permitted and excuses were accepted. Roberts was finally caught up with and on March 21, 1845, was called in by President Woods about absences from prayers. "He said," Roberts notes, "I had overrun the extreme limit allowed—namely 36 prayers as I had 40 against me. He then stated the law. If a student is absent 12 times he is to be spoken to, if 26 times he is more formally spoken to, and if 36 times his connection with the college must be terminated. Absences are to be carried over from one term to another, but not from one year to another, and in carrying the absences from one term to another 8 are deducted. So this law allows about 50 unexcused absences for a whole year, and an absence from church ½ day is reckoned 5 prayers—a whole day 10 prayers." Roberts had failed to hand in any excuses and refused to do so, although he was willing to give verbal excuses. He maintained that: "Every week a student put his imagination at work to frame excuses—when no real excuse existed—and falsehoods were sent in writing, and I thought that when a person renders his excuse to his officer face to face the truth was more likely to be exhibited." President Woods, with understanding insight, allowed that as Quakers did not take an oath but gave testimony on their own fashion, he too would take oral excuses, and Roberts promptly gave verbal excuses "for the amount of 18 prayers last week."[48]

As always when there are requirements, there will be some student opposition and attempts to circumvent them. Thus Roberts noted on October 22, 1841:

"Nothing worthy of note occurred during the [day] unless the throwing of pumpkins in the chapel during prayers is considered so — this was carried on so thoroughly that the President's prayerful voice was drowned by the continual noise and racket. Thus it is easy to see that the compulsory attendance of prayers tends to no good, but rather otherwise — if prayers must be had better order should be preserved meantime, but the very fact of the confusion generally made augurs that students pay no attention, nor wish to. I forgot to mention that in the morning two dead hens were nailed up over the Chapel inner door."[49]

A week later Roberts and an accomplice decided to hook the bell rope, hide the Bible, and secure the door of the bell ringers. While they were in the chapel the student bell ringer came and locked the chapel door. The prisoners finally escaped through a window, but, still bent on their mischief, plugged the keyhole of the chapel and fastened the door of the bell ringer. The laconic diary entry for the next day simply noted that prayers were delayed.[50]

A favorite target for student pranks was the chapel bell. If it were silenced there would be no rising bell and no call to early prayers; students could enjoy the luxury of extra time in bed. In April 1827 the chapel bell was carried off, apparently the climax of a whole series of irregularities, and as a result two seniors were required to leave college and go home.[51] Again in 1836-1837 the bell was taken down by some students and thrown into the Androscoggin.[52] In March 1842 some students, having removed the balustrade on the bell deck, attached a rope to the bell and pulled it down. A hole was broken in the roof, and when the bell hit the ground the wheel of the bell was broken in pieces. Alas, their efforts were not rewarded, for "early in the morning old Professor Smyth came over and with others succeeded in getting the bell mounted upon some stakes and so prayers were not escaped."[53] The next day the old bell was elevated to its proper place amid much confusion among the students. At the beginning of the fall term in 1844, a more serious assault on the chapel bell occurred. The belfry of the chapel was sawed off and pulled to the ground and the next morning was carried off for kindling wood by the students.[54]

The assaults on chapel bells were part of the college mores of the time. Students at Colby sent the tongue of their bell to Bowdoin, no doubt as a joke and an attempt to force a vacation from prayers.[55] Attacks on the college bell did not end with hanging it in the north tower of the new chapel. One Wednesday night in October 1854, the bell was removed and dumped into the river. Through the "agency of Professor Upham" it was recovered and deposited in the chapel on Friday, only to be carted away again. The faculty now took steps to procure a new bell of not less than 500 pounds.[56] Undaunted, the students again removed the bell from the tower in October 1863 but returned it two nights later, before the vote of the faculty to "buy a bell weighing from 160 to 200 pounds more than the former" could be carried out.[57] There is a tale that two students one Halloween night inverted the bell and filled it with water so that it froze solid.[58] This was not a mean accomplishment considering how high the bell was hung in the new chapel tower and how often a ladder had to be moved from one beam to another to get to the bell. All this effort to prevent a single chapel service! In 1878 the *Orient* editorialized, in regard to the many recurring pranks in classroom and chapel: "It is useless to speak of the folly and childishness of such tricks, but if mischief must be perpetrated we hope something more original than spoiling blackboards and cutting the bell rope will be devised."[59]

On October 12, 1844, three days after the belfry of the chapel had been torn down by the students, "some rowdies of the lower classes" carried off all the windows from the chapel.[60] These acts caused a furor on campus and led to an extended investigation by the faculty, but the perpetrators were not discovered. The assaults on the chapel continued. The Visiting Committee, in its report in 1845, took note of these activities and wrote: "There has been unusual and most wanton destruction of glass during the last year as well as cutting and deforming the seats in the chapel. No one can have approached the Old Chapel without being struck with the vast amount of broken glass around it. About 1300 panes have been broken within the year."[61] The students were in a rampageous mood, and 1844-1845 brought the most costly destruction of property of any years between 1831 and 1847.[62] These costs were apportioned among the students and charged to them on their term bills. In spite of the vigilance of the faculty, the students never stopped trying to outwit them. On the night of April 8, 1852, all seats were removed from the chapel "by some student burglars," which the faculty countered by holding morning prayers in the chemical laboratory.[63]

The punishments which students might incur for their "pranks" and for the violations of the numerous regulations were precisely defined in the 1825 edition of the laws of the College. Article 13 stated:

> The punishments, which may be inflicted, are the exaction of study in hours for exercise and relaxation and in vacation, private admonition, official notice of delinquency to the parent or guardian of a student, public admonition in the presence of the whole college, suspension, dismission, degradation to a lower class, rustication, and expulsion. The frequency and repetition of offences shall aggravate the punishment.[64]

Omitted in this statement was the whole system of fines which had become established at the College. The laws then added, as in the earlier edition, the assurance, "but if any student shall speedily evince penitence for his fault, it shall be in the power of the Executive Government, on his private or public confession, to pass over the offence without entering the case on their records."[65]

The routine admonition involved a student being called in to see the president or some other member of the faculty. Public admonition was another matter. It could be before the faculty or before the whole College. In the latter case it was held in chapel and was a very formal and solemn occasion. There were words of admonition for the offence committed and exhortations for repentance. The ceremony was ended with a prayer, as for example, the instance when two students had got into a fight:

> We feel it our duty to exhort you to repentance and we pray God to work in you sincere contrition of heart for this and all your sins, to clothe you with humility, and to put upon you the ornament of a meek and quiet spirit, that putting away all bitterness and wrath, and anger, and clamor, and evil speaking, ye may be followers of God, as dear children and walk in love as Christ loved us and gave himself for us.[66]

Suspension in 1825 was never to exceed six months (reduced from nine months in the 1817 and 1824 editions.) The student was given a definite period of time to leave Brunswick, and if he stayed longer he was subject to additional punishment. While away from college he was to carry on his studies under a person agreeable to the faculty, and if on his return he produced "testimonials of good conduct during his whole absence," and passed an examination, he was readmitted to his class. If he had been indolent and failed to meet the above conditions he might be suspended for a further term not exceeding four months. If then he was not qualified for readmission to his class he was to be degraded or dismissed. If a student was rusticated he was forced to leave Brunswick for a period of twelve months.[67] If his testimonial of good behavior and evidence of diligence in study were then satisfactory to the faculty, he was permitted to rejoin his class on probation, during which period he could be dismissed at the discretion of the faculty. A student dismissed could not return as a member of the College in less than nine months. If his testimonials of good conduct were satisfactory and he passed the necessary examination he could be restored to his class. Notices of suspensions were regularly given in chapel, and at times were received with protest by the students. Thus there is this notation in Peleg W. Chandler's diary in October 1832: "There was a tremendous scraping in the chapel this eve. when Prof. Smith [*sic* William Smyth] went to read a suspension bill against a sophomore (Briggs); he had to stop and did not read it."[68]

The numerous laws and regulations bear witness to the attempts of the college authorities to enforce standards of conduct and uphold religious concepts and practices. They bear ample evidence that the men in charge at Bowdoin adhered to the belief that there was no separation between religion and morality. President Timothy Dwight of Yale, a firm upholder of this doctrine, summarized this position well when he wrote:

> Morality, as every sober man who knows anything discerns with a glance, is merely a branch of Religion; and where there is no religion, there is no morality. Moral obligation has its sole ground in the character and government of God. But, where God is not worshipped, his character will soon be disregarded; and the obligation, founded on it, unfelt, and forgotten. No duty, therefore, to individuals, or to the public, will be realized, or performed. Justice, kindness, and truth, the great hinges on which free Society hangs, will be unpracticed, because there will be no motives to the practice, or sufficient forces to resist the passions of men. Oaths of office, and of testimony alike, without the sanctions of religion are merely solemn farces.[69]

This belief lay behind all the rules and regulations concerning conduct; it was generally held at all colleges at this time and was accepted at Bowdoin by the students as well as by the college authorities.

V.

Religious Societies

SOME OF THE STUDENTS undertook to further religion and morality at the College by forming special societies. The first and oldest of these was the Theological Society, which was founded in the spring of 1808 with a membership of seventeen out of a student body of approximately thirty. Its formation was due to the efforts of Tutor Jonathan Cogswell, with the encouragement of President Appleton and the assistance of a student whose name we do not know but who was generally considered as the only "undergraduate whose character was decidedly religious."[1] The society was primarily for the study and debate of religious topics; "for cultivating," as Cyrus Hamlin, Class of 1834, put it, "some historical knowledge of the heresies and orthodoxies of the past ages and of the present times. We aimed at nothing above our reach."[2] The society had its ups and downs. Professor Smyth, in his lectures on the religious history of the College, remarks: "During the first term of the academic year 1811 to 1812, — the whole number of students being upwards of thirty, — there was not one among them who had made a profession of religion. The interest in the Theological Society became nearly extinct, and few, if any came forward to take the places of those of its members who had graduated. It was regarded by most with feelings of bitter opposition. The greater part of the students appear to have been thoughtless. Not a few were reckless and openly immoral, some of whom formed habits of intemperance which clung to them in later life and brought them to a dishonored grave."[3] But there was a revival of interest. Professor Smyth goes on to report that after President Appleton had read the narrative of the death of the backslider and free-thinker Sir Francis Newport to the students, the next morning twelve to fourteen members were obtained without difficulty for the Theological Society "not one of whom before had been willing to join it."[4]

All the early records of the organization were destroyed in the fire of February 12, 1836, which devastated Maine Hall, but the new constitution adopted at that time no doubt mirrored the society as it had been functioning up to then. The preamble of the new constitution as adopted on March 9, 1836, stated:

Deeply interested in the inquiry 'What is truth?' and sensible that a free interchange of thought by means of friendly discussion is one of the best adapted instruments for obtaining correct principles, we, therefore, form ourselves into a Society governed by the following Constitution.[5]

There were the usual officers of all student societies. "Persons sustaining a good moral character, and who would be interested in theological discussions having been members of the College, at least, one term [could] be elected to the society by a vote of two-thirds of the members present, having been proposed two weeks previous by the nominating committee."[6] The initiation fee was a dollar and dues twenty cents a term. Meetings were held every two weeks on Wednesday evenings, and the regular program called for two original dissertations and two debates on a question proposed two weeks earlier and accepted by the society. The meeting was then thrown open for general discussion. It was up to the president to appoint the participants, and frequent postponement to a later time would indicate that at times there were lapses in preparation. The votes on which side won the debate—not always recorded—show that attendance normally ranged between fifteen and thirty. The records state there was no meeting from July 21, 1847, to March 1, 1848, when a committee of five was appointed "to devise means to resuscitate the society."[7] They revised the constitution—a favorite prescription of students then as now—and sought to collect money to pay accumulated debts. Money was no longer available to continue subscriptions to magazines. Their efforts failed; meetings continued to be poorly attended and not held regularly. On July 12, 1850, there is this notation in the minutes:

As there are now so many other societies in college, in which students exercise their talents at forensic disputation and so many other ways to take up their time, the President thought best not to have any meeting called for some time past....And for these reasons it was moved and voted to suspend the operations of the society to some indefinite future time.[8]

At this meeting it was also voted to put the society's library in the hands of the college librarian. Some of the older members objected to this; another meeting was called on July 16, 1850—the last of the society—and this time the library was entrusted to the care of the Praying Circle. It had gradually been built up to where it contained over seven hundred volumes. For reasons of safety the new custodians transferred the books to the college library that very year.[9]

The subjects for the dissertations or essays read at the meetings of the Theological Society are not given in the records. No doubt they were related to the subject being debated; the latter were regularly voted and recorded. A sampling of the topics will indicate what concerned the students of that day, many of whom were headed for the ministry: "Are extemporaneous sermons preferable to written ones?"; "Is the present division of Christian denominations beneficial to the cause of religion?"; "Will there ever be a time when all people upon earth will become righteous?"; "Ought the young men preparing for the ministry in this state who are natives of the state to remain in the state?"; "Is immersion essential to baptism?"; "Is it generally practicable for ministers to spend their lives in one church?"; "Is the cause of religion promoted by voluntary associations?"; "Is any infringement of the principles that all men are born free and equal consistent with Christianity?"; "Does baptism take the place of circumcision?"; "Are infants proper subject of baptism?"; "Is the doctrine of total depravity taught in the Bible?"; "Have the efforts of infidels retarded the progress of Christianity?"; "Resolved that the sublimated philosophy of the present day styled Transcendentalism is essentially unsound"; "Ought missionaries under any circumstances to defend themselves by force of arms?"; "Should the testimony of those who disbelieve in the existence of a God be received in our courts of Justice?"; "Are the Protestants less guilty in withholding the Bible from the slaves than the Catholics in withholding it from the common people?"; "Are there any innate ideas to the mind?" The last subject debated by the society, "Is France prepared for a Republican form of Government?" indicates along with others of the later years of the society that the interest of the members had shifted to more secular than theological subjects.[10] The society had served its day; it is remarkable that it had been able to maintain itself so long amidst the activities of the broader based Peucinian and Athenaean literary societies and other smaller organizations.[11]

In addition to the Theological Society there was another organization at the College even more religiously oriented. In September 1812 Frederic Southgate, Class of 1810, returned to the College as a tutor. Since his graduation he had undergone a conversion, and he was instrumental in forming small discussion and prayer groups among the students. He had a strong supporter in a transfer student from Middlebury College, James Cargill, Class of 1814. Professor Smyth reports that "in 1813 came three other men, Messrs. Dennis, Cheever, and Pratt, who had the ministry in view, and who had come here not only to receive good but to do good in Christ's name."[12] These men laid the groundwork for Bowdoin's joining a religious movement that had sprung up at various colleges. In 1815 the Praying Society of Brown University sent a letter addressed to the Praying Society at Bowdoin. Since no such society existed at the College, a small group of "professors of religion" met and decided to form such a society for prayer. They were six in number and on July 17, 1815, they adopted a constitution and elected officers. The preamble summarizes well their thoughts and purpose:

In consideration of the alarming prevalence of wickedness in this institution, and a lamentable indifference to the things of religion; believing that a change in the conduct and hearts of the students can be affected in no other way, but by an effusion of divine influence; and also believing the promise of God, that he will answer the requests of those, who call upon him in spirit and in truth; we whose names are recorded toward the end of this book do form ourselves into a society by the name of the Praying Society of Bowdoin College.[13]

The constitution had certain unique features as far as student societies go. The member who had the highest grade of the highest class was to be president without resorting to a vote. To join, a new member had to have the consent of all existing members, and he had to give "charitable evidence that he is a real Christian, and on being admitted shall, in a brief manner, state the reason of his hope, and give his assent to the fundamental doctrines of the gospel." The society was meant to bring "together the religious element of the college without any distinction"; in it there were "neither Congregationalists, Baptists, Methodists, nor Presbyterians."[14] Meetings were to be held after the ringing of the first bell on Sunday morning and before the start of regular church services. These were open meetings and attended by many who were not actually members of the society. They were not recorded, and no business was transacted at them. This was reserved for a Wednesday evening meeting, and the constitution enjoined that "no members shall divulge any of the proceedings of the Society."[15]

The object of the society was "to pray for the influences of Divine Grace upon ourselves, upon this institution and upon the world at large."[16] This purpose it retained to the very end, but its activities were broader than that. It helped to keep Bowdoin in touch with the academic world in general, for, particularly in the early years, the society corresponded regularly with similar societies at Brown, Harvard, Yale, Princeton, Dartmouth, Middlebury, Union, Williams, Amherst, William and Mary, and Waterville [Colby].[17] An amendment to the constitution as early as August 1815 provided that the society "join the concert of prayer for the missionary cause held on the first Monday in every month," an observance practiced at various colleges and churches.[18] A record of prayers being held "for the prosperity of Zion among the benighted heathen" is specifically noted on May 19, 1819.[19] The society led in the support of the missionary movement which manifested itself in the United States in these years and led to the establishment of the Board of Commissioners for Foreign Missions of which Rufus Anderson, Class of 1818, was the longtime foreign secretary.[20] Not only did the society pray for and support missions, but a goodly number of its members went actively into the field. In 1910 there was a revival of missionary interest at the College when the students undertook to support the work of A. S. Hiwale '09 in India. At that time the *Orient* ran an account of what Bowdoin men had done in the past in the field of foreign missions. It reflects so well this important aspect of the interests of the Praying Society that it merits quotation in full.

Here, briefly stated, are the records of a few of these brave men. Words do not tell adequately what they have done. Asa Dodge, '27, went to Syria as a missionary and physician in 1832; three years later he died of fever in Jerusalem, because he had hurried too fast to the bedside of a sick man. Samuel Munson, '29, went to the East Indies in 1833 and the next year was killed by cannibals. Horatio Southgate, '32, devoted the fifteen years of his life to mission work in Turkey and Persia. Daniel Dole, a fine teacher, went to the Sandwich Islands in 1841; took charge of a school and later was President of Oahu College. Elias Bond, '27, went to the Sandwich Islands and Hawaii in 1841 and gave forty years of his life to the work there, in that time taking a vacation of two weeks in 1869. Crosby H. Wheeler, '47, was sent to Harpoot in East Turkey in 1855 and there founded Armenia College. B. G. Snow, '46, was assigned to the Island of Kuaie in Micronesia in 1852. He was the first to reduce the island language to a written form. He issued in it a primer, spelling books, readers, a hymn book, and translations of the Gospels, Acts and some of the Epistles, and a church manual. James S. Phillips, '60, was the son of a missionary, born in India, and gave himself to the work in that country. Perhaps the most famous of Bowdoin's missionaries was Cyrus Hamlin, '34, whose model steam engine is now in the Physics laboratory. He went out to Turkey in 1839. His skill was tried many times as he had to thwart Jesuit and French [and Russian] intrigues. It is a matter of history how he improved the sanitary condition of the military hospitals during the Crimean War, how, to provide employment for poor Protestant Armenians, he started a bakery and supplied the whole British army in Armenia with bread. He turned over the profits of this enterprise, $25,000, to the Missionary Board. His greatest work was the establishment of Robert College in Constantinople, which he accomplished after a hard conflict of skill and diplomacy. The magnificent site and buildings and grounds of the college constitute a splendid monument to the energy and foresight of this Bowdoin alumnus....

Joseph K. Greene, '55, is still in Constantinople, just now in charge of the publication of periodicals in Armenian and Turkish in the Armenian alphabet, and Turkish in the Greek alphabet, after fifty years of service, from 1859 to 1909. Americus Fuller, '59, who went to Aintab, Turkey, in 1874, who has taught in Central Turkey College and who has been President of Euphrates College, has but recently retired from active work. Dr. Charles S. F. Lincoln, '91, is at the present day a useful Medical Missionary at St. John's College, Shanghai, China. Last and best known to undergraduates is A. S. Hiwale, '09. He has returned to his native district of Ahmednagar in India....[21]

Great as was the interest of the Praying Society in foreign missions, its greatest concern was with religious life on the campus. To this end it provided student leadership and participation in the religious revivals which were characteristic of Protestant America in these decades of the nineteenth century.[22] Members of the society also led in observance of the generally observed days of prayer by the churches for colleges,[23] and in the observance of state-wide fast days. For example, there is a notice in the minutes of the Praying Circle on February 27, 1833: "Some of the pious students met this morning at 8 o'clock to commence the duties appropriate to a day of fasting and prayer for the descent of the Holy Spirit on our college."[24] The fast days came to be freed from classes, and in preparation for fasting the student body in general celebrated by having a bonfire the night before. A sixty- to seventy-foot pole was raised, around which brush and tar were heaped to a great height. It is said it took from four to five hours to build a good bonfire.[25] Sophomores supposedly had this duty, but others helped. They were not careful where they obtained their material so long as it would burn. In 1842 they took much from the old gymnasium. According to college rules the bonfires were illegal, but for a while the faculty had relented, hoping the students would lose interest. This was not the case. In April 1842 Professors Packard and Smyth, helped by some town boys (Jaegers), caught at least one of the participants at the big bonfire of that year. He was duly called before the executive government, but as a freshman he was able to plead that he did not know the faculty objected, and nothing happened to him.[26] This was the time when a sophomore threw sulphuric acid in Professor Goodwin's face, and for a time it was feared the professor would lose his sight. The student was most contrite and explained he had meant to throw the acid only on the professor's clothes. He was, however, expelled from the College.[27]

This serious episode tempered the pre-fast bonfire mania for a time. There were no bonfires in 1843 and 1844, but the next year, in lieu of one, the Temple (privy) was set on fire. This was wanton destruction of property, and the cost of replacement was passed on to students on their term bills. But traditions and customs have a way of lingering on. For April 14, 1852, there is this entry in the diary of Benjamin Browne Foster, Class of 1855:

> Evening, the "Circle" met in Chamberlain's room where Professor Stowe conducted a prayer meeting. He in his odd, blunt, picturesque and uneuphemistical style told us about temptations which would "roll off us like drops from a cabbage leaf"....
> Tomorrow being Fast Day, by old custom, it is expected that the sophomores will have a bonfire, drunk, bell-ringing, and general jubilee night. <u>Nous verrons.</u> It is said a deputy sheriff and a posse will guard the meeting house bell and that the Yaggers [town boys] are ripe for a fight.

About 10 the chapel bell rung, the docile faculty having permitted them (rather than the doors should be smashed) to have the key. I went out and found some of the students collected around a heap of slabs, fence rails, benches from the recitation rooms and other lumber, and others dragging fences, boards and brush and carting upon the wheels of the engine, "hooked" for the nonce, the ruins of an old building which by far the most part were engaged in pulling down. They were disguised and many very drunk. Soon the chapel bell, and the fire, with yells, fish horns, thumped funnels and other instruments simultaneously struck up. At the cry of "The Church" a gang rushed thither and, like a Parisian mob in the Reign of Terror, battered down its sacred doors and rushed in. They clambered up the tower for the bell rope which had been wound around the wheel, and soon its deep voice was "keeping time, time, time, in a sort of Runic rhyme...."

The fire was quite bright, though not large, and [the] lofty, granite chapel towers cast a dark shadow out and up into the brightened space. I did not actively participate but with my coat turned, handkerchief around my face, and old slouched hat, stood and sauntered about. Bed at 1.[28]

Clearly Fast Day at Bowdoin was not given over entirely to prayer, sackcloth, and ashes.

The Praying Society at various times revised its constitution. The revision of 1827 had a more concise preamble: "Sensible that we are under infinite obligations to God for the privileges we enjoy and that we need his assistance in all things; believing also his promise, that the prayers of two or three united shall be heard; we therefore form ourselves into an association to be called the Praying Society of Bowdoin College."[29] This time all officers were to be elected by ballot, and there was to be "a committee of three chosen at the beginning of each year whose duty it shall be to ascertain who are hopefully pious and invite them to join the society." By 1830 the term "Circle" began to be used in reference to the society, and in the constitution adopted in 1835 the name "Praying Circle of Bowdoin College" became the official name of the former "Praying Society."[30]

The new constitution was more detailed, and rules were laid down for the conduct of members. Members for the first time were required "to abstain from all intoxicating liquors, except wine at the Lord's supper—or prescribed by a temperate physician." "Any immoral conduct, such as engaging in noisy and boisterous plays, scraping, or in any way disturbing good order, breach of the covenant of the churches, to which we may respectively belong, neglect of religious or relative duties or denial of any of the fundamental doctrines of the Bible, as held by the evangelical churches and this circle, and professed by its members at the time of their admission, shall be censurable offences."[31] This was certainly a broad and non-modern definition of immorality. Censures were to consist of admonitions, suspensions, or expulsions, and were administered by a vote of the circle, two-thirds of the members present concurring. Conviction required confession, the testimony of two credible witnesses, or equivalent circumstantial evidence. Offences strictly personal and private were to be settled according to the directions given in the eighteenth chapter of Matthew, that is through forgiveness and brotherly reconciliation. Occasionally members withdrew; it is surprising how few were ever dismissed.[32] In 1861 the circle passed the resolution "that in the opinion of the 'Praying Circle' drinking intoxicating liquors, card playing, dancing, and habitual absence from our regular meetings are inconsistent with the Christian character and we do hereby express our disapprobation of the same."[33] It was with shame that they felt "it necessary to record such a resolution, but the conduct of some of our members absolutely demanded it." The resolution resulted in the resignation and purging of a number of members.

In the late 1830s the circle began to hold Saturday evening meetings given over to lectures by ministers and members of the faculty.[34] In the fall of 1850 Professor Stowe, appointed that year as Collins Professor of Natural and Revealed Religion, gave a series of Saturday evening lectures on the "Life of Christ."[35] In 1854 the circle voted to hold prayer meetings on those Saturday evenings when there was to be no lecture. The "ringing of the chapel bell should indicate a prayer meeting, and ringing and tolling of the same would indicate a lecture."[36] A new shorter constitution was adopted on May 26, 1855, and an amendment adopted a month later provided that the secretary should make a concluding annual report on the condition of the circle during the previous year.[37] These are valuable in tracing the activity of the organization. Alternating lectures and prayer meetings apparently became an established practice, for on June 27, 1856, there is an entry in the minutes stating that "Professor Packard and Professor Smyth have delivered fortnightly instructive and interesting lectures to large and attentive audiences."[38] The circle was flourishing, and the annual report of 1857-1858 records a "good year" with twenty conversions, twenty-nine new members, and well-attended meetings.[39] In 1859-1860 Thursday morning prayer meetings were permanently established.[40] Another new constitution was adopted on May 26, 1865.[41] The Civil War apparently did not touch the circle. The only reference to that conflict in the records is this entry on June 1, 1865: "The continuance of our lives, while death has taken many, perhaps, some dear to us, calls for our gratitude and adoration."[42]

Religious services of the circle were for a time shifted from Sabbath morning to Thursday evening, and then to Friday evening. Class prayer meetings were instituted, with periodic all-college meetings.[43] In 1874-1875 it is noted that two exercises which had long been omitted were restored. These were the Saturday evening lectures by members of the faculty and the Wednesday noon prayer meetings. It was, however, a small group of devoted members who kept the circle going. In a college which was increasing in enrollment, the membership hovered around forty. The record book for 1867-1882 gives the number of new members recruited annually from 1867 to 1881. These ranged from a high of eighteen in 1872 to a low of one in 1875, with an average of about twelve. To the very end members were required to give an account of their religious experiences before being admitted to the circle.[44] The last recorded meeting was on June 19, 1882, when officers were elected for the coming year. By that time the circle was sending delegates to the Intercollegiate Branch of the Young Men's Christian Association (Y.M.C.A.).[45] On October 19, 1882, there was the first business meeting of the Bowdoin Y.M.C.A., and a week later the constitution was read and signed. At this latter meeting it was voted "that all who were members of the Praying Circle be admitted to active membership in the Y.M.C.A."[46] With this action the circle adapted itself to more modern ways.

In addition to the Theological Society and the Praying Circle, there were a number of other societies at the College with a religious orientation. They left few if any records. One of the earliest of these was the Lockhart Society, devoted to the cultivation of sacred music. We know it existed in 1813 and was active in the next decades. In 1832 at an expense of $300 it purchased and placed in the chapel an organ, with the proviso, accepted by the college Trustees, that it should never be disposed of unless replaced by an organ of equal value.[47] The society recruited the musical talent within the College and did much to enhance the chapel services.

There was also a Missionary Society of Inquiry of ten to twelve members which was active in the 1830s. Cyrus Hamlin, Class of 1834, mentions it in his autobiography.[48] A Bowdoin Unitarian Society was founded in the 1820s, and Henry W. Longfellow wrote to a friend in November 1824 in regard to it. "I wish something could be done for us; we are small as a grain of mustard seed. There are but six members now in college, and our library is limited to a hundred or two volumes."[49] The society sought to strengthen itself by recruiting honorary members. In 1829 Charles S. Daveis, a prominent Portland lawyer and member of the Board of Overseers, was invited to become such an honorary member. The letter of invitation to him is about the only archival material the library has on the society. By then the "immediate" undergraduate members numbered twenty, and the secretary stated: "Our objects are the awakening of attention to the great truths of religion and of a spirit of free inquiry into them, and the diffusion of liberal views. We have a library, which though small, contains much useful matter. It has increased very rapidly within a year, chiefly by donations. As the Society becomes more known we trust that its means of being useful will be increased."[50] How long the society continued to exist is not to be determined.

There was also a "Christian Union" which stressed its liberalism in religious matters. Hatch in his *History of Bowdoin* makes no reference to it, and the library apparently has no records of its activities. However, in the diary of Charles Phelps Roberts, Class of 1845, on April 21, 1844, there is this entry: "I received an election to the Christian Union a society in college composed of liberal Christians of all denominations. I intend to accept the invite believing it a good association, calculated to the promotion of morality and religious feeling. No narrow mindedness and bigotry creeps in here. Goodness and religion which to my mind, are synonymous terms are recognized wherever found and under whatever name." There are several subsequent entries which mention the union. On May 8, 1844, they adopted a constitution and debated "Is conscience an infallible guide?" On April 3, 1845, there is a notation "Had a glorious meeting of Christian Union. Thirty were initiated." The union had a library, and the observation is made: "Will do good if anyone reads volumes."[51] The entries in the Roberts diary whet a person's appetite; one would like to know more about the Christian Union and its reaction to the climate of opinion prevailing at the College.

Because of its name and purpose, the Benevolent Society should be mentioned.[52] It was organized on November 22, 1814, by twenty-nine members who met in the college chapel and adopted a constitution. Its object was: "To assist indigent young men of promising talents and of good moral character in procuring an education at this college." No person was "to receive pecuniary assistance from this Society, until he shall have been a member of the College at least one term." This latter rule was carried on by the College, with one brief exception,[53] down to the institution of the State of Maine Scholarships in 1930.[54] President Sills was wont to tell the Scholarship Committee, over which he presided, that the College expected a student to have enough money to get through at least his first semester, and then if he did good work the College would do its best to see that he did not have to drop out because of a lack of finances.

A person could become a member of the Benevolent Society by paying a dollar and annual dues of a dollar a year, or a life member by paying twenty dollars at one time or thirty dollars in four years. The society was to receive donations in books, college furniture, and money. A committee was established, including members of the junior and senior classes, which was to make appropriate awards "with the advice and consent of the Executive Government of the College."[55] Here was established the long-standing principle that the faculty should have the controlling voice over the distribution of scholarship funds.

A considerable number of emendations were made to the constitution in September 1817, but the society apparently conducted its affairs in a rather haphazard manner. There is a recorded vote of November 11, 1825, which stated: "That in consequence of the careless manner in which the records have of late been kept, and the danger to which the Society are exposed of having them lost, the Secretary be empowered to commence a new book, and to copy such facts, as the standing committee may think best to preserve."[56] At this same time—why is not stated but apparently to bring more order into the affairs of the society—a committee was appointed to look into the "expediency of corporation." They reported favorably, and the Act of Incorporation was passed by the legislature and approved by the governor on January 24, 1826.[57] On September 6, 1826, the society voted to accept the Act of Corporation and to dissolve itself. The following October a number of students met and formed the "Auxiliary Benevolent Society of Bowdoin College." A strictly student organization, it was to have regular meetings with public exercises in the fall and spring terms "consisting of an oration and poem or dissertation." A committee was appointed "to advise with the board of directors of the incorporated society, whenever requested, relative to the appropriation of disposable property, and the individuals who may need and merit assistance." The new Corporated Benevolent Society also drew up a constitution, which is undated but must have been adopted some months later, as it refers to the Auxiliary Society existing among the students.[58] Brief minutes of both society meetings for 1827 are available, but after that no records have apparently survived of either the "Corporated" or "Auxiliary" Benevolent Society of Bowdoin College.[59]

The Theological Society and Praying Circle supported the temperance movement, and drinking by the students was always considered by the authorities as one of the major immoralities. Professor Cleaveland in 1814 and President Appleton in 1816 delivered and published lectures in favor of the "Suppression of Intemperance." This was well before the temperance movement began to arouse wide attention. Professor Smyth reports that "in the Fall of 1827, a Temperance Society was formed in College, which embraced a large proportion of the students and operated very happily in encouraging habits of sobriety."[60] We know little about this society, but we do have "Records of the Temperance Society of the Maine Medical School at Bowdoin College" covering the period 1829 to 1840, when it simply voted to adjourn sine die. Its chief activity was sponsoring lectures, especially a formal annual lecture. The last entry in the record book in April 1840 is the note: "Had an address by President Woods of Bowdoin College on the subject of Temperance at Mr. Adams' Meeting house."[61] Within the next decades the temperance movement gathered momentum. Temperance pledges were circulated by local churches, and they received their quota of student signatures. In 1854 a group at the College formed a new temperance society. It, however, had a short existence, and the minutes of the last meeting, on October 30, 1855, note that few members were present and the existing officers resigned.[62] Although replacements were elected, they were unable to keep the organization going, and the last mention we have of the society is a call for a regular meeting in the Senior Recitation Room at seven-thirty on February 19, 1856.

In the 1830s and 1840s there was a strong movement of spiritualism in Maine, which had its repercussions in religious circles. Phrenology became a popular subject for lectures. The movement did not pass Bowdoin by. In 1833 a Phrenology Society, or Enigma Society, was formed. They were few in numbers, but they "persevered in their noble undertaking regardless of the ignorant and the sneer of those who were unable to solve the Enigma." By April 1835 the society had eighteen active members, and it was busy recruiting honorary members, who by that time numbered fifteen. It had a library of twenty-six volumes devoted to the study of phrenology, psychology, anatomy, and mental characteristics of men and animals. For some reasons, probably because of scoffing remarks, members of the Peucinian Society were not permitted to join. The last record we have of the Enigma Society is for 1835.[63]

With so many religiously oriented societies at the College, it is not surprising that there were others with different orientations. These were kept under strict surveillance, as is manifest by this notation in the faculty records: "As it is made the duty of the Executive Government to prohibit the meetings of clubs and societies in college, which in their opinion have a tendency unfavorable to science and morality; therefore voted, that the Meetings of the Glee Club, so called, be forbidden."[64] The two old and strong literary societies, the Peucinian going back to 1805, and the Athenaean to 1808, were, one might say, religiously neutral. They were certainly not hostile and accepted the general position accorded religion on the campus. But religious issues did not leave them untouched, as is shown by this entry in Charles Phelps Roberts's diary: "It has been the hobby of the latter (Peucinians) to claim all the religion and decency and bequeath vice and immorality to the Athenaeans. The Athenaeans, however, make their own bargains and are not such dupes as to receive the character which the very good Peucinians would grant willingly to them."[65] The Greek letter fraternities, when they came to be established in the 1840s, were not anti-religious, although as they became stronger they did become a force in transforming customs and practices at the College.

There did exist for a time at the College a most secret organization whose aims seem remote from those of the Praying Circle. This was the "Dole of the Raxian," the name taken from the Hebrew *Raxis*, signifying brotherly love. Its emblem was a skull and crossbones, with the motto "Liberty, Truth, Death to Traitors." Its object was to foster and increase good will, happiness, and brotherly love among its members. Founded in 1826, the society never had a large membership. In 1832 the offices became vacant, but the society was resurrected in 1845. A new constitution was adopted and officers elected. But within a few years interest declined, and the last minutes in its record book are dated August 5, 1859.[66]

In comparing the College of 1825, when he left Brunswick, with the College in 1850, when he returned to teach, Professor Calvin E. Stowe wrote later:

> To me the whole religious atmosphere of the place was as different from what it had been twenty-five years before, as June is from November. It was perfectly delightful to me, and though exceedingly depressed in health, I never had a more uniform religious enjoyment than while I was in Brunswick during the years 1850, '51 and '52. If the religious character of the College gains as much from the years 1850 to '75 as it did from 1825 to '50, it will be all that the most ardent friends of the Lord Jesus can reasonably hope for before the millennium.[67]

What had produced this remarkable change? The able and religiously oriented leadership of Presidents Allen and Woods, building on the foundations and course set by Presidents McKeen and Appleton, no doubt played an important part. They had strong support from members of the faculty and the Boards. In September 1831, the presidency of the College was vacant, pending the decision on the status of President Allen, who had been removed from office as a result of an act passed by the state legislature providing that college presidents should be elected annually and requiring for election or re-election a two-thirds majority of the votes cast by the Boards. The act also ended the practice of regarding diploma fees as presidential perquisites. President Allen had aroused the opposition of some members of the Boards, and as there was no procedure for impeachment, they sought to obtain his removal through an act of the legislature. The Boards voted to abide by the law, but President Allen was not so easily cowed. He moved his family to Newburyport, Massachusetts, and brought suit for the recovery of his salary and fees in the Federal Circuit Court. The suit was tried in Portland in 1833, and in the case of *Allen v. McKeen* (the latter being the treasurer of the college) Justice Story ruled that Allen could recover his fees but not his salary. However, the court went further and ruled that the action of the legislature in respect to the College was unconstitutional, in effect freeing Bowdoin from the control of the legislature and restoring President Allen to his office.[68]

At the time when the president was removed from office, the faculty voted that the person "who officiates at chapel, in view of the amount of duties required should receive additional compensation."[69] Moreover, they taxed themselves to provide this compensation, for it was considered an obligation of the faculty as a whole to carry on the religious services. On September 4, 1832, they voted: "that the services of the chapel and sabbath be assigned to Professor Newman, for which he is to receive a compensation of $200 a year, each member of the Executive Government paying one sixth part of the same; providing, however, that any Professor is at liberty to officiate himself instead of paying his proportion of the aforesaid sum."[70] The Boards must have known of this arrangement when they voted the next day that a committee was "to distribute the duties formerly performed by the President of the College among the other officers of the college and said officers of the college be required to perform such duties as shall be assigned to them respectively by said committee."[71]

A remarkable unity prevailed about Bowdoin being a Christian college and religion being a vital factor in education. In general the students accepted this religious focus of the College;[72] they participated in religious societies and supported their activities. While the students were not always jubilant about required attendance at the many chapel and Sunday services, there was also no great hostility or rebellion. This change in religious atmosphere which Professor Stowe noted at the College was also a reflection of the society of which the College was a part. In spite of oft-repeated aphorisms about "ivy towers" and "the outside world," a college mirrors the climate of opinion and the life of the people from which it draws its clientele and support. There was a general religious revival in the United States in the first half of the nineteenth century, and this was manifest also at Bowdoin. Nothing showed this more than the efforts and interest that went into building a new chapel for the College. It was conceived as being the very center of Bowdoin.

VI.

The Building of the New Chapel

SEVEN YEARS AFTER THE CHAPEL had been moved to higher ground and turned to face Massachusetts Hall, the Boards undertook to replace it. On February 23, 1825, a joint committee of inquiry was appointed "to prepare and present at the next meeting, a plan for a chapel of brick and to ascertain in the most effectual manner for what sum it can be built and report same."[1] The committee apparently did its work promptly, for the next September another joint committee was appointed to apply to the next legislature for a grant to enable the College to erect a new chapel. At the same time a building committee was appointed "with authority to consider and adopt a plan for a new chapel, with suitable public rooms and to determine the site of the same and in case the Legislature shall lend the necessary aid to erect said chapel, the ... committee shall forthwith proceed after giving further notice in two of the public newspapers for proposals to make the necessary arrangements and contracts for erecting said chapel."[2] The Trustees also voted at the same meeting to enlarge the old chapel by adding eighteen feet to the southerly end, and that the second floor of this addition "be finished in proper form as a place for the meeting of this board." A sum not exceeding three hundred dollars was to be appropriated for this purpose. The Overseers did not concur, and the vote was dismissed.[3] Instead another committee was appointed to study the enlargement of the old chapel.

The College petitioned the legislature for funds, first for $9,000 to be paid in three installments, then for $5,000, and President Allen suggested further that the legislature might be asked to grant a township of land which the College could then sell. The president argued: "We need a chapel for various reasons; for convenience of the College and Medical School, for security against fire, for protection of the Library against water. At present the Medical students have no room to attend religious services in the chapel, nor is the chapel sufficiently large for exhibitions. The library is now hardly large enough to contain the books and it is often inundated with water by reason of the junction of the cupola with the descending roof." The legislature, however, could not be persuaded to make a grant.[4]

At the meetings of the Boards in September 1827, the Trustees voted that it "is expedient to erect a building for a chapel and other public uses." The Overseers did not concur, and a conference committee was appointed. This resulted in a more positive proposal to appoint a committee to prepare a plan, make estimates of expense, and choose a site for "a building for a chapel and other public uses and to report at the next meeting of the board."[5] The committee never considered the erection of a one-story building, but like the existing chapel it was to house the library and "a room for the paintings more suited to their character and value and better adapted to a favorable arrangement for exhibition of them." They foresaw the expansion of the student body and the necessity of building new dormitories. "This idea," they stated in their report, "has had its influence upon the opinion of the committee in fixing on the proper site for the Chapel; and their opinion is that it should be erected on a line with the present college buildings or Halls, fronting west, and south of these Halls at a suitable distance, so that when two more Colleges or Halls shall have been erected on the same line and fronting in the same direction, the Chapel shall form the center building."[6] They recommended that the chapel be built of brick according to the plan drawn up by Mr. Melcher, a Brunswick contractor. They did not give an estimate of the cost of the building in their report. This proposal for the site of a new chapel was a change in previous plans, where it had been designed that the dormitories (at that time called colleges) should be in line, while the new chapel was to be built somewhat to the south and west of them, in line with Massachusetts Hall and the old chapel.[7] The problem of building a new chapel and dormitory remained quiescent for the next few years, during which the vexing problem of the control of the state legislature over the College was clarified.[8]

With President Allen restored to office (1833) and the College again carrying on in normal fashion, the need for a new chapel, more space for the library and the gallery of paintings, more lecture and classroom space, a place for the Boards to meet, and a new dormitory was stressed by the Visiting Committee in its 1834 report.[9] Although the membership of the Visiting Committee was changed each year, the committee for 1835 agreed with its predecessor about the need to build a new chapel and recommended that a committee be appointed to report on a plan for the chapel. This recommendation was accepted by the Boards, and a committee consisting of President Allen, the two secretaries of the Boards, and the treasurer of the College was authorized to procure the aid of an architect. On September 7, 1836, the very day the Boards were meeting again, the committee received the plan for a chapel. President Allen drafted the report for the committee, saying they approved the plan but of course had not had time to get estimates. They believed, however, that it would cost from eight to ten thousand dollars. Their report is interesting and noteworthy, for it is more exact about the location of the chapel. They adopted the general recommendation made by the committee in 1828 and concluded:

> They are of opinion, that the chapel should be placed one hundred feet south of Maine Hall, and project equally in front and in rear of Maine Hall, standing with the cupola in front. The next college building for the residence of students, they think, should be placed one hundred feet south of the chapel, when built; and such a new college building would cost about twelve thousand dollars.
> In behalf of the committee.
> Sept. 7, 1836   Wm. Allen, President[10]

This report was accepted by the Boards.[11]

For the next two years nothing was done about carrying forward the building, but the project was not forgotten. In 1833 the Trustees had voted forty dollars for putting a stove in the chapel, which up to then had been unheated.[12] The Overseers did not concur with the vote, but a stove apparently did make its appearance. The library had a stove which was heated during the hour assigned to receipt and delivery of books. The librarian, in his report for 1838, not only called attention to the danger of fire from this stove, but more especially from the stove in the chapel. Here "great fires" were built for morning and evening prayers, and after one was kindled it "was left entirely to itself." This was "tenfold more dangerous" than the stove in the library.[13]

It was clear that something needed to be done about providing more space, and this was one of the first problems tackled by President Woods when he assumed office in September 1839, on the generally welcomed resignation of President Allen. In October 1839 he inserted in the newspapers an invitation for friends of Bowdoin to meet at Brunswick and consult about raising funds for a new building. The meeting was held in the college library on October 30, 1839, and Robert P. Dunlap, Class of 1815, was appointed chairman and Asa Cummings secretary. After "free consultation and an explicit statement of the reasons which render another College edifice necessary," they adopted resolutions expressing the need of a building to contain a chapel, a library, and a gallery of paintings. As "the finances of the College do not admit of an expenditure for this object," an "appeal should be made to the benevolence of the friends of the College." A committee of twelve was appointed to carry forward the project. It consisted of "Gen. Wm. King, Rev. President Woods, Hon. R. P. Dunlap, Robert H. Gardiner, Esq., C. S. Daveis, William Richardson, John D. Kisman, Honorable Daniel Goodenow, Hon. Alfred Johnson, and John Appleton." The list, headed by General King, is the first indication we have of the latter's interest in the erection of the chapel which for a brief time was to bear his name.[14]

A very succinct statement of "Reasons for the erection of a Building to contain a Chapel, a Library room and a Gallery of Paintings" had been drawn up preparatory to the meeting. It stressed that the old chapel was not large enough for the accommodation of students at morning and evening prayers, that exhibitions by students had to be held in one of the village churches, and that the chapel could not be heated without incurring considerable risk of losing the library, which was over the chapel, by fire. The crowding of library shelves and gallery walls was mentioned. Providing a new gallery would also permit the enlarging of the existing cabinet for the exhibition of minerals and shells. Over 2,000 specimens had recently been received, which were now stored in boxes. There must have been some question at the meeting about the advisability of launching on a fundraising project. At least President Woods received such words of caution in several letters written to him. The suspension of specie payments and many bank failures had caused a scare throughout the business community. John Appleton, Class of 1822, wrote him from Bangor: "Those able are unwilling and those willing are unable—from the pressure of the times to render you any more than good wishes."[15] A subscription paper combining portions of the minutes of the friends of Bowdoin meeting and the reasons for the erection of a new chapel was prepared and sent out by members of the committee to various individuals.[16]

The difficult financial situation of the country apparently delayed the solicitation of funds. The Visiting Committee in 1841 stated that the absolute necessity of erecting a chapel was obvious to all. If the number of students should increase as anticipated they would have to "attend prayers in sections or worship in a crowded manner wholly inconsistent with due solemnity and decorum."[17] The college finances, however, were in a precarious state, incurring a $1,000 annual deficit. The Boards appointed a retrenchment committee to consider reductions in salaries and see where instruction could be turned over to tutors and the services of professors dispensed with. The faculty was requested to devote their winter vacation to procuring subscriptions and donations to aid the College, "principally with a view to obtain means for the erection of a building for a chapel, library, and gallery of paintings."[18] The faculty took this assignment seriously and secured subscriptions of about $6,000 to be paid over the next four years. The subscriptions, however, were never all paid, and in the end only a little over $2,000 was realized from the 1842 efforts.[19] In this financial crisis we have the first mention of "Bowdoin Women" coming to the aid of the College. The Visiting Committee in 1842 gallantly reported:

> We are further advised that our female friends have taken measures to aid the same object [raising funds], by appropriating to our use the proceeds of the sale of beautiful articles wrought by their own fair hands, directed by the elegance and taste, for which the sex is distin-

guished. If the amount thus obtained should not fall short of their expectations, it may come up to near a thousand dollars. The ladies fund is to be applied to the erection of the chapel, but may be borrowed for other purposes, until wanted for its proper destination.[20]

The committee estimated the cost of a new chapel and dormitory at $22,000, of which sum $10,000 would be necessary for a new dormitory. As the College was paying out nearly $1,000 a year for room rent, the dormitory could well be financed by borrowing the money at 6 percent.

The Visiting Committee the following year again stressed the need for a new chapel. This time it reported that about $4,000 had been received for the chapel and $500 from female friends.[21] Apparently the sale of fancy work had taken a slump. Litigation about the rights of the College to certain properties entailed to it under the will of James Bowdoin made it difficult to raise funds.[22] It was generally thought that this might be a large sum and would provide all the money needed. President Woods, however, in his report, stressed the need to go ahead with raising funds for a chapel without waiting for the settlement of the Bowdoin estate. The Boards in 1842 and 1843 voted that the Building Committee should go ahead when it was certain that subscriptions sufficient "to cover the expense of such a building, not to exceed fifteen thousand dollars," were at hand.[23] The receipt of $31,696.69 from the negotiated settlement of the Bowdoin estate, while it did not extricate the College from all its financial difficulties, did provide some funds for various projects.[24]

The Building Committee applied to Richard Upjohn of New York, the most renowned church architect of the time, about plans for a chapel. At the end of January or beginning of February 1844, President Woods and Joseph McKeen, the treasurer of the College, were in New York to consult with Upjohn, having a letter of introduction from Robert H. Gardiner, of Gardiner, Maine.[25] Upjohn was troubled by the problem of designing a building "large enough between those great College Halls to appear respectable" and stay within the appropriation voted by the Boards. He was also concerned about the material to be used in its construction and had about "concluded that the building must be of brick." Mr. McKeen noted in a letter of February 9, 1844, to R.H. Gardiner, that "the President appeared to be more reconciled to it [use of brick] than I expected he would be."[26] In this letter McKeen drew a sketch of the design which Upjohn had in mind, and it was subsequently not basically changed. It shows clearly how greatly the need for providing library space affected the plans for a chapel.

On March 9, 1844, President Woods reported in a letter to Charles S. Daveis that good progress had been made "in obtaining a plan for the Chapel while I was in New York...."[27] The committee of the Boards had made it an "invariable condition" that the proposed plans for a chapel "be capable of execution within the sum appropriated by the Trustees." President Woods believed a chapel in either Gothic or Romanesque style could be erected for $15,000. He was "driven, though very reluctantly, to the conclusions, that we cannot afford to build of granite." Upjohn had promised to come to Brunswick sometime in April, and President Woods set about alerting various persons to meet with him. Upjohn, however, was unable to come to Brunswick on schedule. He was a busy man, and as Mr. Gardiner wrote to President Woods: "The truth [is] that Upjohn has more business than he can well accomplish in fact or it is wanted. He is now building 5 new churches and is attending some others and doing sundry small jobs."[28] Upjohn sent along his plans and in August promised to come to Brunswick in a week or two. It was not until the first days of September that he arrived just in time for the meeting of the Boards on September third and fourth. At that time he also consulted with representatives of the First Parish about plans for erecting a new meeting house.[29]

Meanwhile President Woods had continued his efforts to raise money for the chapel. In June 1844 he approached Mr. Amos Lawrence, a philanthropist in Boston, and asked him to get in touch with the Appleton family about calling the new chapel the Appleton Chapel. Mr. Lawrence promised to give $1,000 if the chapel was so named, but he was unable to interest the Appleton family in the project. Professor Alpheus Spring Packard, son-in-law of President Jesse Appleton, was an intermediary in this proposal. The Appletons pointedly gave no reason for their refusal, but Professor Packard and Mr. Lawrence speculated it was because the Appletons were prejudiced against the College in the dispute over the Bowdoin estate, and that Bowdoin "was an institution in which Boston people have no special interest." As Mr. Lawrence wrote to President Woods, he supposed the "Appleton Chapel will have to be cut down."[30]

Having failed to tap the textile fortunes of Boston, Lawrence, and Lowell, President Woods approached General William King about calling the new chapel King Chapel, as many friends of Mr. King desired.[31] He informed King of his failure to enlist support from the Appletons and then went on to say that several of King's friends had "intimated it might be inconvenient for you to make an immediate donation, but that it might meet your views, to leave to the College in the ultimate disposition of your property, such a sum in real estate or otherwise as in connexion with other smaller sums which might be raised in the interval, would authorize the Boards at their next meeting to direct that we should proceed with the chapel according to Upjohn's design, under the name of King's Chapel." Woods felt that "such a promise of future payment would be as satisfactory to the Boards as an immediate bequest, since they can easily command the ready money necessary for erecting the chapel." President Woods in his appeal did not forget Mrs. King, for he wrote: "Mrs. King also I trust would not be displeased to see in Maine another King's Chapel, not inferior to that in which she worshipped in her younger days." President Woods offered to meet with Mr. King some evening and discuss the matter further. Just what General King's reaction was to the appeal at this time is uncertain. On August 21, 1844, President Woods wrote to Robert H. Gardiner urging his attendance at the coming board meetings, "especially with reference of the right arrangement of the part of the Report of that Committee relating to the Chapel." Woods rejoiced that Gardiner was pleased with the plan of the chapel and wrote: "Though we have not as yet obtained any definite provision for the plans necessary to complete it, I do not despair of being able in some way to effect this object."[32]

At the meeting of the Boards in September 1844, the Visiting Committee reported that the appropriation of $15,000 which the Boards had made conditionally for the erection of a new chapel could now be made absolute, thanks to funds from the Bowdoin estate. They went on to say:

> The Building Committee proceeded according to their instructions to procure a plan for the Chapel, and applied for this purpose to Mr. Upjohn of New York, whose reputation as an architect is unrivalled. The Plan furnished by him, and which is exhibited to the Boards, is thought by competent judges, to sustain fully his reputation. The order adopted by him is the Romanesque, which is distinguished from the Gothic, by greater simplicity, and is consequently capable of being executed at less cost. This is the same style as that adopted by him in the "Church of the Pilgrims" which he is now erecting in Brookline, and which has been highly commended. His plan provides for a Chapel 90 ft in length, 28 in breadth, and 56 in height, occupying the central part, and lighted from the second story, for the College Library, and a Gallery for the Paintings in the rear; for two Society libraries in the wings; and for various offices over the side entrances. After careful estimates, it is thought this large edifice may be erected of granite furnished from a neighboring quarry for about $21,000.[33]

The committee felt that the additional $6,000 beyond the $15,000 appropriated by the Boards could easily be raised. It recommended "to expend so much of the appropriation of $15,000 as may be necessary to complete the outside of the building in the course of the present year." The committee went on to propose:

> And in consideration of the valuable services of the Hon. William King, as President of the Convention which formed the constitution of this State, and as its First Governor, in promoting the course of science and learning within the State, and of his high regard for the welfare of the College the Committee recommends that the Chapel when erected, be called and known by the name of
> "King Chapel"[34]

The Boards followed the recommendations of the Visiting Committee, accepting Upjohn's plans for the chapel and directing the Building Committee "to proceed immediately to the erection of the same according to said plans, and to have the outside completed by the first day of September next."[35] They also voted to call the new building "King Chapel," although they as yet had in hand no written statement from Mr. King in regard to a gift. This was in line with the precedent set at the time of the founding of the College, when the Boards gave the name of Bowdoin to the institution and only later received the patronage of James Bowdoin. The Boards were always concerned lest they give the impression they were granting an honor in return for a monetary consideration.

The Building Committee lost no time in starting construction, and Mr. I. R. True of Richmond was soon at work on the foundation of the chapel. By November 11 the foundations were "so far advanced that another week of good weather will enable us to do all the work that is necessary to an early start in the spring."[36]

Meanwhile, Mr. King took his time about completing formal arrangements about his proposed gift of $6,000 to the College. On November 11 and again on November 25, 1844, President Woods wrote Mr. Gardiner asking him to intercede with his friend Mr. Evans to get in touch with General King.[37] "Nothing," President Woods thought, "would be as likely to induce General King to carry his good purposes into immediate effect as a letter from Mr. Evans, such as was talked of between us, when I was recently at Gardiner. There is danger that otherwise he may put off making the arrangement until it will be too late." No record is at hand of intervention by Mr. Evans, but in early June 1845, President Woods again visited General King "and found that he had made up his mind to bring the matter [of a gift] to a definite settlement at the time of the laying of the corner stone."[38] In order to do this more effectively, King wanted the laying of the cornerstone put off a few weeks to give him time to sell some of his townships so that he could "lay down the money on the corner stone." "If he should fail to make the sale he would set a portion to be deeded the College on that occasion." At all events, President Woods reported, "he will take pains to secure to the College some five or six thousand dollars before that time, to be announced at the ceremony of laying the corner stone." The cornerstone laying was accordingly delayed until July 16, 1845. The exact date on which General King did get around to acting is uncertain, for the letter promising a gift is undated. However, in his address at the cornerstone laying, the Honorable Charles S. Daveis publicly thanked General King on behalf of the Trustees and Overseers for the disposition "that you have this day given" to aid the College in completing the chapel.[39]

General King wrote — in line with the original proposal made to him by President Woods:

To the President and Trustees of Bowdoin College
Gentlemen —
　　Having understood that the sum appropriated by the Boards for the new College Chapel is not sufficient to finish it, and being desirous that this noble work should not be unnecessarily delayed for want of means, therewith enclose to you for this object my security for the sum of six thousand dollars.

　　The interest I feel in the cause of education in general, and especially in the welfare of Bowdoin College, having been connected with its affairs for more than forty years, leads me to embrace the present occasion to congratulate you, Gentlemen, upon the present good condition of the College, and its animating prospects.

　　Much has already been done by it to qualify our young men for the different departments of the public service, and there is reason to hope, that with the higher advantages it will possess when the improvements now in progress are completed still more will be accomplished by it for the best interests of the State.
　　　　　　　　　　With Respects and esteem
　　　　　　　　　　Your friend
　　　　　　　　　　William King

　　The original of this letter is in Special Collections in the Hawthorne-Longfellow Library at the College, and there is a copy of it, again undated, in the Trustee Records of September 3, 1845.[40] The Boards placed the letter on file and voted:

That the Trustees and Overseers of Bowdoin College return their thanks to the Hon. William King for the liberal donation in aid of the erection of the chapel called by his name. That they accept the same and will proceed to complete the chapel out of the resources of the college, to be reimbursed by the avails of the donation before referred to.[41]

　　President Woods applied to the Masonic lodge in Brunswick to make arrangements for laying, "according to Masonic Form," the cornerstone of the new chapel. On June 28, 1845, the lodge acceded to this invitation and appointed a committee of three, Robert P. Dunlap, Abner B. Thompson, and Isaac Lincoln, to make the necessary preliminary arrangements. It was further voted to request the grand master to cause a "Grand Lodge to be held in Brunswick at such time" as the College might designate for the laying of the corner. A committee of five was named to receive such Masonic groups as would attend the Grand Lodge and participate in the ceremonies. It was arranged that Mr. Dunlap would actually perform the ceremony.[42]

　　The cornerstone laying was designed to be a gala occasion. The faculty gave an adjournment to the senior class on the day before the cornerstone laying so that they could erect a triumphal arch decorated with evergreen on the walk leading from the chapel to the front road. That evening the students staged an informal celebration, marching under the triumphal arch to the site of the new chapel. Here Charles Phelps Roberts, a senior, delivered a short speech and recited a poem beginning:

> Till you fix the corner stone,
> It won't erect itself alone

"After a great deal of tumult, hilarity and dancing the crowd dispersed to their separate abodes in expectation of the great day of the laying of the cornerstone."[43]

On the morning of July 16, 1845, a steamboat brought many Masons and others from Portland to the wharf in Maquoit Bay. It was a beautiful warm day. At about two-thirty the Masons formed their procession at the local Masonic Hall and marched to the campus. Here they were joined by President Woods and other college officers, and the procession marched to the chapel. The students led the way as escorts, followed by the president and other college officials; then came the Trustees and higher dignitaries of the Masonic Order, followed by the Portland Brass Band, the Grand Lodge of Maine, the Boston Brigade Band, the Knights Templar of Boston, the Brunswick Band, and last of all the Brunswick lodge. The Masons were all in full regalia and carried numerous banners. Staging had been built and "many spectators were seated on the building stones which were heaped about." Some of the Knights Templar had managed to bring along a jug with "wine of refreshment" which they kept beneath the seats and did not fail "to partake of."[44]

President Woods began the ceremonies by reading Psalm 122: "I was glad when they said unto me...," and then made some opening remarks. There followed a prayer by Rev. Mr. Dwight of Portland, after which President Woods "alluded briefly to the munificence of the distinguished gentleman" who had enabled the College to erect the chapel. According to the *Maine Democrat*, he then spoke of the circumstances under which the Ancient Order of Masons had been invited to lay the cornerstone, observing in substance,

> That in the old world, for many centuries of the Christian era, all the great edifices, civil and ecclesiastical, and especially the great Gothic Cathedrals, have been devised and erected, from base to spire, by the ancient fraternity of free-masons; and that in our times and country the corner stones of all our great national Monuments, from the Capitol at Washington downwards, had been laid by their hands; and that in compliance with this long established custom and out of regard to the wishes of some of our patrons and friends, an invitation had been extended to the Grand Lodge in this State to lay the Corner

Stone of King Chapel; that this invitation had been promptly and courteously accepted by the Grand Lodge, and that we were happy on this occasion to commit this work, as we then did, to the hands of those to whom of right and by custom it belonged.[45]

There is no need to examine critically the historical accuracy of President Woods's statement. No doubt it was "out of regard to the wishes of some friends and donors" that the Masons were invited to take over the ceremonies. General King had been the first grand master of the lodge in Maine and ex-Governor Dunlap, who was a member of the building committee, was a member of the Brunswick lodge, as were many other local friends of the College.

"After various Masonic formalities, the Most Worshipful Grand Master John T. Paine...assisted by ex-Governor Dunlap proceeded to lay the Corner Stone." In the small tin box nineteen inches long that was encased in the cornerstone, there was placed a Bible, the Constitutions of the United States and the State of Maine, the laws of Bowdoin College, a triennial catalogue, a current catalogue, catalogues of the Athenian and Peucinian Societies, and two silver plates. On one of the plates was inscribed in Latin the names of the president and the professors, the date, and other particulars as to the edifice, on the other a Masonic Memorial. "Corn, wine, and oil were poured upon the stone, the Grand Master repeating, — Corn, Wine, and Oil, emblematical of Health, Plenty, and Peace—and may the all-bounteous author of Nature bless the inhabitants of this place, with all the comforts of life—assist in the erection and completion of this building, protect the workmen against any accident, and long preserve this structure from decay, and grant us all a needed supply [of] the Corn of Nourishment, the Wine of Refreshment, and the Oil of Joy." The square was then applied in all directions, and a Masonic hymn sung.[46] The cornerstone was laid, and the Honorable Charles S. Daveis, a member of Bowdoin's second class and an influential leading member of the Board of Trustees, then gave a long flowery oration on the history of the College, devoting a good part of it to a description of Gothic and Romanesque architecture and thanking General King for his generosity.[47]

The day was hot, the ceremony drawn out, and it is not surprising that students wandered off to inspect the wax statuary exhibit which was showing in Brunswick for a week. Finally, at about six o'clock, the events were over except for the final processional exit. The steamer was supposed to return to Portland at five o'clock, but by the time the passengers arrived "the fog was so dense that the boat could not leave, to the great disappointment of the passengers."[48]

The erection of the chapel went well during the next year.[49] The granite was obtained from a local quarry, and masons from New York did the work. The Visiting Committee, in September 1846, reported that they were pleased with the progress that had been made but noted that an additional $10,000 would be necessary to finish the interior. Faced by the need for more money, the Boards, nevertheless, voted "that the outside of King Chapel be completed forthwith including doors, a gutter agreeable to the plan of Richard Upjohn, but not including the windows and excepting the towers above the tops of windows, but be protected from the weather and that the sum of $3,650 in addition to the $21,000 already appropriated be appropriated for the above."[50] They further authorized the president and the Committee of Finance to proceed to obtain further funds for the completion of the chapel and the use of the College. Realizing that there would still be money needed to complete the chapel, the Boards authorized the Building Committee "to expend a sum not exceeding $10,000 in addition to the sums already appropriated [$24,650] in completion of King Chapel, provided the same can be procured from other sources than the present college property."[51]

President Woods had anticipated the need of a fund drive and had asked Professor Upham to visit Boston and certain other places to see if funds could be raised. On August 1, 1846, the latter reported on his efforts:

> I am sorry to say I have obtained nothing. But, I think I have ascertained this, that the Congregational Denomination would be found ready as a body to meet all the reasonable demands of the College, beginning with the sum of fifty thousand dollars, if they felt a little more confident as to its denominational position. The Baptists a few years since made an effort to raise 50,000 Dollars for Waterville College, the Congregationalists of Maine would cheerfully, I think, make a similar effort and would be likely to succeed in it, if they could be made to see that the responsibility of sustaining Bowdoin College rests upon them, much in the same way and for the same reasons that the responsibility of sustaining Waterville College rests upon the Baptists. I have no doubt myself that a majority of both Boards, differing as they conscientiously do in religious sentiments, have come to the conclusion that under the force of circumstances now apparently uncontrollable, Bowdoin College, in a few years, will take the position of the Congregational College of Maine, in the same sense and on the general principles that Waterville is known as the College of the Baptists of Maine, as Yale and Trinity are known respectively as the College of the Episcopalians [Trinity] and Congregationalists [Yale] of Connecticut and Harvard is known as the College or University of the Unitarians of Massachusetts. I suppose that they believe such is the tendency of things; and that they are ready to acquiesce in it, by means of gradual and conciliatory movements. Perhaps I am mistaken. But if such is really the feeling of both Boards, as I suppose it is, and if this feeling can be a little more definitely ascertained and authenticated so as to be laid before some of the leading men in the denomination, I suppose that the

money can be raised. And at present I do not know where else to look for it. At your suggestion I have thus laid the subject before you in writing, that you might consider of it and lay it before some members of the Boards. If nothing can be done, I hope no offence will be given, as I am certain that none is intended.[52]

This letter has been quoted at length, for there is no other document which explains so well the origin and intent of the "Declaration" on Bowdoin's relation to Congregationalism.

With the authorization of the Boards to proceed with the solicitation of funds, a statement was drawn up and submitted to various members of the Boards for their reaction to it. This paper did not meet with general acceptance and was particularly objected to by George Evans, Class of 1815, of Gardiner, long an Overseer of the College and recently made a Trustee. Professor Upham went up to see him and requested him to alter the paper so as to make it unobjectionable. On the basis of the former draft, Evans sketched out a statement and took it to Robert H. Gardiner, another Trustee, who made several alterations. Both men returned to Mr. Evans's office and "conversed with [Professor Upham] freely and fully upon the whole subject." One of Evans's chief objections to the original draft was not that it gave control of the College "to the Orthodox Congregationalists; but because it gave that control expressly, for the consideration of fifty thousand dollars to be contributed by the denomination to the college." He "objected to the idea of a bargain or contract which he deemed inadmissable, but proposed to accomplish precisely the same object by means of a Declaration or expression of opinion binding in honor the parties and effectually securing the end desired." Professor Upham, who had spent a whole Saturday discussing the proposed changes with Mr. Gardiner and Mr. Evans, was in the end quite satisfied with the suggested alterations. The following Monday Mr. Evans drew up a sketch of what he proposed to say and showed it to Mr. Gardiner, who again made a few alterations. A clear copy was then made by Mr. Evans of the statement.[53] It soon came to be known as the Declaration and was circulated to the Trustees and Overseers. It was signed by eleven of the Trustees, three refusing, and by thirty-four Overseers.[54] The text of the statement reads as follows:

DECLARATION

Whereas, It has been deemed desirable by some of the friends of Bowdoin College that its position in relation to the religious instruction which shall be given in the college, and in regard to the denominational character which it shall profess, should be clearly understood, and also that some reasonable assurance of its future policy should be furnished to those who are disposed to contribute to its support: now, the undersigned, members of the trustees and overseers of the college, do hereby declare, —

First, That they regard it as a permanent principle in the administration of the college that science and literature are not to be separated from morals and religion. Against such a separation the charter of the college has guarded, by requiring that its funds shall be appropriated, not only for improvement in the "liberal arts and sciences," but also in "such a manner as shall most effectually promote virtue and piety."

Second, That they are of opinion this object can be most fully accomplished, and at the same time the pecuniary ability of the college increased, by a known and established denominational character and position, whereby the college may be entitled to appeal for support to some particular portion of the community, by whom the corresponding obligation to afford it is recognized.

Third, That although there is nothing expressly said in the college charter which requires it to have any particular denominational position; yet, from its foundation, it has been and still is of the Orthodox Congregational denomination, as indicated by the state of the religious community in Maine when the college was established, by the religious instruction which has heretofore been given, and by the opinions of its former and present presidents, and of a large portion of those who have been engaged in its government and instruction.

Fourth, That they consider any attempt to modify or change the character which it has so long maintained, unwise and inexpedient, and they have no purpose or expectation of making such an attempt.

Fifth, That in their opinion the boards of trustees and overseers and the academic Faculty should be composed of those who are competent and willing to perform their respective duties in a manner not to impair or restrain, or in any degree conflict with the moral and religious instruction which is designed to be given in the college, in harmony with its denominational character as herein defined, care being taken that such instruction be given by officers of that religious faith.

Sixth, That although no purpose or expectation is entertained of attempting any change in the character of the college in the foregoing particulars, yet if, in the progress of opinions and events, it shall result that the "liberal arts and sciences, virtue and piety," can be more successfully advanced by some modification or changes, nothing herein expressed is to be understood as forbidding the trustees and overseers of that day from adopting such measures as shall best promote the ends of the college, and the advancement of religion and knowledge, a proper regard being always had to the circumstances and motives which induced this Declaration.

Seventh, The undersigned make this Declaration as a basis of action, in the expectation and hope that it will secure the highest results of literature and piety; and that it will not only furnish a basis for pecuniary aid, but will also effect a conciliation of different views and interests, and thus present the college in the most favorable and satisfactory light before the public.

President Woods was pleased with the Declaration and evaluated it as follows:

> It seems to me all that could be asked by the orthodox friends of the College, and as I hear is quite satisfactory to them. It leaves the Boards as they are and only provides that the religious instruction of the College should be in accordance with the sentiments of the Orthodox Congregationalists, which is certainly best in the present state of things. Even in this particular I feel assured from what I see of the disposition of many of the Overseers and of the present officers of the College, there will be nothing intolerant or exclusive. On the contrary I shall expect to see and think I can see already, in some degree, a relaxation of the jealous and bitter spirit of sect; just as far as the question of the denominational position of the College is settled. I can give you some evidences of this which will not be unpleasant to you when I see you.[55]

Armed with this Declaration, Professor Upham, with the aid of Reverend John Wallace Ellingwood from Bath, an Overseer, went out to solicit funds. The latter was particularly entrusted with the task of collecting what he could from the subscriptions raised in 1842. These early subscriptions became so blended together with those of 1846 that it became impossible to separate them, "the subscriptions of 1846 having been made with the understanding that the payments of '42 were to be allowed as payments in part of their subscriptions in 1846." The trustees, on July 1, 1852, directed that an alphabetical list of all donors with their titles and places of residence be made. A handsomely bound copy of this report shows that Professor Upham led the subscribers with a gift of $6,062.50, followed by Mrs. Amos Lawrence with $6,000.00 and Mrs. Susan Collins with $5,000.00.[56] There was a further subscription of $3,100.00 and twelve of $1,000.00 or slightly better. Much of the money, however, came from small donors, many from Massachusetts. In all about $70,000 was raised, which included $5,725.00 given specifically for the chapel, $8,000.00 for the Education Fund, and $17,435.00 for the establishment of a professorship in natural and revealed religion. Although no record is available of the denominational affiliation of the donors, it is clear that they were mostly Congregationalists. This important acquisition of funds rescued the College from disaster. It provided money for the payment of salaries, the completion of the chapel, the payment of loans contracted for the erection of Appleton Hall (in 1843 at a cost of $9,000),[57] and the establishment of the Collins Professorship of Natural and Revealed Religion, Bowdoin's first endowed professorship.

While the Declaration was beyond doubt of real significance in raising funds for the College, it brought bitter controversy between the Board of Trustees and the Overseers. The former was composed of a good number of non-orthodox Congregationalists, largely of Unitarian persuasion, while the Overseers had a substantial majority of orthodox Congregationalists. If the College was to be truly Congregational, in line with the spirit of the Declaration, it was held by the Overseers that both boards should have a majority of orthodox Congregationalists.[58] A majority of the Trustees held to the contrary. Three Trustees had refused to sign the Declaration, and a number of the thirteen who did, maintained they had never bound themselves to such an extent. They held that "in the choice of president or theological professor, they were, as individual signers of the paper, under obligation to vote for an orthodox Congregationalist. Beyond this, and especially in filling their own vacancies, they felt at liberty to take such a course as would, according to their best judgement at the time, be most for the interests of the college."[59] Some of the Trustees were also concerned that there would be an attempt to restrict appointments of the faculty to orthodox Congregationalists. They considered themselves the exponents of liberalism. A crisis arose when the Trustees elected new members and the Overseers refused to concur; the seats on the Board of Trustees remained vacant. Finally, in 1857, the Boards appointed a conference committee consisting of five trustees and seven overseers to study the matter; this committee met in the vestry of the Congregational church in Brunswick on November 24, 1857. The meeting resulted in the "removal of some misunderstandings between the two Boards and...the general influence of the discussions had been good."[60] A step towards the ending of the crisis had already been taken when in 1855 the Trustees elected Josiah Pierce, Class of 1818, an orthodox Baptist lawyer and an Overseer since 1831, as a member and he was approved by the Overseers. Two orthodox Congregational clergymen were elected in 1859, and the subsequent elections of two prominent laymen in 1860, William Pitt Fessenden and James Ware Bradbury, stabilized the situation.[61]

With funds at hand, work on the chapel was carried forward. At Commencement in 1847 the Visiting Committee could report that the exterior of the chapel, with the exception of glazing and the spires, was completed.[62] The imminent use of the new building raised the problem of what to do with the old chapel. In the spring of 1847 the woodshed had been set on fire, and the Visiting Committee, in view of the fact that "a taste for material illuminations seems to be on the increase among the students," recommended offering the old chapel to the medical faculty on condition that they remove it from its present location where it endangered the safety of other buildings.[63] This the Boards did by formal vote on August 31, 1847, with the proviso that if the medical school did not want the old building, it should be sold and removed from the college grounds.

Since the medical school refused the offer, the old chapel was sold and removed.[64]

The eastern end of the chapel building was the first to be completed, and by Commencement of 1848 the library had been moved into it. That year the Trustees met for the first time in the new library. The south wing was also far enough along to be used as a temporary chapel. By 1849 the north wing was finished sufficiently to be used as a lecture room for the professor of mathematics and as a picture gallery. A quantity of black walnut lumber had been obtained at favorable terms for the finishing of the chapel and was now seasoning.[65]

At Commencement in 1850 the Boards authorized the Building Committee to finish the chapel from money already appropriated and from donations. They further voted that the east end of the chapel, being used as its library, should "be called Banister Hall in honor of Hon. Wm. B. Banister, a distinguished citizen of Newburyport—whose friendship and influence have been kindly and effectually exercised in behalf of the College."[66] The family, particularly his daughter Mrs. Sarah W. Hale, had contributed generously to the funds of the College. The sum of $1,000 having been donated for the completion of the chapel by Mr. Theophilus W. Walker, a highly respected merchant of Boston "who associates his domestic and filial remembrances with his friendship for the College," the Boards authorized that "the room containing paintings shall be known as the Walker Building in commemoration of the name and virtue of the departed mother of the Donor."[67] Subsequent gifts from the family led to the erection of the beautiful Walker Art Building at the College.

The spires of the building were now completed and the outside substantially finished. One troublesome problem remained. Upjohn had recommended the use of tin for the roof. It had been used successfully in Canada, but local workers were not used to working with this medium. The roof leaked badly, and even after repeated attempts to repair it the Visiting Committee in 1855 reported that the roof needed to be painted as there were small leaks.[68]

Decorating the interior of the chapel caused much concern. Here the Building Committee got involved in dicussions with a Mr. Gervase Wheeler of New York in regard to decorating the library and the chapel. An agreement was made with him to submit designs, and the library was decorated under his direction. His proposals for the chapel were, however, not accepted, and the College broke relations with him. It is clear that he and Mr. Upjohn were at odds. In July 1851 Mr. Upjohn drew up designs for the interior of the chapel and invited Samuel Melcher of Brunswick, who was to do the interior work, to come to New York so he could show the plans to him. It was first proposed that the carving of some of the decorative pieces be done by men in New York City, but in the end they were done more simply and at much less cost locally.[69]

Lack of available funds had been responsible for the delay in chapel construction, largely because the College received none of the principal or interest from the promised gift of $6,000 from General King. As early as July 1847, although King was still in relatively good health, President Woods and Mr. Upham were concerned about the safety of King's donation and sought to obtain security for the same. They were assured by the Reverend John W. Ellingwood of Bath, who made inquiries, that King's note was "perfectly safe for years to come, and that if his affairs were now to be wound up, he would pay every debt and leave fifty thousand dollars."[70] This optimistic report of King's financial strength did not allay President Wood's fears. In July 1850, after King's mental capacities had begun to fail, Woods wrote the following letter, to whom is not clear, since it is headed only "My dear Sir":

> As the note of General King to the College has now become due; and as you have been intimately connected as a friend of the family, in the recent arrangements for the settling of his estate, you are hereby requested to join the Treasurer of the College in taking such immediate steps as may be necessary both to serve the interest of the College, and at the same time to meet the views and interests of the respected family of the honored donors.[71]

Nothing is known of what became of this initiative, but it is clear President Woods was attempting to safeguard the interests of the College. The recent litigation over the settlement of the Bowdoin estate had not been well received by many, and in attempts to secure the King bequest the College proceeded very circumspectly.[72] In March 1852 the commission which was appointed to settle the King estate decided against the College's claims, leaving it, as President Woods wrote to Mr. Upjohn, "eight thousand dollars minus of the sum [gift plus interest] which we had counted upon for completing the chapel. This adverse decision has thrown us into the greatest embarrassment and it still remains undecided whether we shall proceed to contest in the higher courts, or shall abandon the claim and seek elsewhere for the necessary means of finishing our work. If unsuccessful in either of these efforts we may be obliged to suspend the work again before finishing."[73]

Members of the King family were already considering a way out of the impasse. On March 26, 1852, James G. King, a nephew, wrote to his aunt, Mrs. Porter, in Camden:

> My dear aunt,
> I duly received your favor of 8th ins. and its contents have been read with great interest. I think it is due to my Brothers and myself, as well as to your impressive and affectionate appeal to us—to say, in

reply, that we do not arrive, at the same conclusion, as yourself in regard to the subject presented to us.

The name of King, was worthily given to a prominent Building of Bowdoin College, of which Uncle William was an early, constant, and influential friend—and would, if his mind had been preserved, have proved a munificent Patron. If the College, being disappointed, in receiving his money should be willing to withdraw his name, and substitute that, of another, who would pay for the distinction—it would be quite clear, that it was not intended to confer an honor—but to offer an equivalent for his gift.

We, who cannot but feel pride, in the name and character of Uncle William—would not desire his name should be continued, to this Building under such circumstances—as we think that we should do it, no honor, if we would consent to pay for its being retained.

What, however, we do desire, and have proposed is to appropriate whatever may be necessary to insure the comfort and well being, in all respects, of our uncle and aunt, at Bath—for the remainder of their troubled days—so that, in any event, in addition to their already aggravated sorrows, that, of dependence upon strangers, may be spared to them.[74]

On June 17, 1852, General King died. He was "nearly 85 years old and had been failing outwardly about a fortnight, the light within had long been extinguished." The funeral was held in Bath on the nineteenth, attended by many public personages and representatives of the College. "Flags and black drapery ornamented the custom house and a great many other buildings and many lines with like embellishments were stretched across the streets." "Minute guns were fired whilst the procession moved and Masonic rites were performed at the grave."[75] By the time of his death the commissioner in charge of his estate had notified the College that no funds were available and had rejected the claims of the College on the estate. The college authorities were still undecided as to whether they should try to collect through the courts.[76]

The matter of the King bequest was, however, settled without resort to the courts when Mrs. King wrote the following letter:

To Leonard Woods D.D.
President of Bowdoin College

Sir:
    Entertaining the best wishes for the prosperity of Bowdoin College and believing were my late husband alive, and in full possession of his faculties, it would be his earnest desire to have such measures adopted, as would relieve the college from pecuniary embarrassment arising from the outlay on the chapel, I express it as my desire the name of King be withdrawn from the Chapel and that of some future generous Donor, or the name he may suggest, be substituted; pro-

vided the $4,000 are not raised in the manner now contemplated.
Respectfully
Anna N. King

We approve of the above request
   C.W. King
   C.N. Porter
   E.T. Bridge
   A.F.K. Bridge[77]

Professor Upham was confident that he could easily obtain $4,000 if the donor be permitted to name the chapel. The Visiting Committee, however, objected to putting the chapel "up for auction," and the Boards, following their recommendation in the meeting on August 31, 1852, voted:

> That the proposal of the widow and only son and other relations of the late William King that the name of King Chapel be no longer appropriated to that building, be acceded to, and that the Chapel remain without any other designation until the further order of the Boards, and that the Treasurer of the College be authorized to deliver up the note of the late William King for the sum of six thousand dollars, the estate being insufficient to pay the same and to afford a competent support for the widow and to pay all other debts.[78]

Work on finishing the interior of the Chapel proceeded slowly. At first it was thought the dedication could be held in September 1854, on the old commencement day. November first was then suggested, which elicited the observation of Charles S. Daveis of the Board of Trustees, who was scheduled to give the dedicatory address, that this was "the most Catholic day in the calendar." For "many reasons" President Woods thought it best to postpone the dedication. After consultation with Daveis it was decided in May that the dedication would be held on Thursday, June 7, 1855; it had to be a Thursday because the train from Portland ran only on alternate days.[79]

The Committee of Arrangements consisted of President Woods, John S.C. Abbott, William Smyth, and Rev. George Adams. Invitations were sent to a long list of distinguished citizens. In spite of threatening weather, many guests arrived on the morning train. At a little after ten o'clock the procession moved from the library to the Chapel proper which "was well filled, though by no means uncomfortably crowded." The Reverend Dr. George Adams of the First Parish Church in Brunswick opened the services by reading appropriate passages of scripture and offering a prayer. A hymn was then sung by the choir from First Parish, whereupon President Woods made timely remarks and then "proceeded to dedicate the house to 'Him without whom they labor in vain who build it,' in a peculiarly fervent and appropriate prayer." Professor Roswell D. Hitchcock, Collins Professor of Natural and Revealed Religion at the College, then preached a long dedicatory sermon on Colossians 2:3: "In whom are hid all the treasures of wisdom and knowledge." He made reference to the three main purposes for which the building was erected. "In its Gallery of Paintings, it proclaims the legitimacy of Art; in its Library, the worth of knowledge; in this grave and lofty room, with its glowing windows and its starry roof, it proclaims the dignity of a rapt and reverent Communion with God." He went on to speak of the "evangelical doctrines in relation to God—to Nature—and to man, which are drawn from those treasures of wisdom and knowledge to which the text refers." The eloquent sermon apparently made a great impression. The two-hour ceremony was concluded by a prayer by the Reverend Dr. Dwight of Portland. In the afternoon, in spite of heavy rain, a large audience attended the address by Charles E. Daveis on the history of the College, before a meeting of the Maine Historical Society. Mr. Daveis, being in feeble health, made only a few introductory remarks and then handed his manuscript to Rev. John S.C. Abbott, who read the long address. The *Brunswick Telegraph* concluded its account of the proceedings with the statement: "To the friends of the College and of education generally in this state, the occasion was a memorable one, as marking the erection of a building in which generations yet unborn will doubtless worship, and explore the 'treasures of wisdom and knowledge.'"[80]

The Chapel had been a long time in planning and building, largely because of the difficulty in raising the necessary funds. A building which was first estimated to cost $15,000 soon required $21,000, and in the end cost $46,791.22. On July 28, 1855, when the Building Committee made its final requested report, $2,173.22 of this sum remained uncovered by either appropriation or donation.[81] This led the Boards to vote:

> Whereas the accounts for the expenditures on the chapel have been duly examined, allowed and approved by the proper committees: Therefore, however objectionable the practice of spending more for any object than the sum appropriated, yet under the circumstances of the case that the Treasurer be authorized to credit the chapel account with the balance due therefrom of $2,173.20 and that he charge the same to the general funds of the college.[82]

There was no mention of thanks being extended to the Building Committee.

Although the Chapel was dedicated, it was not completely finished. During the following year the room over the library was fitted out with chairs, settees, and carpet at a cost of $273, and the Boards were requested to make a further appropriation of $70.[83] This room was to be used as a meeting place for the Overseers, but it was soon found to be inconvenient. It was open to all sounds from the Chapel, the stairs were too steep, and there was not enough light. The Visiting Committee recommended further changes and $100 was appropriated.[84] There were two furnaces in the cellar of the Chapel used to heat different parts of the building. Long stove pipes to apertures in the walls and the presence of much combustible material constituted a fire hazard. The Visiting Committee in 1858 recommended converting the furnaces to the use of coal. Nothing was done at once, but in 1860 and 1861 the Boards appropriated money for a new furnace to heat the Chapel and the library. The College was beginning to convert to the use of coal and in 1861 built a coal house for the deposit of coal near the depot at a cost of $90. Formerly what coal had been used was stored in the cellar of Massachusetts Hall.[85] The expense of heating the Chapel seemed large during the austerity of the Civil War, and the Boards voted that in the cold weather when a fire was needed the chapel services were to be held elsewhere.[86] In 1868 the Boards voted $250 for a new furnace to warm the library. But there were still difficulties. In 1870 the Boards voted $50 for the repair of the chapel chimney, as well as for a stove for the college library.[87]

Along with the heating of the Chapel, the stopping of leaks in the roof was a continuing problem in the following years. In 1857 the Visiting Committee reported the Chapel was made tight. Three years later they found the repairs on the roof of the south wing were not properly made and there was need for repairs also on the north wing. In 1861, in addition to reporting on the need of pointing up the mortar on the east end of the Chapel, they found such bad leaks in the library roof that it was necessary to remove books from the shelves in every storm. A year later they found the leaks over the library nearly all stopped.[88] In 1863 the Visiting Committee reported the south wing "not yet made tight" and the carpet in the Chapel worn out. The Boards promptly voted $130 for repair of the roof of the south wing and $120 for a new carpet. But the leaks were not stopped, and in 1865 the Boards voted $200 for shingling the south wing. In 1869 the upper side windows were found to leak so badly in driving storms that the water ran down over some of the pictures on the walls. This time the Visiting Committee thought that an appropriation of only $20 would "remove the trouble."[89] Leaks in Brunswick roofs were not a rare phenomenon and were taken in stride.

The chapel building had from the beginning been meant to serve multiple purposes. In 1849 the north wing had begun to be used as the art gallery, and a year later it had been named the Walker Gallery.[90] The Boards had been concerned about the paintings and in 1847 had appropriated $200 to obtain the service of a competent artist "to make examination of the paintings and take measures to preserve and guard them from injury." They also voted to authorize the president to exchange such paintings as in the opinion of the faculty were unsuited for public exhibition for other works of art of worth and merit. They took steps to see if the families of donors would object to the sale. In 1850 the Boards authorized the sale of those pictures which in the judgment of the president and Robert H. Gardiner were unsuitable for hanging. Money from the sale was to be used to pay for cleaning the paintings, and if any money was left over, for the purchase of more pictures.[91] By 1852 the Visiting Committee could report that $829.50 had been paid so far for cleaning the pictures, and that the pictures bequeathed by James Bowdoin had all been cleaned. They recommended that certain pictures should be sold to pay for the expenses incurred. Three paintings which still remained in Boston were the prime candidates for sale. One was *L A and His Daughter,* a "picture of no merit of any kind and only fit for a brothel." The other two were a picture of nymphs bathing and a copy of Titian's *Danae and the Golden Shower.* They felt that the last two had considerable merit as works of art, and they wrote: "In Europe where the eye has been long familiar to the exhibition of naked statues little hesitation would be made to admitting them into respectable galleries, but the *Danae* is certainly designed to excite improper ideas, and objects which might be viewed with impunity by persons of mature age might have bad effects upon youth by exciting life passions yet dormant." They recommended that the president be left to deal with the problem. In 1857 the Visiting Committee was able to report that the pictures had been cleaned and brightened and that the collection made a good impression and was "one of the best in the country."[92]

The long sought place to display the art collection was not a success. In 1884 the Visiting Committee reported: "The Picture Gallery is a misnomer. It is simply a store room for paintings, and not a safe one at that." The leakage about the windows had already injured some of the pictures, and there seemed to be no way of preventing this. This harsh verdict was affirmed by the Visiting Committee the following year.[93]

As is often the case, libraries are no sooner built than they are found cramped for space, and this was true of the new library. The Visiting Committee in 1856 reported that while the library could make do that year, something would have to be done the next. They recommended that the entry between the library in the east end of the building and the picture gallery in the north wing be fitted out for the expansion of the library. It took some time to accomplish this, and it was not until 1861 that the Visiting Committee noted that the "new room in [the] north wing has been furnished in neat style and will furnish accommodation for increase of the library for some years to come." A new furnace to warm this addition still had to be supplied, and this was acquired the next year. It did not solve the heating problem, however, and later changes were necessary.[94]

Such repairs and alterations are more or less to be expected in a new building and are made currently. There was one anticipated completion which took much longer. The six panels on each of the side walls were to be filled with appropriate paintings. As the Visiting Committee noted in 1858: "It is expected and was originally intended that they be filled by private munificence."⁹⁵ The project indeed started promptly and well. In the first year after the Chapel was dedicated, two panels were completed. They were painted by Mr. Mueller, a German artist from New York, after cartoons by Raphael. The first panel on the north side and immediately to the right of the lectern represents the Apostle Paul preaching on Mars Hill. It was the gift of Mr. Jared Sparks, president of Harvard University, and Mrs. Sparks. The next panel represents the miracle of the lame man healed by Peter and John at the beautiful gate of the temple. It was the gift of the Honorable Bellamy Storer of the class of 1813, and later the recipient of an honorary degree from the College.⁹⁶ He was a lawyer who for many years served as a Superior Court judge in Ohio and taught at the Cincinnati Law School. The third panel to be filled is the fifth on the north side and represents the *Adoration of the Magi*. It was also painted by Mueller after a painting by Peter Cornelius (1783-1867), a founder of the Duesseldorf School, in the Ludwigskirche in Munich. It was apparently painted in 1857-1858, for the Visiting Committee in 1858 noted in respect to this painting that the College "was indebted to generous liberality of a graduate of the college, whose name, at his own express request, has not been made known to us, and is not to be made public."⁹⁷ This donor was Harrison Otis Apthorp, Class of 1829, who provided $250 for the painting of the picture but steadfastly insisted that his anonymity be maintained.⁹⁸ He offered also to contribute if an effort were made to fill a fourth panel. No such subscription was undertaken, but in 1860 President Woods engaged an artist, who remains unknown, to fill the panel next to the entrance on the north side with a copy of the *Annunciation* by the French artist Jalabert. The president had hoped to pay for the painting by selling the copy of Titian's *Danae and the Golden Shower*, which the Boards had authorized him to do. The picture proved difficult to sell, and President Woods now induced the Honorable Nathan Cummings, Class of 1817, who had advanced money to pay the artist of the fourth panel, to take the *Danae* as satisfaction for the debt.⁹⁹

There were now four panels filled on the north side, with pictures depicting New Testament scenes. A start was made on filling the south side with Old Testament scenes when the 1866 graduating class presented a picture based on Raphael's *St. Michael Slaying the Dragon*. It is immediately to the speaker's left. It was done by a New York painter, Charles Otto, who apparently was in a hurry, for he requested permission from President Woods to finish the painting on Sunday so he could take an early Monday morning train to New York. The president, with a twinkle in his eyes, replied. "While I, myself, may not have any personal objections, yet I fear that the sense of the community would be that the Dragon was rather getting the upper hand."¹⁰⁰ There must have been some general plan to provide historical sequence, for the next panel filled was the third one on the left. This picture was given by the class of 1877 on its graduation and is a copy of Raphael's *Moses Giving the Law.* It was painted by Francis Lathrop, and many Brunswick people served as models. That same year the panels on the north side were completed. One was presented by Mrs. William Perry of Brunswick in memory of her husband and is a copy of part of Raphael's *Transfiguration;* the other was given by friends of Dr. John D. Lincoln, Class of 1843, of Brunswick and depicts the *Baptism of Christ* after the picture by Carlo Marotti. These last two paintings were also done by Francis Lathrop.

After this flurry of artistic activity it took thirty-six years to complete the four remaining Old Testament panels on the south side. In 1886 Henry J. Furber, a member of the class of 1861, gave the picture *Adam and Eve,* copied after the painting by Hippolyte Flandrin in the Church of St. Germain-des-Pres. It was done by Frederic Vinton of Boston and unlike the other chapel paintings was painted on canvas and then fastened to the wall. It is often rated as one of the best of all the panel paintings. In 1908 Dr. Frederick H. Gerrish, Class of 1866, a professor at the medical school, presented the picture *David with the Head of Goliath and the Maidens of Israel Singing Songs of Joy,* after the painting by Tissot. It was done by J.B. Kahill, a resident of Maine but a native of Syria. Mr. Kahill was his own model for David. He had himself photographed in the desired pose and worked from this photograph for his final study.[101] The last two panels were also the gift of Dr. Gerrish and were painted by Miss Edna T. Marrett of Brunswick.[102] One, finished in 1913, given in memory of Professor Henry L. Chapman, who taught at the College from 1869 to 1913, is a copy of Michelangelo's *Isaiah* in the Sistine Chapel in Rome. It is the next to the last painting on the south side near the entrance. The other, finished in 1915, was given in memory of Dr. Gerrish's brother William Little Gerrish, Class of 1864, an officer in the Union Army who lost his life in battle at Petersburg, Virginia, in 1865. It is a copy of Michelangelo's *Delphic Sibyl* in the Sistine Chapel and is an exception to the south side panels representing personages from the Old Testament. The angels after Fra Angelico (from the *Madonna of the Linaiuoli* in the Uffizi in Florence) which fill the half-panels on each side of the rostrum were also done by Miss Marrett and were given by members of the class of 1906.[103]

Although the interior decorative panels were unfinished, the Chapel was an imposing structure when it was dedicated in 1855. The twin towers rising to a height of 120 feet were a village landmark. The arrangement of the interior, with three tiers of benches parallel to the main aisle, was unique for New England. The benches on the rostrum were to become the accustomed seats for the faculty and the student choir. Seniors sat in the forms nearest to the rostrum, the juniors, sophomores, and freshmen next in order, the freshmen being required to remain standing in their places as the upperclassmen, starting with the seniors, filed out. This was not the only disadvantage the freshmen had to sustain; they were handicapped so far as hearing was concerned. As Professor Little observed in his history of the College: "The majority of New Englanders believed that meetinghouses, including college chapels, should be erected according to the laws of acoustics. President Woods held that a church should be erected according to the law of optics. The Bowdoin chapel was so erected."[104] The acoustics in the Chapel were bad,[105] and subsequent attempts to remedy this have alleviated but not solved the problem. Two small balconies at the rear and front of the Chapel provided additional space and made it possible later to install a large organ. The rich black walnut woodwork is a thing of beauty and apparently early impressed the students. To the surprise of the Visiting Committee in 1855, they could spot not a single jackknife mark on the benches or panels, and they wrote: "If such should continue permanently to be the moral effect of the costly and exquisite finish of this structure, the generous friends who have aided in its erection will feel themselves abundantly repaid for their outlay."[106] These aspirations and hopes have been justified, for the benches and panels remain unblemished to this very day. Instead of carving up the benches, the students began inscribing their names on the inner door to the north chapel tower. "On it are written," the *Orient* noted in 1903, "the names of nearly every student in the last twenty-eight years and still there is room for more. It should be regarded as a simple duty demanded by college custom, that everyone put his signature there, for his children and admirers later to pick out. Is yours there?"[107]

The campus including the First Parish Church with the original tower designed by Richard Upjohn.

The campus showing belfries on both Massachusetts Hall and the old chapel, 1818-1830.

The campus and the First Parish Church with spire, 1848-1866.

The interior of the Chapel after the installation of the Curtis Organ in 1927, showing the New Testament panels on the left (north) side and the Old Testament panels on the right (south) side.

The Chapel, designed by Richard Upjohn, built of local granite between 1844 and 1855 during the presidency of Leonard Woods.

The art gallery in the north wing of the Chapel after the acquisition of plaster casts of antique sculpture in the late 1870s.

The library in the room at the back of the Chapel, officially named Banister Hall by the Governing Boards in 1850.

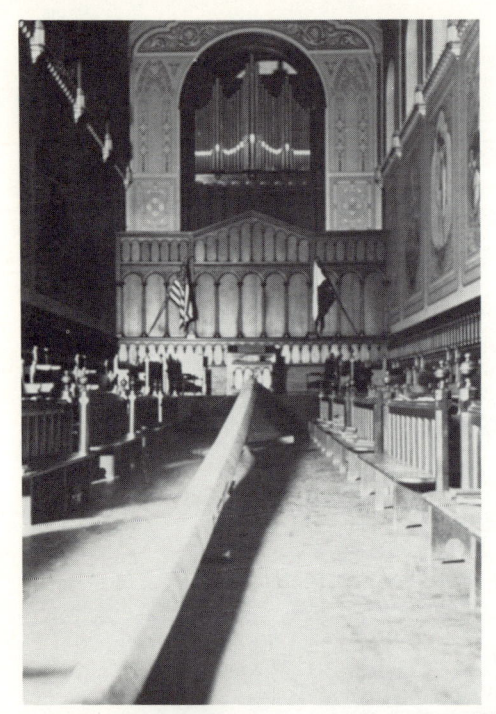

The Memorial Flagpole as it rested in the Chapel, placed there in protest by the students on April 12, 1930.

President Sills and the grounds crew hastening to remove the flagpole in time for vespers the next day.

VII.

Endowments and the Issue of Denominationalism

INSTRUMENTAL IN THE BUILDING of the Chapel was the receipt by the College of two important funds, the one from the residue of the Bowdoin estate, the other from the 1846 solicitations of aid, primarily from the Congregational churches of Maine. The latter campaign had involved the issuance of the Declaration calling attention to the relationship of the College to the orthodox Congregational denomination. There were different ideas as to the nature and depth of this relationship, and the problem of denominationalism became an issue in the succeeding decades. Apart from the Declaration, which has been quoted in full above, there were other events and statements which tended to affirm that Bowdoin was a Congregational college, in the sense that most colleges in the United States in these years were church-related. The establishment of the Collins Professorship of Natural and Revealed Religion was considered to be a manifestation of this relationship.[1]

With the election of Leonard Woods to the presidency of the College in May of 1839, currents of change were soon noticeable. The tensions and strains of the years of Allen's administration were happily ended. The young president was a bachelor, and it was soon evident that he cultivated a different relationship with the students from that of his predecessors. The old parietal rules which had existed ever since the College was founded were not annulled, but they were now more leniently administered. Scholarly, devout, genial, President Woods was not a disciplinarian. President Hyde was later to write of him:

> In his mild and charitable eyes, robbed hen-roosts, translated live stock, greased blackboards and tormented tutors, were indeed things to be perfunctorily deplored; but they were not deemed specimens of total depravity, or cases of unpardonable sin: nor was he as insistent upon meting out a just recompense of reward to the culprits, as his more strenuous colleagues thought he ought to be. This mingling of austerity on the part of the faculty which made mischief of this sort worth doing, with extreme leniency on the part of the President, which insured immunity from serious penalty, made the college from 1839 to 1866 probably the best place there ever was in the world for

boys to be boys, and to indulge that crude and lawless self-assertion which was the only available approach which the colleges of that day afforded to manly courage and ordered independence.[2]

If students at Bowdoin seemed to manifest their independence more ardently than in the past, this was but an expression of the spirit of the times, not unlike the political activity of the students in Europe which came to a climax in the revolution of 1848. Greek letter fraternities came to Bowdoin in the early 1840s, and new ties of loyalty were being formed; the old Bowdoin was changing and renewing itself.

The Boards even more than the faculty took a dim view of the behaviour of the students. The students were wont to "liberate" wood from the woodyard, and in 1845 the Visiting Committee recommended moving the woodyard to prevent stealing. "They [the students] may deceive themselves by the use of cant phrases and thus indulge themselves in the habitual breach of the 8th Commandment, but God is not mocked and your committee cannot too strongly urge upon the executive government [faculty] the necessity of bringing the students to a right understanding upon this subject and inducing their pupils to refrain from practices dishonorable to them as Christians and as gentlemen."[3] In the spring of 1847 the woodshed with the remaining supply of wood was set on fire. This wanton destruction of property, the most flagrant of a whole series of depredations, aroused the Visiting Committee. They made a study of the annual destruction of property from 1831 to 1847; the lowest amount apportioned to individuals being $10.87 in 1837, the largest amount $74.01 in 1843, with an average of $33.04 per year.[4] The committee concluded that the vices and morals at the College needed attention. The sad conditions were the result of the lack of proctors from the executive committee in the dorms at all times, especially at night, the influence of secret societies, and the lack of moral instruction, especially in the first two or three years of a student's life at the College. The committee was convinced that a separate department devoted to ethical and moral subjects could no longer be delayed. Until that great need was supplied they wanted the president to lecture to incoming classes one or two times and "point out to them the duties they are required to perform, and the dangers and temptations to which they will be exposed, admonishing them of the consequences to themselves, which a course of disorder and vice must certainly bring."[5]

Even before this report was written, a subscription paper dated March 15, 1847, was drawn up and circulated. Its purpose was to found a professorship of theology subject to certain stated regulations. The interest on the funds subscribed should be permitted to accumulate until it amounted to at least $15,000, when the professor should be appointed. He should "at all times be selected from ministers or ordained clergymen in regular standing of the trinitarian orthodox congregational denomination of

Christians."[6] The paper went on to spell out the unique position contemplated for the new professor:

> The Professor shall not be a member of the executive government of the College nor be required or allowed to communicate any knowledge of the character, opinions, or conduct of any student of the College obtained by intercourse or conversation with the students.
>
> It shall be his duty to endeavor to cultivate and maintain a familiar intercourse with the students, and to visit and converse with them at their chambers; and by conversation as well as by more formal teaching and preaching to impress upon their minds the truths of the gospel of our Lord Jesus Christ, and their suitableness to promote the happiness of the present life, and the necessity, that they should be cordially embraced to secure the happiness of a future and endless life.

The Boards were to be able to "regulate" the manner in which these duties should be performed, including ordinary instruction in the College, but were not "to prevent the performance of the duties enjoined or...to cause the professor to teach or conduct in any manner inconsistent with the faithful performance of those duties."

The next year the Visiting Committee reported that certain persons had subscribed $16,500 for an appointment of a theological professor and recommended that the Boards accept the fund with the conditions as outlined by the subscription paper. This the Boards did on September 6, 1848, and officially established the Collins Professorship of Natural and Revealed Religion.[7] The usual salary for professors at this time was $1,000, and the Boards voted that, whenever the interest exceeded this sum, it should be added to the principal.[8] Mrs. Ebenr. (Susan) Collins had subscribed $5,000 to the fund, the principal to be secured by a note with the interest being paid semiannually. Judge Ether Shepley, who had written the Visiting Committee report calling for the establishment of a theological professorship, contributed $1,000, as did Professor Thomas C. Upham, Benjamin Tappan, Class of 1833, and Mrs. Ebenr. Hale, Jr. There were a number of $500 and smaller contributions. In all $17,435 was subscribed for this purpose, just about a quarter of the total of around $70,000 raised by the 1846 financial drive.[9] Some of the gifts were in the form of notes on which the interest was not always paid, and the fund varied considerably during the succeeding years.

The Boards sought immediately to fill the chair. In September 1848 they elected the Reverend George L. Prentiss, Class of 1835, of New Bedford to the chair, but he declined the appointment. The following year they chose the Reverend Daniel J. Noyes, and he also refused their offer.[10] Meanwhile, President Woods continued his practice of holding on Sunday evenings a Bible class for seniors who wished to attend voluntarily.[11] At a special meeting on March 21, 1850, the Boards elected Rev. Calvin E. Stowe, Class of 1824, then professor of Biblical literature at Lane Seminary in Cincinnati, the first Collins Professor at a salary of $1,000, the moving money not to exceed $400.[12] President Woods was strongly in his favor and spoke of his ample qualifications. After two years—long enough for his wife to write *Uncle Tom's Cabin*—Stowe resigned his post to become professor of sacred literature at Andover Theological Seminary. Industrious and able, Professor Stowe fulfilled his obligations very satisfactorily. He was backed by the Boards, who at their meeting in September 1851 voted: "That all students of the College are required to attend at least one general exercise in each week conducted by the Collins Professor of Natural and Revealed Religion and on such day and at such time and with such arrangements as may be designated by the President."[13]

Professor Stowe was succeeded as Collins Professor by the Reverend Roswell Dwight Hitchcock of Exeter, New Hampshire. The Visiting Committee, after his first year at Bowdoin, reported most favorably on his work as Collins Professor.[14] And well it might. In his annual report to the committee in 1854, Professor Hitchcock related that he had invited the freshmen to his home and visited them in their rooms. Throughout the fall and part of the spring he gave the freshmen three recitations a week on Paley's *Natural Theology* and also worked with sophomores and juniors. Once a fortnight on Saturday evenings he gave lectures on religious topics; attendance was voluntary, and the lecture room was filled. In addition, he gave some ten to twelve discourses on the Sabbath at the First Parish Church. In all he thought his work had gone well.[15] This was exactly the kind of activities the donors had in mind when they established the Collins chair. The Visiting Committee was enthusiastic and reported in 1855 that morals at the College were in good condition, and the faculty recognized the influence of the Collins Professorship.[16] This was the year the Chapel was completed and dedicated; the importance of religion at Bowdoin was evident to all. In 1855 Professor Hitchcock accepted a position as professor of ecclesiastical history at Union Theological Seminary. Professor Egbert Coffin Smyth, who had been teaching Greek and later rhetoric and oratory at Bowdoin since 1849, was then made Collins Professor and held that position until 1863, when he went to Andover Seminary. In his report of 1859 to the Visiting Committee, Smyth commented on one of the more controversial assignments of the Collins Professors. This was to visit the students in their rooms, and he had done so. "It gives me great pleasure," he wrote, "to state that such visits have always been most agreeable to me by the courtesy with which I have been received, and that my experience is convincing me not only of the feasibility of such a mode of intercourse, which has sometimes been called in question, but also of its salutary influence."[17] The Collins Professorship was continuing to work out well.

Endowments and the Issue of Denominationalism 93

After Professor Smyth, the chair was held from 1864 to 1884 by one of Bowdoin's most devoted and beloved professors, Alpheus Spring Packard.[18] On his death in 1884 the chair was vacant until 1890, when it was awarded to Professor Frank Edward Woodruff, who had been teaching Greek at Bowdoin. By this time the professorship had lost most of its unique features, in large part because the endowment was inadequate, and the holders of the chair had to devote much of their time to other teaching assignments.

In the early 1870s the finances of the College were again at low ebb. Under President Joshua L. Chamberlain, the Boards in 1874 undertook a drive to raise $100,000 for endowment.[19] It was a time to take inventory of what the College had, and the Collins Fund was examined afresh. The Boards found that on September 6, 1848, the Collins Fund had actually stood at $13,300.[20] Since then the note of Mrs. Ebenr. Collins remained unpaid, as did that of Mrs. Elizabeth M. Nelson. On August 2, 1859, the Boards had voted to remit $200 and the interest on the Nelson note.[21] If all other funds had been paid, the principal would have amounted to $8,100. The Boards accordingly voted that this amount be taken from general funds and placed to the account of the Collins Professorship along with the Collins note.[22] This, however, did not settle matters. Interest had not been paid on the Collins note, and on November 18, 1875, this note, on the suggestion of Mrs. Collins, was converted into a bond of $7,500 without interest.[23] It was her intention to pay it off in installments, but if at her death the bond had not been paid off, yearly payments of $500 were to be paid until her estate at No. 20 Chardon Street in Boston was sold. The Boards in 1876 instructed that $16,461.67 be transferred to the Collins Fund along with the Collins bond and a note for $500 of Mrs. Harriet Bell.[24] This latter note was cancelled in 1882.[25] In 1877 Benjamin Delano gave $500 to be added to the Collins Fund; Professor R.D. Hitchcock, then at Union Theological Seminary, gave $80 in 1879, and on June 19, 1893, $500 was paid on the Collins bond by the executor of Mrs. Collins's estate.[26] Thus when the Boards again made inquiry into the fund, the college treasurer, Ira P. Booker, reported that the fund stood at $24,421.67 as of February 3, 1896. One of the assets of the fund was the Collins bond, and in 1896, when the estate of Mrs. Collins was finally settled, the college authorities were happy to receive $7,000, the remainder of the bond, and willingly forgave the payment of some back interest they had claimed due.[27]

At this time President Hyde was advocating important changes in the use of the Collins Fund. It was not adequate for a professorship and besides "systematic visitation of students in their chambers for religious conversation by a person employed and paid to perform that particular function is manifestly impracticable."[28] He suggested using the money to obtain the services of eminent preachers who would visit the campus and preach at Sunday services. He also proposed using some of the money to pay for a

Y.M.C.A. secretary. But the Boards were slow to be persuaded. They did verbally instruct former President Joshua L. Chamberlain to investigate the terms under which the fund had been established. He reported on June 14, 1897, submitting the terms as adopted in 1848.[29]

Nothing was done about the fund until President Hyde sought to provide pensions for the faculty by taking advantage of the program of the Carnegie Foundation for the Advancement of Teaching. That foundation would not extend "its benefits to any institution which imposed a denominational test in choice of governing boards, faculty, or students, or taught distinctly denominational tenets or doctrines."[30] The provision of the Collins Professorship that the incumbent was to "be selected from ministers or ordained clergymen in regular standing of the trinitarian orthodox Congregational denomination of Christians" was held by the foundation to be a violation of its practice. Two other college funds—the Winkley Professorship and the Stone Foundation (to be discussed later)—were also held objectionable. The College sought aid from the courts in setting aside the restrictions of the original terms establishing the Collins Professorship. On April 7, 1908, the State Supreme Judicial Court, In Equity, in *The President and Trustees of Bowdoin College* v. *Hannibal E. Hamlin, Attorney General of Said State,* ruled:

> Ordered, Adjudged, and Decreed that the trust created by the establishment of the fund mentioned in the bill is a public charitable trust; that the administration thereof in the particular manner prescribed by the founders of the fund now is impracticable; and that accordingly, until the further order of this Court, the Plaintiff, The President and Trustees of Bowdoin College, is directed to apply the income of said fund to the payment of the salary of a Secretary of the Young Men's Christian Association of said Bowdoin College, and the residue of said income, if any, from time to time, be added to the principal of said fund, or, at the option of said Plaintiff and the Overseers of said Bowdoin College be applied to the support of the First Parish Church, of said Brunswick or to the support of the service at the College Chapel, or to the purchase of books for the library of said College, of a religious, theological, ethical or philosophical character or to providing speakers for, or otherwise aiding in carrying on the work of said Association. Such disposition of the income is adjudged to be within the general scope of the intention of the donors of the charity fund.[31]

This ruling satisfied the Carnegie Foundation, and the funds of the Collins Professorship have ever since been used in accordance with its direction.

On February 1, 1924, the Boards repealed the vote passed in 1848 providing "That whenever the interest shall exceed the sum of $1000, the excess be invested until otherwise ordered, as part of the capital to compensate or reimburse any losses which in the course of events may occur."[32]

This directive had long not been observed and to right the wrong, the Boards voted: "That the acts of the several Treasurers of the college in failing to add any of the interest derived from said Collins Professorship to the principal be and the same hereby are ratified and approved." To list the Collins Professorship Fund along with the endowed Bowdoin professorships seemed irrational to President James Stacy Coles and at his direction Glenn R. McIntire, at that time assistant treasurer, wrote a memorandum to the bursar asking him "to transfer the Collins Professorship Fund from the "Professorship" group to the "Special Purpose" group.[33] Mr. McIntire added: "It will no doubt save confusion if in the published reports we simply say Collins Fund and omit the word Professorship." The first provision of the memorandum has been complied with, the second not. The fund is still carried on the college books and reports as the "Collins Professorship of Natural and Revealed Religion." On June 30, 1979, the fund stood at $35,697.63, and since 1974-1975 all the income from it has been granted to the library for the purchase of "religious books" separate from and not part of the regular library book budget. The college authorities have kept faith with the terms of the original foundation of the Collins Professorship Fund, as interpreted by the State Supreme Court in 1908.

The history of the Collins Professorship, here given in some detail, not only shows the close relationship of the College to Congregationalism that existed in the mid-nineteenth century, but also reveals the lessening of that bond and the growing secularization of the College. There were other developments that depict in much the same way the decline of denominational ties. On August 2, 1864, Henry H. Boody, Class of 1842, who had taught rhetoric and oratory at the College and had resigned his position in 1854 to enter business in New York, made a gift to the College of $50,000 to be paid in five annual installments, the whole sum bearing interest at 6 percent.[34] The conditions under which the gift was made and readily accepted by the Boards are of interest in indicating the relationship between the College and Congregationalism. Mr. Boody supported the Declaration of 1846 that Bowdoin was a denominational college "as illustrated in the case of Yale, Amherst and Dartmouth Colleges" and in other colleges belonging to the Methodist, the Episcopalian, and other denominations. He went on to state:

> By an Orthodox Congregational College, I understand a college in which a clear and decided majority of its Boards and Oversight consists of that denomination, recognized by and acceptable to the denomination, as fair exponents of its character, views and aims, and who undertake the management of the college with such denominational care and fidelity as may reasonably be expected, and is always deemed proper in analogous cases, yet with a just and generous liberality toward other denominations."

While both Boards enthusiastically accepted the gift under these conditions and Mr. Boody was elected to the Board of Trustees where he served from 1864 to 1871, the Trustees also passed an explanatory statement unanimously.

> That it is the understanding of this Board in accepting the donation of Hon. H. H. Boody upon the letter accompanying the same, that the expression in said letter referring to "character, views and aims" are limited to the religious character, and the denominational views and aims as expressed in the orthodox creed."[35]

Fearing that this vote "might be misapprehended and perhaps misapplied," the Trustees the next year passed another vote striking out the phrase "as expressed in the orthodox creed."[36] Since neither of these last votes were sent to the Overseers for their concurrence, they cannot be considered a part of the agreement with Mr. Boody.

Mr. Boody had some difficulties making his payments. He later withdrew the conditions under which his gift had been made, and on June 29, 1869, he wrote to the Boards:

> Having recently made arrangements for the payment of my donation to the College, I herewith unconditionally withdraw and cancel all and singular the particular stipulations and conditions contained in my letter to the Boards in which I made the proposition to give the sum of fifty thousand dollars, $50,000, to the college, deeming it wiser to leave that fund, in common with the other funds of the college, to be used and appropriated, as the wisdom and piety of those who shall hereafter administer the affairs of the college, may dictate.[37]

This action by Mr. Boody was strongly approved by the *Whig and Courier*, which had repeatedly criticized the Boards for pledging the "conscience of the College in all time to a special belief." It wrote: "This withdrawal relieves the college from the obligations assumed, and never raises a doubt of its religious character, which character not even the most liberal minded man wishes to change, but simply asks that it shall not be offensively thrust into view."[38]

In 1878 the College received a gift of $10,000 from Henry Winkley of Philadelphia "on condition that the college adhere to the religious teachings of the Orthodox Congregational or Presbyterian church."[39] On May 10, 1880, he made another gift of $15,000, the income to be used "as the Trustees may think best." The following September he remitted a further $15,000, which was to be used along with his previous gifts—making $40,000 in all—"to endow the Winkley Professorship of the Latin Language and Literature on the condition that the college adhere to the

Theological teachings of the Orthodox Congregational or Presbyterian Church." The Boards again made no objection to accepting a gift tied to denominational commitments. As in the case of the Collins Professorship, the Carnegie Foundation objected to these restrictions when the College sought to enter its program for faculty pensions. In this case the College applied to a residuary legatee of Mr. Winkley, who granted release from the denominational restrictions made when the professorship was founded.[40] The Henry Winkley Professorship of the Latin Language and Literature continues today as one of the endowed chairs at the College.

That same year, 1880, the College received another major gift which imposed denominational restrictions. Mrs. Valeria L. Stone instructed her trustees to pay Bowdoin College $70,000 on the following conditions.[41] Twenty thousand dollars was to be devoted to the completion of Memorial Hall on condition that ownership be transferred from the alumni to the College, and she later (November 15, 1880) added $5,000 for this purpose. She further directed:

> The remainder ($50,000) of the entire amount given (or so much of it as may be deemed necessary) shall be appropriated to the endowment of the chair of Intellectual and Moral Philosophy which shall henceforth be termed the Stone professorship. But this sum shall be paid only upon this condition, Viz: that the President of the College and a majority of its Board of Trustees and also of its Board of Overseers, as well as the incumbent of the Stone professorship shall always be in doctrinal and religious sympathy with the Orthodox Congregational churches of New England, and at any time this condition is disregarded the endowment of the Stone professorship shall be forfeited by the College and revert to the Theological department of Phillips Academy in Andover, Mass.

The Boards accepted the gift with thanks, and the professorship was established. The terms under which the fund was established were very specific, and the Carnegie Foundation naturally objected to them when the College applied for admission to its pension program. The College could obtain no release from the restrictions imposed by the gift, and the funds were forfeited to Phillips Academy.[42] At that time the fund amounted to $56,118.16. Had it been retained, the restrictions imposed would have had to be circumvented in some way or the fund forfeited on the election of President Sills to the presidency of the College. Neither he nor any of his four successors has been Congregationalist, a clear indication of the decline of the College's denominational connections.

The Carnegie Foundation not only required the removal of restrictive clauses in respect to the endowment funds but also required the Boards to pass a resolution stating:

That no denominational test is imposed in the choice of trustees, officers or teachers, or in the admission of students, nor are distinctly denominational tenets or doctrines taught to students.[43]

Since the members of the Boards felt this had always been the rule, the acceptance of this statement caused no difficulty. Bowdoin now came under the Carnegie pension plan. President Hyde, in making the announcement in chapel on February 11, 1908, hailed "this as the greatest piece of good fortune that has come to Bowdoin in many years."[44]

In addition to these major gifts, the College also received some lesser funds for scholarships which were linked with the Congregational denomination. In 1871 the Shepley Scholarship provided interest from a $1,000 bond of the Androscoggin and Kennebec Rail Road to be applied "to aid students of the college in need of pecuniary assistance and intending to become ministers of our Lord and to preach his gospel as commonly received by the Trinitarian Congregational or by the Presbyterian denomination of Christians to obtain an education." The next year the Mary L. Savage Memorial Scholarship, amounting to $1,000, was given by her husband, Dr. William T. Savage, Class of 1833, "for the payment of the current expenses of some needy student having the Christian Ministry of the Evangelical faith as now understood by the General Conference of the Congregational churches in Maine in view." If any student receiving money from this fund should not enter the ministry he was asked to repay the amount so that it could "be appropriated to the purpose designated." The Stephen Sewall Scholarship was established in 1873 to be awarded "to pious students preparing to enter the ministry of the evangelical Congregational Church. The beneficiary shall be free from the use of tobacco and other injurious drugs and intoxicating liquors, and also free from other immoral habits." In 1875 the Emerson Scholarship was established, the interest of the fund to "be given to the student who is looking forward to the Christian Ministry in connection with the Orthodox Congregational churches." The Benjamin Delano Scholarship was given in 1877 "for the benefit of some deserving young man studying in the college for the evangelical Christian Ministry of the Congregational denomination."[45]

The above five scholarships were for many years grouped together at the beginning of the list of scholarships in the college catalogue with the notation: "The income of the preceding five scholarships is to be appropriated for the aid of students preparing to enter the ministry of the Evangelical Trinitarian churches." In the 1954-1955 catalogue and ever since, the scholarships are listed alphabetically, and there is no indication that these scholarships are designated for students intent on entering the ministry. Hidden away in the Business Office, the restrictions are, however, still maintained on the fund records.

Since the establishment of these scholarships in the 1870s, three additional scholarships for prospective ministers have been provided. Under the Moses R. Ludwig and Albert F. Thomas Scholarships (1884) preference is "always to be given, other things being satisfactory, to such Christian young men as shall hold membership in some trinitarian Congregational church and shall be in course of preparation for the ministry."[46] The Trueman S. Perry Scholarship (1939) is to be awarded "to a student looking to the Evangelical ministry as a profession."

There have been a few other scholarships more recently which state a different religious preference. The Eva D.H. Baker Scholarship (1932) is preferably to go to a Christian Scientist; the John Finzer Presnell, Jr. Scholarship (1947) to "a student of high Christian principles"; the George W.R. Bowie Fund (1965) to "a needy Protestant student, preferably a country boy of American ancestry from Androscoggin County"; and the Simon Family Scholarship Fund (1977) "to students of the Jewish faith who reside on the North Shore of Boston."[47] One other scholarship with religious ties is the G.W. Field Fund (1881), which by preference is to go "first to students or graduates of the Bangor Theological Seminary and, second, to graduates of the Bangor High School."[48]

The financial aid the College received through the Congregational churches was but one of the ties between these churches and the College. The Congregationalists came to think of Bowdoin as their college, much as they thought Bangor Theological Seminary was their seminary.[49] Ever since 1829-1830, the Congregational Conference had sent committees to visit the Bangor seminary and report upon its needs and welfare. It was a step towards cooperation and financial help, not an effort to take over control of the seminary. The Maine Branch of the American Education Society held its annual meeting in conjunction with the meetings of the Congregational Conference of Maine. Bowdoin professors were active in the former, and in 1857 the names of the Bowdoin faculty began to be included in the minutes of the Congregational Conference. Two years before, this practice had begun for the faculty of the Bangor seminary. A closer relationship between the conference and the College was established in 1865 when "a series of resolutions by the Conference commended the College to the churches, since its Board had 'recognized the position of the College, in accordance with the generally acknowledged facts of its history, as Orthodox Congregational....' The mover of the resolutions also suggested that the Conference appoint a Committee to visit the college annually as in the case of the Seminary."[50] But it was not until fourteen years later that, with the warm approval of President Chamberlain, a visiting committee was chosen by the conference to visit the College. It made its first annual report to the conference in 1880, and these were continued until 1902, when Professor Deems notes "for some reason reports were discontinued although names of the Committee continued to be listed."[51] Perhaps the reports were not made regularly after that, but on May 9, 1907, the *Portland Express*, in reporting on a session of the General Conference of the Maine Congregational Churches, stated: "A report was made on Bowdoin College which is a Congregational institution, in which it was stated that the college was in poor financial condition and that many of the professors were greatly overworked."[52] The conference did nothing to remedy this situation, although it did vote to support a drive to raise $150,000 for an endowment fund for the Bangor Theological Seminary.

The appointment of this conference Visiting Committee was but a means of keeping friendly contact with the College on the part of the Congregational churches. Certainly neither the committee nor the conference ever made any attempt to intervene in college affairs, or there would be references to this in college records; I have found none. If the Congregational Conference sought to maintain ties with the College, the College also was glad to rely on the help of the churches. On January 14, 1874, the Trustees voted "That Rev. J. O. Fiske, with such as the Overseers shall join, be added to the Committee to obtain endowment for the college, and that they be especially requested to appeal to the churches of Maine to secure a liberal endowment for the chair of Moral and Intellectual Philosophy."[53] The committee, which hoped to raise $100,000 for endowment, was headed by President Chamberlain and in a letter dated February 25, 1874, wrote:

> To all friends of Christian education, who desire that the study of the Liberal Arts and Sciences shall be prosecuted under the auspices of a pure Christianity, we appeal to attest in this practical manner their intelligent faith. To Congregationalists especially to whom this institution has always sustained peculiar relations, we commend this cause, in the confident expectation that they will meet the call with a liberality which will demonstrate their devotion to sound learning and religion.[54]

The drive for funds was a success, and during President Chamberlain's administration around $300,000 was added to the college funds.[55]

President Woods's independence in religious matters and his refusal to further the entrenchment of Congregationalism at the College had brought him into conflict with some of the Congregational leaders in the state.[56] In this regard President Harris and President Chamberlain shared Woods's views. While recognizing that the College had a Congregational character, neither Harris nor Chamberlain were inclined to stress the connection of the College to the Congregational churches. They were content to recognize, as Chamberlain's subscription letter of 1874 pointed out, that the College and the Congregational church had "always sustained peculiar relations"; there was no need to define and paragraph them.[57] It therefore aroused attention when President Hyde, in his inaugural address, raised the issue of denominational control. His whole address centered on the relationship of the community and the College, and in respect to churches he stated:

> Inasmuch as the Christian church is divided into sects, and in view of the fact that all other religious interests are at present administered by these several sects, it is obviously fitting that the religious control of the College should rest in the hands of some one of these denominations. And that the College shall in this sense be under the control of the Congregationalist denomination is admitted and recognized by all concerned in its government and administration. At the same time, since the College belongs in the widest sense to the community, and to the Church Catholic, every form of sincere Christian faith should be respected; denominational proselyting should never be attempted; and each student should be encouraged to live consistently in the form of faith which parental example and early association has hallowed and made sacred. The religious teaching should be positively evangelical; avoiding controversial attacks on other forms of faith. The College must first of all be loyal to Christ; secondly, it must squarely identify itself with that interpretation of Christianity to which its history and ecclesiastical affiliation commit it. It must do this, however, with all due respect for the various forms of faith prevailing in the community at large.[58]

Considering the general relationship which existed between most colleges and religious denominations at that time, and the history of the College itself, it was not an unreasonable statement. Critics jumped on the opening sentences and tended to overlook the ecumenical qualifications made later. The *Brunswick Telegraph*, commenting on the assertion that the College was under the control of the Congregational denomination, stated: "That is undoubtedly true but it does not *belong* to the Congregationalists as some assert....We have no disposition to try titles, but simply ask that the old fashioned knocker on the front door shall not be constantly rattled."[59] Henry V. Poor, Class of 1835, in a letter to the *Telegraph*, leveled the sharpest criticism of all. Hyde had put an end to his hopes of better days to come for the College. It was going "to remain as it had been, not a University, but a school of theology. It would remain as it has been, the teacher of dogma." What did Hyde mean by the term "evangelical teaching"? Poor continued:

> I know what it [evangelical teaching] was when I was at Bowdoin over fifty years ago. It was the acceptance of the Bible history of creation, not only of the earth, but of all the celestial bodies, some six thousand years ago. It was the acceptance of the dogma that the whole race were under a curse for the sin of Adam and that for such sin nearly the whole of humanity are to suffer eternal torments in hell.... Is the Evangelical doctrine of today the Evangelical doctrine

of fifty years ago? If it is, then good-bye to Bowdoin. If not, then the new President should tell us what it is.... What I complain of is the use of words that convey no adequate idea of what a person in a very responsible public position does believe. I further object most decidedly to the continuing of Bowdoin College as a school for teaching theology."[60]

Poor was not only inaccurate as to what Bowdoin had been in the past, but also as to what Bowdoin was likely to become under President Hyde's leadership.

Under President Hyde, Bowdoin was to become stronger than ever before. It was to remain what it was always held to be, a "Christian college," but the denominational ties to Congregationalism were reduced to a vanishing point. In a study made in 1891, it was found that eleven of the thirty-five so-called Congregational colleges in the United States required that the majority of the trustees had to be Congregationalists, and that in the other twenty-four the charters made no mention of the denominational relations. Bowdoin was among the latter, and in summarizing the situation of each college, the author of the study noted: "Bowdoin's Congregationalism rests on a tacit understanding that its President, and a majority of its trustees, shall be Congregationalists; a good basis, in the opinion of the President."[61] But even this tacit understanding was to be breached once and for all at the end of President Hyde's administration.

During his presidency, Hyde became not only one of the leaders and spokesmen of the college world, but also of the Congregational church and of religion in general. Within the state he kept close contacts with Congregational leaders and was an active member of the First Parish Church in Brunswick. Yet he did not bring denominationalism into the affairs of the College. His sermons and chapel talks were always Christian and ecumenically oriented, never sectarian. In general throughout his administration the trend was away from denominational connections, and it was he, more than anyone else, who pushed for severing what legal ties there were, when the Carnegie Endowment Fund prescribed it as a prerequisite for the College to become eligible for the Carnegie pension plan. Yet there was one proposal during his administration which, while it might not have strengthened denominationalism at the College, would almost certainly have greatly influenced the position of religion on the campus.

In 1899-1900 there was a movement among the trustees of the Bangor Theological Seminary to move the seminary to Bowdoin. Such affiliations were being made elsewhere. Union Seminary had recently become associated with Columbia, the Pacific Congregational Seminary was going to move from Oakland to Berkeley, and there was talk of moving Andover to Cambridge and affiliating it with Harvard. The thought was that the seminary property would be liquidated, perhaps adapting the buildings for the establishment of a new state normal school at Bangor. It was estimated that this would mean that Bowdoin would receive about $300,000.[62] The Bowdoin authorities were approached, and in reply, in June 1900, the Boards voted:

> That they would welcome the advent of the Seminary to Brunswick; that they would permit the erection on college grounds of such buildings as the seminary might wish to erect; that they would allow the students of the Seminary to avail themselves of our Library, Gymnasium, Laboratories and other facilities, and open to the students of the seminary such courses of instruction as they may be qualified to pursue upon such terms as may hereafter be approved by both institutions; and that in general they would cooperate with the seminary in every possible way for the mutual advantage of the two institutions.[63]

The vote gives some indication as to how the relations between the two institutions would have developed had the trustees of the seminary not decided to stay in Bangor. This decision was not made "for good and all" until June 5, 1911.[64] One can only speculate on what the effects of a seminary on the Bowdoin campus would have been, but it no doubt would have led to a very different Bowdoin from the one we have today.

Just as there were changes in the relationship of the College to Congregationalism at large, so there were also gradual changes in the relationship of the College to the First Parish Church in Brunswick. New financial arrangements between the two were worked out. By 1860 the student body had grown to such an extent that they were no longer comfortably accommodated in the south gallery, and the juniors, much to the satisfaction of the Reverend Mr. Adams, began sitting in the north gallery, thus "balancing the house."[65] This raised the question whether the College should not pay a pew tax on the north gallery, and there was also dispute as to whether the College owed a pew tax on the south gallery, which it had been assigned in the new meeting house in 1846. In 1863 the assessors of the parish approached the College for the payment of the pew tax, which it had not paid for the past two years. The college treasurer in turn maintained the College was under no legal obligation to pay the tax. The parish sought some amicable arrangement "by which the rights of the parties in interest may be clearly, and once for all determined."[66] It was not until 1867 that an agreement was reached and the College paid the tax.[67] The College also made other payments. In 1868 it contributed fifty dollars "towards painting the Congregational Church." The following year the Visiting Committee recommended an appropriation not exceeding $100 to repair the cushions in the galleries. During these years the College apparently also kept an insurance policy of $1,000 on the church.[68]

In 1872 the parish began to consider abandoning the raising of revenues by taxes in favor of voluntary contributions. They were slow to give up the taxes and in 1876 again approached the College for rent on certain portions of the church building. The Boards appointed a committee to investigate the matter, and this committee stated in 1877: "We are of opinion that the seats in the South Transept are subject to tax, as other seats in the Church, that the College has no interest in the North Transept, but if it uses it, should pay some compensation."[69] It also recommended that a committee be appointed to investigate and report whether the College had any and what interest in the fee of the lot where the church stands, and the lot east of Harpswell Street. The Boards, acting on this recommendation, appointed a committee to report on "the relations existing between the Congregational Society in Brunswick and the college and particularly as to what interest the college has in the meeting house of said Society and in the fee of the lot on which the same stands and the lot east of Harpswell Street...."[70]

The committee moved slowly, and it was not until July 8, 1879, that it reported. By that time the parish had definitely abandoned the collection of pew taxes.[71] As to the interest of the College in the meeting house, the committee went back to the indenture agreement of 1821, which meant the College owned one-ninth of the lot on which the church stands and the south gallery, the latter having been exchanged for the rights to the north gallery in the old meeting house. Nothing was said about the lots east of Harpswell Street. The committee held further that students were occupying the north gallery on the invitation of Rev. Adams, and the College actually had no obligations in regard to this gallery. The question whether the parish had the right to tax the galleries at all had apparently never arisen. However, as a point of fact, the College for several years had paid the tax. The previous year it had paid fifty-eight dollars in tax on the college pew and sixty dollars on the south gallery. For two years the tax on the north gallery had been twenty dollars annually but this forty dollars had not been paid. "Without admitting any legal or moral obligation to pay" this last amount, the committee felt it should be paid, "inasmuch as the college has been accommodated in various ways by the Parish which has been put to some expense thereby." The church building had been used in ways not originally contemplated, as for example exhibitions and concerts. Since the parish was now no longer going to levy taxes on pews but had decided to resort to voluntary gifts, the committee proposed that in addition to the forty dollars for back taxes on the north gallery, the College make a voluntary gift of $150.[72] The Boards accepted the committee report and ever since has made an annual gift to the parish. The sum has varied and in 1980 stands at $600. In return, the parish has permitted the College to use the building for commencements, convocations, and baccalaureates, and on other occasions when the College has need for a large auditorium. At times the College has made additional gifts, as was done in 1894 when major repairs on the church building were necessary and the College, at the request of the parish assessors, contributed $200.[73] These historic and rather involved relations between the College and parish caused no difficulty when the agreement on pensions was negotiated with the Carnegie endowment fund.

More important than these legal and monetary matters in maintaining ties between the College and the First Parish were the services each performed for the other. The Orient described this relationship well:

> This is a Christian College; such was the intention of its founders and such has been the aim of its overseers and instructors. A Christian College implies a more or less intimate connection with some Christian church, and for that reason it was put in close relations with the old church on the hill. Nearly a century's fruitage of strong men has justified the wisdom of that provision. The church and the College have been a mutual inspiration to each other and have grown strong and vigorous side by side.[74]

The presidents of the College, the Collins Professors, and other faculty as well, often occupied the pulpit at First Parish. Many of the faculty and their wives were leaders in carrying on the work of the parish. First Parish was generally held in the community to be the college church.[75] It speaks to this warm relationship between college and parish that President Joshua L. Chamberlain while in office donated the big stained glass window back of the pulpit in the meeting house to the memory of his father-in-law, the Reverend George Adams, and that the two beautiful transept windows are memorials to two honored and beloved faculty members, Professor Alpheus Spring Packard and Professor William Smyth.[76] And it was by no means a one-way street. The pastors of the church spoke regularly in the Bowdoin Chapel and to student groups, offered innumerable invocations, prayers, and benedictions at college gatherings, and sought always to minister to the students when need arose. Friendship and cooperation between college and parish were the rule as they went their separate ways.

VIII.

Religious Life at the College, 1867-1917

THE COMPLETION OF THE long sought new Chapel did not change to any degree the religious life and practices at the College. The old religion-oriented student societies carried on much as always. The routine of compulsory attendance at daily morning and evening prayers at the College and attendance at morning and afternoon church services on Sunday in the village churches continued. Nor was this pattern changed by the events of the Civil War. In fact, as one reads the documentary record of the College during the war years, one is struck with how few changes were apparent in daily life at the College. Nor did the accession of the Reverend Samuel Harris of Bangor Theological Seminary to the presidency of the College in the spring of 1867, on the resignation of President Woods the previous July, bring about any great innovations.

President Harris, like all the presidents before him, believed firmly that religious training was basic for a sound education. In his inaugural address he stated:

> I have spoken of physical and intellectual training. But as physical training is subordinate to intellectual, so both are subordinate to moral and spiritual ends. The importance of this part of education has been urged by the greatest educators and the greatest minds in all ages....
>
> We are in sympathy, then, with the great Masters of learning, as well as with Jesus and the apostles, when we demand that education aim pre-eminently to cultivate the moral and spiritual side of man's being, and to establish, strengthen and settle the pupil in the principles and practice of Christian character....
>
> To the innumerable evils arising from sectarian jealousy we must not add this more fatal than all, of making college education unchristian through fear lest in teaching Christianity, we seem to teach sectarianism. That would be to sacrifice our own sons to the demon. That could be justified only by a sectarianism so intense that it would leave the educated intellect of the country unchristian rather than have it Christian in any sect not our own. The difficulty has been met by a common consent that every college have a denominational character in the sense that its religious instruction

accord with some one denomination. In this sense Harvard, Brown, Amherst, Yale and in fact every college in N. England, and almost every one in the United States, is denominational. In the same sense and no other, Bowdoin has always had a denominational character. This character has been the same from the beginning. I know no desire or purpose in any quarter to make its character in this respect in the future any other than it has always been in the past.[1]

Harris went on to deplore sectarianism and called for a liberal theology in support of universal Christianity. He made no mention of Congregationalism as such in his address.

In his address he also recommended the addition of more science courses to the curriculum, and this was done. Paley's *Natural Theology*, which for many years had been taught to freshmen for two terms, was now dropped, but Paley's *Evidences of Christianity*, a one-term course for seniors, was continued. President Harris himself took over the chair of mental and moral philosophy when Professor Thomas C. Upham resigned in 1867. There was actually little formal religious instruction at the College. As in the past, it was a matter left to extracurricular instruction in chapel and church services and in meetings of the Praying Circle and other student groups. The Collins Professor of Natural and Revealed Religion carried on much of this work, but it was shared by the president and other members of the faculty.

Under President Harris, some changes in attendance at religious services were made. Already under President Woods, suggestions had been made to alter the Sunday afternoon services. In January 1861 the students had presented a petition to the faculty "that a service on the sabbath be held in the afternoon at the general Lecture Room of the Medical College, at which the students shall attend, which is to take the place of the regular service at the church, the evening chapel service, and the Saturday evening lecture."[2] After careful deliberation, the faculty, because of "the difficulties which embarass the question," felt they could not comply with the petition. However, the next year Professor Egbert C. Smyth, then Collins Professor, in his report to the Visiting Committee, took up the idea of change and suggested that four religious services required on Sunday — morning prayers, morning church service, afternoon church services, and evening prayers — were too much. He wanted to end the requirement of attendance at afternoon church services and to introduce services at the College at "four o'clock or a little later" to be conducted by the Collins Professor.[3] Nothing came of his proposal. Two years later the Visiting Committee, noting that ever since the College opened, morning chapel and the first recitation had been held before breakfast, recommended considering having chapel and classes start after breakfast. They, however, expressed the "fear students would sleep rather than eat breakfast."[4] The Boards were not to be moved to action. When the First Parish Church suspended afternoon services early in the second term of 1866, the faculty decided that afternoon services should be held in the Chapel during the second and third terms, conducted by the Collins Professor. This arrangement appealed to the Boards, and they recommended that it be continued.[5] However, the suspension of the afternoon services at First Parish was but temporary, and the next year Professor Packard, as Collins Professor, reported to the Visiting Committee that it had been "inexpedient to have Sunday P.M. services in the chapel as recommended by the Boards."[6] The old practice of student attendance at afternoon services at local churches was again the established order. By the end of the 1860s, however, because of the ill health of Rev. Adams, the afternoon services at the First Parish had virtually been discontinued. On April 18, 1870, the faculty voted:

> That there be a sermon or informal address (and also singing) as a substitute for the afternoon service in church, and that in consideration of attending this service the students be excused from attending the P.M. service in the several churches; that this service begin at 5:20 o'clock."[7]

The students now had an option. They no longer had to attend afternoon church services if they attended Sunday evening prayers, which were now to take the form of the vesper services which were to prevail at the College until September 1966.[8] In May 1871 First Parish undertook officially to affirm current practice and end afternoon services once and for all. Thanks to the strong advocacy of Professor John S. Sewall in parish meeting and the prospect of installing gas lights in the church building, the parish voted to discontinue afternoon services in favor of an evening service. This was an important shift in policy, for never before had there been an evening preaching service at First Parish.[9] It clearly required action by the college authorities, and on July 1, 1871, the faculty having taken note that the Sunday afternoon service at the Congregational Church had been transferred to the evening, voted "that the evening service is not one of the usual meetings for public worship according to the meaning of the college law, and that the students are not required to attend it."[10]

Likewise under President Harris there was an attempt to suspend evening prayers. In his report to the Visiting Committee in 1870, Harris had pointed out that evening prayers had been omitted at Harvard, Yale, Amherst, Dartmouth, Union, and Hamilton, and even at Union and Andover Seminaries. All considered the step a wise one. He reasoned:

> The evening prayer follows immediately an hour's session in recitation and is liable to be attended with more or less inattention and restlessness. We do not think the observance is beneficial to the students' habit of reverence. We believe that all the moral and religious influence of daily chapel prayer may be more effectually

secured by morning prayer alone, than by both morning and evening prayers. We recommend omission of evening prayers.[11]

Harris's assessment was no doubt correct, but the Visiting Committee was not prepared to recommend the abolition of evening prayers.

President Harris resigned at Commencement in 1871 to become professor of systematic theology at Yale, having held office for only four years. The Boards did not make a long search for a successor. They immediately and unanimously chose a member of the Board of Trustees, Joshua Lawrence Chamberlain, to be president of Bowdoin. He had graduated from the College in 1852 and three years later from Bangor Theological Seminary. However, he was never ordained, but returned to Bowdoin as an instructor, holding in succession the chairs of rhetoric and oratory and modern languages. In 1862 he was granted leave of absence to serve in the Union forces. He won recognition for his role in the defense of Little Round Top in the Battle of Gettysburg, was twice severely wounded, rose to the rank of brigadier general, and was commissioned to receive the surrender of Lee's army at Appomattox. After the war he returned to teach at Bowdoin and served as acting president of the College on the resignation of President Woods until President Harris took over. In 1866 he was elected governor of Maine and was thrice reelected to annual terms by large majorities. In 1867 the College conferred on him the honorary degree of doctor of laws, and he was chosen to the Board of Trustees.

Professor Little writes: "On entering upon his administration President Chamberlain under the authorization of the Boards and in response to a wide-spread demand and expectation, inaugurated several changes in former college methods and a distinct and considerable enlargement of the curriculum."[12] Little does not cite evidence for the "authorization of the Boards" and "wide spread demand" for reforms, but one need only read President Chamberlain's inaugural address to realize that changes were about to be made at Bowdoin. He declared the College was charged with being "behind the times," and went on to say:

> The college had touched bottom not so much by the fault of men, as by the fate of things. But how to rise again? and how to begin? Young men passed by the college because they demanded a kind of education she could not give. To meet this exigency, to carry out the wishes of the friends of Bowdoin and the votes of the Boards, devolved a labor which I did not err in calling a task....
>
> It is a stupid thing to think we should cut entirely loose from the past, or indeed to fancy we can do it if we will; but it is equally unwise to shut ourselves up in the past, and to see with its eyes rather than our own....
>
> But the spirit and fashion of the past have been full strong in our systems of education. The monastery is not exactly the proper train-

ing school for the times. It was good in its day and place; and the world owes much to the faithful hands that kept the cloister lamp alive through age of night. But the day is come now, in which men can work.

It was the cloister spirit, after all that made most mischief with the old college. Its tendency was away from life; the natural affections rebuked; the social instincts chilled; the body despised and so dishonored; woman banished and hence degraded, so that even to admit her to a place in the higher education is thought to degrade a college. The inmates, separate, secluded, grown abnormal and provincial, came out into the world strangers to it, and in its own simple phrase, fools. Now that is not exactly what the college wants of men.[13]

It was clear that Chamberlain had visions of transforming "Old Bowdoin." He went on to discuss the advantages of having more study of German and French, and above all of the sciences. He found no cause to fear any conflict between science and religion. He did not neglect reference to religion, but it was in a different vein than in past Bowdoin inaugurals:

This leads me to one thing higher. No society, no study, no science, no philosophy is sound and complete which does not recognize the highest in man — his relations with the Supreme. Therefore I pray for the highest blessing that can rest upon this college, that it cherish true religion. I see a banner with a legend half obscured and forgotten. I take it up. I lift it to the face of day. I set it boldly and high on yonder towers. *Christo et Ecclesiae!* "To Christ and the Church." Not — O man of many fears and little faith — not the church of sect and dogma; not the church with a stake in its creed; not the church of the Pharisee or the fanatic; but the church of brotherly love, the church of the Redeemed on earth, the church Universal! Not to Christ the peer of Confucius and Zoroaster and Plato, but Christ the peerless one! Not the Christ that frowns on sinners, but the Christ that died for them![14]

This is not the place to discuss Chamberlain's broadening of the curriculum, the increase in the study of German and French, the establishment of a scientific department with courses in engineering, the admission of women to some classes at the College, the introduction of military training and the consequent military rebellion of the students, the extension of physical training, the gradual introduction of the elective system, and in general the modernization of the College.[15] Here are to be considered the changes in respect to religious life at the College.

Changes in regard to Sunday afternoon services had just been made, and others had been proposed. It was therefore no revolutionary action when in September 1871, immediately on Chamberlain's assumption of office, the faculty voted to change the time of the morning chapel to half-past eight, after breakfast. Recitations were then to follow at consecutive hours, and there were to be no Saturday classes, Saturday being reserved for field trips, preparation of themes, and other tasks.[16] The Boards had long been reluctant to act in this regard, but now the Visiting Committee without murmur accepted Chamberlain's opinion:

> The reasons for this [change in hours] are easily seen. When the attendance on prayers was the first duty, and that often at an unseasonable hour, the tendency was not favorable towards fostering those religious impressions which the service was intended to promote. Neither conscience or consciousness could be hopefully appealed to, and even bodily absence from both this exercise and the recitation immediately following was by no means a rare occurrence; and the excuses "Slept over" and "Sickness" seem to have acquired a peculiar local meaning from which the original element of seriousness had apparently been eliminated. Both evils rapidly disappeared when the first duty was breakfast and that at 7 o'clock in the morning. Prayers followed at half past 8 in the Winter and at 8 in Summer. The four hours immediately following were devoted to the recitations of the day.[17]

The first academic year under President Chamberlain started with changing the time of morning chapel; it ended by the faculty recommending unanimously to the Boards the abolition of evening prayers.[18] The Boards were loath to act, and on August 29, 1872, the faculty inasmuch as "the Boards did not dissent, but virtually left the responsibility with [them], therefore voted that evening prayers, except Sundays, be omitted until further notice."[19]

This left the students with compulsory attendance at daily morning chapel service, Sunday morning service at some church in the community, and Sunday evening prayers. If a student preferred to attend some afternoon services which were still being held in the community he was excused from attending vespers on Sundays.[20] There was also a regular religious service by the Collins Professor or by another faculty member on Saturday evenings to which all the students were "invited but were not required to attend."[21] In addition, there were also voluntary prayer meetings under the direction of the Praying Circle on Sunday mornings and Friday evenings. Evaluating the changes, President Chamberlain reported in 1874:

> I am confident that the moral tone of the College has never been better, — in any recent time at least....The omission of evening prayers, which was only reported to the Boards, was not owing to a weakening of moral tone or religious conviction but to a deliberate opinion, formed by years of careful observation and inquiry under the administration of my predecessor, that the best interests of the college — moral and religious — would be promoted by omitting even-

ing prayers and holding morning prayers at a reasonable hour and after breakfast. No member of the Faculty has a personal objection to attending or holding evening prayers, but the result of the present plan has fully confirmed them in the belief that we should be right in following all other colleges—theological seminaries—of equal rank with ours, in this regard.[22]

While the time of holding chapel services was changed, other things connected with chapel remained the same. The juniors had begun to leave before the seniors, a major violation of "decorum and discipline," and consequently President Chamberlain on November 7, 1871, issued a circular to the class insisting "as a point of good order" that the juniors must remain in their places until every member of the senior class had departed.[23] The decorum of the students continued at times to be unsatisfactory. On January 27, 1873, the faculty voted to give two demerits to a student for reading in church.[24] The College at this time had a whole scale of demerits for various offences. Fifteen demerits resulted in a warning to students and parents, a second fifteen demerits in a second warning, a third fifteen demerits to being dropped or dismissed from college. Absence from church resulted in four demerits, absence from other exercises two, delay of theme for each day one demerit. Tardiness brought half the demerit given for absence, except for prayers, where this rule did not apply.[25] Checking on attendance and decorum in chapel was a duty of the faculty, and to this end they sat interspersed among the students. The students did not like this, and the *Orient* recommended that the faculty sit apart by themselves, and not "as sentinels among the students, for it looks as if they come to prayers for no other purpose than to watch the students."[26]

The taking of attendance at chapel and church services remained a problem as it always had been. In 1880 printed lists were made for the monitors at the Episcopal and Unitarian churches of the students who signified their intentions to attend services there. A year later, on the motion of Professor Charles H. Smith, the faculty voted that "attendance at all the churches except the college church be kept" by the student filling out a blank form stating: "I was present at the _____ church on Sunday _____ when the exercises opened and remained until they closed." The signed blank was then to be handed to the student's class officer on the following day.[27] The number of students attending services at other churches than the Congregational varied, of course, and there is no way of ascertaining how many there were. Professor Egbert C. Smyth, in his report as Collins Professor in 1862, stated that one-half to one-third of the students attended elsewhere.[28] The *Orient* on March 24, 1873, reported that "a number of our College boys form the choir for the Episcopal Church on Pleasant Street."[29] And then on March 13, 1878, noticed that "the Episcopal church still continues to be the worshipping center Sunday evenings, which leads to remark upon the coincidence that so many young ladies and gentlemen should meet for a common purpose."[30]

While not all, clearly the majority of the college students attended the Church on the Hill. Here they were by right and custom assigned to seats in the galleries. This segregation of students, apart from the rest of the congregation, led at times to problems of decorum. In 1877 a faculty committee consisting of President Chamberlain and Professors Charles H. Smith and Jotham B. Sewall were appointed to consider the propriety of transferring the seats of the students from the gallery to the body of the church. No change was made at this time nor in 1889, when another committee was appointed for the same end.[31] Actually, the students preferred sitting in the galleries. The *Orient* jokingly noted that a student could save money by going to the Church on the Hill, for they never passed the contribution box in the galleries.[32] Here in the galleries the students could look down on the congregation, eye the young ladies, sleep if so inclined, and above all read. As a bit of Bowdoin verse put it:

> A prayer-book's all that can be seen
> (The railing serves him as a screen
>   and hides this naughty youth).
> He's nearly bubbling o'er with glee,
> For down below, upon his knee
>   He reads the latest *Truth*.[33]

The Reverend Adams, on being asked to respond to a toast "To the South Gallery of the Old Church and its Occupants" at the first annual reunion of the Bowdoin Alumni Association of New York, held at Delmonico's on January 19, 1871, recalled:

> As to ... the South Gallery.... Speaking literally I should say there was little to be seen there, except a row of boots, more or less highly polished, generally less, resting on the bulwark in front. Whether there were human feet in those boots, and human bodies connected with those feet, and heads attached to those bodies, and brains to those heads, this deponent will not now venture to determine. The whole Congregation knew about the boots; they were obvious to the meanest capacity: the brains, not so obvious.[34]

This row of feet on the railing was often referred to as "Dr. Adams' Boot and Shoe Display."[35]

The deportment of the students in the galleries naturally bore some relation to the man who was occupying the pulpit. Rev. Ezra Hoyt Byington, who succeeded Rev. Adams at First Parish, was not liked by the students, but they apparently listened to him nevertheless. One Sunday, in speaking on the good effects of the temperance crusade in the West, he remarked that the price of whiskey had fallen several cents to the gallon.

"At the same time he glanced up to the galleries filled with 'the boys' who manifested their appreciation of the fact by 'audible smiles' and by wooding up."[36] Byington resigned his pastorate on October 1, 1878, and the *Orient* promptly carried a local news item: "It is not so hard to go to church now, for we have a little curiosity to see who will preach."

> The sweetest sound that greets our ears
>   When our vacation's spent
> Is when some Brunswick damsel says
>   "Herr Byington has went."[37]

There no doubt was resentment on the part of students against compulsory church and chapel attendance, more so in respect to the former than the latter, for chapel was considered part of the College. You went to chapel as you went to classes and professors presided, but church services were different. Other people were not forced to go; why should students be? It is not surprising that opposition to required attendance existed; it is remarkable how little there was. There was no student rebellion such as took place against President Chamberlain's sponsorship of compulsory military training. The *Orient*, the weekly college newspaper, started publication in 1871, and periodically there were editorials and letters protesting compulsory church and chapel attendance.[38] But there were also articles and letters in favor of existing practices; there was no concerted campaign to change existing rules.[39]

Yet the climate of opinion in general, and particularly in colleges, made changes inevitable. The introduction of the elective system shattered the old concepts of what constituted an education. Changes in relation to chapel services at the College in the first years of President Chamberlain's administration have been noted. In 1880 a faculty committee was appointed to make improvement in religious conditions at the College. It recommended (1) discontinuing the Saturday evening lecture; (2) requesting the Praying Circle to cancel their Sunday morning prayer meeting in favor of a meeting on some other evening in the week when faculty and students could meet together for prayer and discussion; (3) asking the Boards for money for possible Sunday speakers, new singing books, and a new chapel organ; (4) singing at morning prayers. The report was discussed by the faculty and indefinitely postponed.[40]

The new Chapel was inadequately heated. A father who was a physician went so far as to request that "his son be excused from chapel attendance in very cold weather, on account of the low temperature in the chapel."[41] His request was honored. The Boards sought to remedy the situation by installing a new heating system. Chapel services were also moved to the lower room of Memorial Hall during the winter months.[42]

With the advent of President Hyde in September 1885, the faculty voted that prayers no longer be held on Sunday morning. This left but two required Sunday attendances: the morning religious service at some church in the village and vesper exercises, now to be held at four o'clock Sunday afternoons.[43] Other reforms were undertaken. In the fall of 1889 the faculty held prolonged discussion on the problems of church services and chapels. Monitors, not faculty, were now to take attendance and report them to the registrar. He was to keep record of all absences, ascertain their causes, and report them to the president when necessary. He was also to make separate mention of church and chapel absences on the term bill to parents or guardians. Again a committee was appointed to see if sittings could be obtained for the students in the main part of the church. The posture of students during chapel services was discussed, but no action was taken by the faculty on this perennial problem. The faculty also voted that a list be sent each term to every pastor in town of the students who intended to attend Sabbath service at his church.[44] Efforts were also made to put more life into the chapel services. The *Orient* noted on December 18, 1889, "President Hyde spoke in chapel last Sabbath evening upon Robert Browning with eloquence that had a soul in it....We are having great chapels this year, and the boys are tending out for all they are worth."[45]

But old problems also remained. In February 1891 the *Orient*, in a critical editorial on student behavior, stated:

> A few are not interested in chapel. During reading of scripture they are preparing for the next hour or whispering to the man in front or behind. [This] may or may not go on during singing. If prayer is longer than they think it should be, there is that incessant thumping against steam pipes.[46]

The problem of tardiness at chapel did not vanish. The bell ringer had difficulties closing the chapel doors so the services could start. The *Orient* reported in 1890 that, to deal with this situation: "The Saint Peter (S.P.) degree has recently been conferred upon our esteemed college janitor. Mr. Booker has been appointed guardian of the chapel door, and now it is only those who get there in time that succeed in gaining admittance to the place of morning worship."[47] Again, in June 1891, the faculty considered the problem of attendance at chapel and church services. Faculty class officers (one faculty member for each class) were now given general oversight of attendance and deportment at all religious exercises.[48] In an effort "to consider whether some changes might not be made in the religious services of the college so as to increase the general interest in them among the students," the faculty, on the motion of Professor George T. Little, voted to appoint a committee to study the matter.[49] This committee unanimously recommended that the order of chapel services be slightly changed to begin with a hymn, during which all stand, and then proceed to a reading of scripture and prayer with all seated. A majority of the committee recommended further than the faculty consider requesting the Boards to make attendance at church services on Sunday optional. This, however, was "not to be interpreted as at all anticipatory of similar action in regard to attendance at chapel."[50]

Nothing was done in respect to the last proposal until four years later when, on January 22, 1900, it was moved "that the Faculty express to the Boards their opinion that after this year the students not be required to attend church."[51] The motion must have aroused opposition, for it was up for discussion in four subsequent meetings, and it was not until February nineteenth that the faculty passed a more circumlocutory statement:

> That the Faculty express to the Boards their opinion that the college should no longer be expected to enforce the attendance of the students at church on Sunday, but that the obligations of the college in the matter of church attendance will hereafter be best discharged by the published announcement that such attendance is expected and that a record of attendance will be kept and transmitted to parents or guardians.[52]

It was clearly a compromise solution in respect to changing a century-old policy of the college. Church attendance would henceforth be voluntary, but the College would still check on it and notify parents of the conduct of their sons. The Visiting Committee and Boards accepted the proposal.[53]

The change was welcomed by the students, and the *Orient* reported the following October that "more students are attending the Congregational Church Sunday mornings, under the new regulations, than they did when church attendance was compulsory."[54] While order among the students seemed better, there were, however, still some who read and studied during the services. President Hyde, in his annual report for 1902-1903, paid tribute to the support of the College by the ministers of the town and concluded that church attendance by the students was "materially increasing, and the attitude towards religion is quietly, though fundamentally, improving."[55]

But attendance soon slacked off. On February 24, 1905, the *Orient* reported that few were attending the services at the college church, although they were of the highest quality and the sermons of Rev. Mr. Jump were always of the very best.[56] Perhaps this *Orient* comment on poor attendance led to a proposal at the faculty meeting two weeks later to stop taking attendance at church services. It was, however, not until the following November that the faculty voted: "To include no longer in official reports to parents the record of church attendance."[57]

There was no thought of discontinuing compulsory attendance at chapel services, and in connection with them old problems remained. An article in the March 20, 1902, issue of the *Orient* states them well.

It is gratifying to note that students who own dogs have been considerate enough of late to attend chapel without them. However, there is still much room for improvement in the spirit of students while in the chapel forms. Some students feel called upon to carry on a noisy conversation and to emphasize their remarks with a continual thumping of their feet; others lounge about on the seats with their feet stretched over the form in front of them, and have not the courtesy to rise during prayers. More than once, this term, a hat has been scaled across the aisle in front of the pulpit. Such conduct cannot but merit positive censure from every thinking student, who has been brought up to reverence the laws of God and respect the laws of common decency.

It is also customary for students in certain forms to busy themselves with their lessons during the services. This should not be....When we realize that for years the students at Bowdoin were required to attend two chapel services each day, we must feel degenerated, if we cannot carry ourselves becomingly at *one* ten-minute service....Surely undergraduates can have no excuse for treating this, the only common gathering for the worship in a common religion, with such apparent carelessness and disrespect. We hope that a change may be made for the better.[58]

The Visiting Committee noted this article with approval, but went on to say that at times there were no faculty at prayers, and it was the duty of the faculty to see that the students maintained a proper attitude. "The College is a Christian institution and is so administered. And though a seemly demeanor at public worship is not a certain proof of Godliness, the failure of it is a clear instance, of an absence of gentlemanliness — not to speak of its more serious relations...."[59]

The faculty had also noted the *Orient* article, for at their meeting on March 24, 1902, they discussed the question of inattention at chapel exercises.[60] The report of the Visiting Committee apparently also struck home, for on June 22, 1902, they appointed a committee of two to secure regular attendance of the faculty at chapel exercises and devise some plan for breaking up the chapel rushing, i.e., attempts of the sophomores to keep the freshmen from leaving.[61] Today a small plaque on the chapel doors still bears witness to damage done in one of these rushes. It reads: "These Doors Presented to Bowdoin College by the Class of 1900 by Request." The Visiting Committee in 1903 found that there was less to complain about than in the previous year, yet conditions were not completely satisfactory. The Trustees passed a formal vote that the portion of the Visiting Committee's report referring "to the behaviour of students at chapel be communicated to the President and Faculty with the hope that regulations may be made to prevent such irregularities in the future."[62] There is no record of any such regulations being made, but the faculty did, in February 1905 and in September 1906, pass new regulations in regard to absences and excuses at chapel.[63] At this time twenty-three unexcused absences from chapel a semester were permitted, which tempered considerably the obligation of daily attendance.[64]

While this recital of events connected with attendance at religious services may leave a rather negative impression of religion at Bowdoin, there are other happenings during the Chamberlain-Hyde years which give a much more favorable picture. Among these are the greater use of music in chapel services, a greater effort to provide more varied and appealing chapel programs, and the establishment of a dynamic Young Men's Christian Association (Y.M.C.A.).

Nehemiah Cleaveland in his *History of Bowdoin College* writes: "Music, vocal and instrumental, has been always cultivated more or less in the college."[65] The words "more or less" are indeed a true characterization of the situation until well into the twentieth century. It was the students, not the faculty, who took the lead in sponsoring what music there was. Cleaveland, who graduated in 1813, goes on to say that there was a society for the cultivation of sacred music during his college years. We know little about this "Lockhart Society," what it did or how long it existed. An attempt to form a glee club was frowned upon by the faculty. The faculty records of September 2, 1831, state: "As it is made the duty of the Executive Government to prohibit the meetings of clubs or societies in college, which in their opinion have a tendency unfavorable to science and morality: therefore voted, that the meetings of the Glee Club, so called, be forbidden."[66] It was exactly at this time that Charles C. Taylor, Class of 1833, took the lead in soliciting funds of around two dollars each from the members of the classes of 1832, 1833, 1834, and 1835 for the purchase of an organ which was placed in the old chapel in the summer of 1832.[67] This was three years before an organ was placed in the First Parish Meeting House — again the result of private solicitation.[68] It was a period when the singing of hymns rather than psalms became established. A choir was organized at Bowdoin, and it apparently began to take part in some of the chapel services. In a poem read at a meeting of alumni in Bangor in February 1877, Dr. Edward M. Field, Class of 1845, remarked about the chapel services:

> The chapter read — the fervent prayer
>   The hymn both sweet and clear;
> These like the precious things of earth
>   Are still to memory dear![69]

But it apparently was the choir rather than the congregation who sang the hymn. In 1872 the *Orient* noted "the choir gave us some admirable music on the day of prayer for colleges."[70] The choir apparently sang on special occasions and not regularly. On March 24, 1875, the *Orient* commented:

"The singing Sunday evening in the chapel was a great success." But four years later it asked "Why don't we have singing at Sunday evening prayers?" In June 1880 the *Orient* carried with apparent approval a clipping from the *Princetonian:* "Our chapel choir's singing is like drift wood floating on a stream—it drags on bars, but don't amount to a dam."[71] Something needed to be done. In proposals to improve the religious condition at the College, a faculty committee recommended that singing at morning prayers be introduced as soon as possible, and that to this end the College should procure a suitable pipe organ for the Chapel.[72] The next year Professor Packard, in his 1881 report as Collins Professor to the Visiting Committee, remarked: "The chapel service has of late been made more impressive by the introduction of singing by the college body led by the organ and choir."[73] The choir at this time was a very small group. The *Orient* speaks of unusually fine music by the five members, and the faculty on December 17, 1883, voted that beginning with the next term the organist be paid his tuition and the four singers five dollars each for their services.[74] This was the first mention we have of paying the organist and choir. The faculty also asked for a new organ.[75] But in view of the state of the college finances, the Visiting Committee did not see how either could be done. Pay or no pay, the choir apparently now shared regularly in the chapel services. The *Orient* in September 1886 mentioned that chapel was now at twenty minutes past eight, and the editors were "glad to see the chapel choir in their places on the second morning of the term."[76]

Basic for improving the music and thereby the whole chapel program was acquiring a new organ to replace the one originally supplied by the students in 1832. Under President Hyde's leadership, the faculty on June 25, 1887, appointed Professors Henry L. Chapman and Charles C. Hutchins "a committee to take whatever action they deem best towards securing an organ for the College Chapel."[77] What efforts they undertook we do not know, but in the spring of 1888 Oliver Crocker Stevens, Class of 1876, and his wife gave to the College in memory of Mr. Stevens's grandfather, Oliver Crocker, and the latter's son, George Oliver Crocker, money for a new organ.[78] On March 26, 1888, the faculty voted that the president thank Mr. and Mrs. Stevens for their gift and assured them of the readiness of the College to comply with the stipulations Mr. Stevens had made. According to the vote of thanks tendered by the Boards to Mr. and Mrs. Stevens, these conditions were: "that the organist be compensated for his services and that the organ be available for practice by students at proper seasons."[79] Professors Chapman and Hutchins selected the organ, which was built by Messrs. Cole and Woodberry of Boston. They took six weeks for their work, and the organ cost $1,200. It was 8 feet wide, 5½ feet deep, and 15 feet high, finished in walnut, the front pipes richly decorated in gold and colors. There were two manuals with 61 notes and foot pedals with 27 more, and all together 381 pipes. Things moved swiftly for once.

On April thirtieth the faculty voted that the old chapel organ be placed in lower Memorial Hall, possibly to be used at times for "winter" chapel. On May twenty-first the faculty asked their committee to arrange, if possible, "for an organ concert for the present week." The committee was equal to the task, and on Saturday, May 26, 1888, the organ was played for the first time in public in a recital and concert at which Mr. Kotzschmar and Mr. Stockbridge played and the Glee Club sang two selections. The *Orient*, in describing the organ four days later, enthusiastically but incorrectly prophesied: "With these attractions, the 15 rule [allowable cuts] can soon be abolished, as each man in college will undoubtedly, hereafter, attend chapel regularly."[80]

The faculty kept up its efforts, and in June 1889 recommended to the Boards the employment of a choir of eight, who were to receive fifteen dollars each, and a leader, who was to receive sixty dollars, to provide music for the chapel exercises. The Boards, at the recommendation of President Hyde and the Visiting Committee, had appropriated $100 for instruction of the choir in 1888. Mr. William H. Stockbridge was to be employed for that year. The next year the president, in line with the faculty vote, advised that rather than an appropriation of $200 for the instruction of the choir he preferred $180 "for the maintenance of the choir." This would allow using some of the money to pay the choir members. The boards met his wishes; by 1894 the sum had been increased to $200.[81] To great applause, President Hyde told the Boston alumni in 1890 that the new organ and an organized choir had greatly enriched the chapel services.[82] New hymnals were purchased, and the old ones given to the Maine Missionary Society. At last the "blowing" of the organ was recognized as a paying college job, and the student who performed this service was to get "ten dollars ($10) per term."[83] But problems remained.

In his report of 1901, President Hyde stated that the appointment of a quartet and leader had partially solved the problem of music at chapel services. It was satisfactory at Sunday afternoon services, but at daily services, when the quartet was joined by a fluctuating number of volunteers, it was not satisfactory. He felt it would be best to eliminate the volunteers and "employ with proper renumeration to the leader and his seven associates, a double quartette, which shall be expected to make the same careful preparation by rehearsals and the learning of new music, for the morning chapel, which the single quartette now makes for Sunday afternoon."[84] But his proposals were not carried out. In October 1901, the *Orient*, which had editorialized in May that the choir was too large and only good singers should be admitted, reported that the chapel choir numbered twenty-two members plus the organist.[85] At times the choir functioned well, at other times not so well. In the fall of 1907 the choir members had got into the practice of appearing in the choir loft just in time to sing the hymn and then leaving immediately. On November eleventh the faculty undertook to stop this practice. They voted that a choir monitor be appointed and paid fifteen dollars a year. The immediate result was a strike on the part of the choir, not for more pay—for they got no pay—but for shorter hours, as the news report put it. Only the leader appeared, the other eleven members sitting with their classes. It says something about the state of "congregational singing" that the absence of the choir led to the cancelling of the hymns that morning. The strike aroused much attention on the campus, but Dean Sills was able to settle the matter by calling in the members of the choir and talking things over.[86] The size of the choir fluctuated; in 1913 there were sixteen members, but we know little about how they were selected or if they regularly received compensation. The leader was appointed by the faculty. On November 5, 1917, the faculty voted that the Committee on Student Aid was to apportion $120 among members of the choir, certainly not a great remuneration.[87]

The greatest step, no doubt, in upgrading the music in chapel was the appointment in 1912 of Edward Haines Wass as instructor in music. He not only offered the first music courses given at the College, but took charge of the choir and served as the organist until his death in 1935.[88]

The improvement of music in the chapel was but one of the changes for the good brought about by President Hyde. More important, no doubt, was his own personal contribution to vitalizing the chapel program. Professor Burnett, in his fine biography of Hyde, writes: "The character of these [Sunday chapel] services was a problem which the new president had to take up immediately.... He immediately began a practice that he continued throughout his life, of choosing for Sunday afternoon some theme in practical ethics that had current interest and limiting his discussion of it to about twelve minutes. The effect upon the attitude of the students was well-nigh instantaneous."[89] It was a new type of sermon, a new type of theology, always biblically centered but presented in a way that appealed to youth. This was the period when the Social Gospel movement was having a great impact in the United States.[90] "The Christ of the twentieth century," wrote Hyde, "is not exactly the same as the sectarian Christ of the nineteenth, or the dogmatic Christ of the sixteenth, or the official Christ of the thirteenth, or the metaphysical Christ of the fourth, or even the Christ after the flesh, which Paul had already outgrown in the first century. The Christ of the twentieth century is preeminently the social Christ, and is greater than all that has gone before."[91] As one reads accounts in the *Orient* and other papers of Hyde's chapel talks and his excellent baccalaureate sermons, it is easy to see why there was a new awakening of religion on the campus. He modestly noted in his presidential reports of 1903 and 1904 that "the attitude toward religion is quietly, though fundamentally, improving."[92]

Some old traditions were maintained, others altered or dropped, and new programs added. Just when the custom of "Seniors' Last Chapel" began it is impossible to say. On that occasion, more were in attendance than usual, and at the close of the service the seniors locked arms and while marching out they sang *Auld Lang Syne*. They had a special verse to be sung as they passed out the chapel door:

> Farewell, farewell, dear chapel walls,
>   And classmates true and kind;
> Those mem'ries fond we'll ne'er forget,
>   And days of auld lang syne.[93]

At the entrance they waited for the other three classes to pass out, who then formed two lines and the seniors marched through. The president of the junior class proposed three cheers for the seniors, and they in turn responded by cheers for Bowdoin, the faculty, and others. As the *Orient* noted: "Not a remarkable scene indeed, for display and formality but for simplicity"; it is justly called "the most important ceremony of the College course." From then on the seniors were excused from attendance at chapel.

The "Day of Prayer for Colleges," which had long been observed in many churches, was retained under President Hyde. In 1898 the observance was moved from the last Thursday of January to Sunday. The custom of cancelling classes on that day was thus ended. When the World's Student Christian Federation appointed a Sunday in February as the Universal Day of Prayer, Bowdoin went along with this practice.[94]

In his second presidential report to be printed, that of 1892-1893, President Hyde wrote that "it is the duty of a college founded and maintained so largely in the interest of piety and religion to do all in its power to awaken and sustain the religious life of the students." The use to which the Chapel was put, he continued "was not commensurate with its possibilities. If we could devote five hundred dollars to the payment of ten persons who should give an address on a Sunday of each month, the effect on the religious interest of the students would be marked. With such an appropriation we could secure the most prominent ministers in New England. I suggest this as a legitimate way of expending a portion of the Collins Fund."[95] The Boards did not take up the idea nor did they when he repeated his appeal in even more urgent terms the following year. It was not until March 17, 1907, that this pet project of his could be implemented. Professor and Mrs. George T. Files provided funds whereby outstanding preachers would from time to time be invited to occupy the pulpit at First Parish in the morning and conduct the college Sunday chapel services in the afternoon. The preachers would then in most cases meet with the students informally in the evening "to answer questions on any subjects connected with life or religion."[96] In addition the *Orient* regularly reported on the chapel addresses by these distinguished guests, so that it must have been a rare student indeed who did not come in some contact with what these men had to say.

The program of "College Preachers" was to be administered by President Hyde and Rev. Herbert A. Jump of First Parish. It was planned to have such a minister once a month, and he was to be a man of national reputation who had a message for young men. All denominations were to be represented. The program was welcomed by the parish and College. Actually, the number of college preachers was never large. They were a distinguished group as a whole and were regularly listed in the college catalogue down to the catalogue of 1917-1918, when the program apparently came to an end.[97]

Not only were the chapel services revitalized in these turn-of-the-century decades, but new student societies were formed. Students assumed the leadership in furthering athletics at the College. The fraternities came to play a greater part in the social life of the College, having largely displaced the loyalties which were long associated with the Athenaean and Peucinian Societies. In 1882 the old Praying Circle transformed itself into the Young Men's Christian Association. This was exactly at the time when the Y.M.C.A. was expanding its work in the student field and stimulating new interest in religion on college campuses throughout the United States. The Bowdoin Y soon became one of the largest and most active organizations at the College.

The constitution adopted in 1882 stated that the object of the Young Men's Christian Association of Bowdoin College "shall be to promote growth in grace and Christian fellowship among its members and aggressive Christian work, especially by and for students."[98] There were to be two classes of members. To be an active member a student had to be a member in good standing of some Evangelical church and be elected by a two-thirds vote of members present at any regular meeting. Only such active members had the right to vote and hold office. Any student of good moral character could be elected an associate member by a majority vote of members present at a regular meeting. Partial membership rolls showing this distinction of membership are available until the class of 1900. A new constitution was adopted on June 8, 1899, but as no copy has come down to us, we do not know what henceforth were to be qualifications for membership.[99] As late as October 24, 1901, a distinction was still being made between active and associate members, but starting with November twenty-first of that year, the records refer simply to admission to membership.[100] Whether the requirement of belonging to an Evangelical church was dropped at this time is not clear, and the minutes never refer to this matter. However, we have mention in a report of the association to the Visiting Committee that the requirement of church membership was done away with in 1906.[101] It seems clear that membership was now open to any student who would participate in its activities and pay the modest dues. At least in the autumn of 1906, when the association was in debt, they set out to recruit 200 members at one dollar each; if they succeeded they were promised a gift of an additional $200. Apparently able to enlist only 156 members, they nevertheless were able to clear their debts.[102]

The association met with success from its very beginning. Professor Packard, in his 1884 report as Collins Professor to the Visiting Committee, stated that he had met occasionally with the association in their weekly meetings and did "not doubt that the influence has been important on the moral and religious life of the college."[103] On November 3, 1887, the association took over quarters which the College had refitted for them in South Winthrop Hall. The seating capacity was about doubled over their previous quarters, but at the first meeting was "filled to overflowing." The *Orient* wrote with approval:

> The new room is well lighted with gas, is neatly papered and carpeted, and its windows opening on each side of the building are tastefully curtained. In fact, there seems nothing further to be desired in the line of improvement or additions.[104]

When Winthrop Hall was remodelled in 1898, the association met for a time in Professor Chapman's room in Massachusetts Hall. President Hyde promised that the association would get a room of its own when the new library was built. By 1904 the association was established in Banister Hall, and two years later in a new room in the north wing of the chapel.[105]

The student Y associations, like the Y in general, "sought to devise a religious and secular program to supplement but not compete with the activities and goals of the churches."[106] To this end they held prayer meetings and Bible study groups, sponsored both religious and secular lectures,[107] sent out deputations when invited to take over services in churches of all denominations,[108] took up collections for Thanksgiving and Christmas baskets, ran a book exchange, etc. In developing a program, the students were helped by the travelling secretaries of the Y movement and the literature coming from headquarters.[109] Bowdoin early fell in with the general Y program of providing a freshman handbook (1892)[110] and holding a reception in the fall to welcome the freshmen to college. At the latter, various professors were invited to speak as well as some students. The Bowdoin association from the very start participated in state YMCA conventions and in the Northfield and other conferences established by the national Y. The record books contain little information aside from the names of officers, committee members, and delegates to conferences.

The Y movement always placed great emphasis on Bible study. Actually, there was little or none of this in the regular Bowdoin college curriculum, and the Y undertook to fill this gap.[111] This was often part of their regular prayer meetings. On November 1, 1893, there is a note in the *Orient* that the Y.M.C.A. hoped to revive the Tuesday evening Bible study. In 1903 there was a revival of interest. Rector E. D. Johnson of the

Episcopal church undertook to lead the juniors and seniors, Professor Chapman the sophomores, and David R. Porter '06 the freshmen. President Hyde mentioned these classes in his 1904 report, and in 1906 he again saw fit to mention the Bible classes conducted by Rev. Jump of First Parish and by Rev. Leroy W. Coons, the new minister at the Universalist Church. In that academic year, Bible classes were also organized in the fraternities.[112] At Commencement in 1908 the Boards undertook to fill a long-felt need by appointing Mr. Roderick Scott, who held both A.B. and M.A. degrees from Harvard, as assistant in English and Christian Association secretary.[113] With his appointment, Bible study took on a new lease of life. Promptly the next fall he organized three Bible classes: "Studies in the Life of Christ" for freshmen and sophomores and "Studies in the Social Significance of the Teaching of Jesus" for juniors and seniors. Both of these were to have student leaders. He himself would teach an elective, "Studies in the Teachings of the Earlier Prophets."[114] The next year Mr. Scott was succeeded by James Lukens McConaughy, who soon was also to add professor of education to his title. He remained at Bowdoin until the fall of 1915, when he went to Dartmouth. Miles Erskine Langley, who had been at the College one year as instructor in surveying and mechanical drawing, took over the secretaryship of the Christian Association. With the entrance of the United States into World War I, the Y adapted itself to army life at Bowdoin. A secretary of the Y was never again appointed, faculty advisers thereafter providing what leadership the College furnished the students.

In 1903-1904 the *Orient* had begun to head its weekly religious items "Religious Notes" rather than "Y.M.C.A. Notes," and used the name "Christian Association" rather than "Y.M.C.A.," although the latter was never completely displaced. The name was apparently changed at some time, for in the spring of 1910 a new constitution was adopted changing the name of the Christian Association back to the Young Men's Christian Association of Bowdoin College. The constitution also provided for an alumni advisory committee.[115] President Hyde, in his report for 1910, cited with approval the *Orient*'s statement that "this had undoubtedly been the most prosperous year in the history of the Y.M.C.A., and with plans already formulated next year will even surpass this year's record." He went on to mention the new constitution and then summarized the work of the Y. Its membership stood at 198, larger than ever before; it published 500 handbooks and gave one to each student; Bible study enrolled 113 with an average attendance for two months of 52; missionary study and missionary giving at Bowdoin had set a record; the Y had raised $300 to support A. S. Hiwale '09 as a missionary in India; a boys' club had been established at Pejepscot, and forty students were active in this project; a Sunday school class had also been established there; the students had raised $20 by a collection in chapel for Thanksgiving Day dinners; weekly meetings were held every Thursday evening with an average attendance of 54; in addition there were four special meetings during the Week of Prayer; four Wednesday noon meetings during Lent, and four special Sunday evening meetings conducted by the college preachers. Arrangements had also been made for students to take out temporary membership in the Church on the Hill. Obviously proud of the work being done, President Hyde mentioned that "when the present Secretary came here he was told by the General Secretary of all the Associations for America, that Bowdoin was one of the discouraging fields for student Y.M.C.A. work in the country." Opinion at national headquarters had changed.[116]

The work of the Y continued to expand. In 1911 the *Orient* wrote: "Under the splendid leadership of Mr. McConaughy the association has completed the most successful year's work in its history. More men have been reached, more work has been done, and more interest in the association has been stimulated than ever before."[117] That fall it was planned to have twenty-two groups of five to ten members with student leaders to study the social significance of the teachings of Jesus (seniors and juniors), the life of Christ (sophomores and freshmen), and men of the Old Testament. The final Bible study report stated that actually seventeen classes had been underway with an enrollment of 141 and an average attendance of 86—certainly a very respectable showing. The interest in Bible study finally led the College to offer a course for upperclassmen in biblical history for the second semester of 1914-1915, to be given by Professor McConaughy.[118] It was taught only once, for when Professor McConaughy left Bowdoin in 1915 the course was dropped.

President Hyde always threw his support behind the Y, and during his presidency the association took a leading part in religious affairs at the College. In 1914 nearly 75 percent of the student body were members. Hyde mentioned the Y regularly in his reports and in 1915 wrote: "Bowdoin is probably the first college to incorporate in its annual reports any statements of the religious activities of the year."[119] The descriptive paragraphs in the college catalogue on the Christian Association—Y.M.C.A. (the names were used interchangeably) stressed that membership was open to all students. In the catalogue for 1910-1911 a new phrase was added—it was "an undenominational student organization membership in which is open to every undergraduate."[120] This of course had always been true, but stressing its undenominational character was no doubt in line with other statements made when the College entered upon the Carnegie pension plan. It perhaps was also made in an effort to get non-Protestants to join in the activities. Some Catholics did share, and the students established both a Catholic and a Protestant Sunday school at Pejepscot.[121] But Catholics on the whole tended to stay apart from the Y. In the fall of 1911 they organized the Gibbons Club with about twenty members. The purpose of the club was "to assist each other in the performance of religious duties and in keeping up interest in the Catholic

Church."[122] For a time at least it was fairly active and in 1912 gave a play, *Our Jim*, in the Town Hall to raise money to build a new Catholic church in Brunswick to replace the one that had burned down in a recent fire. There had, of course, been other such denominational organizations or groups associated with various churches in the community. The College never supported these financially; it did aid the undenominational Y, and the latter received money from the Blanket Tax (student activity fees) when that system of supporting campus organizations was established in February 1912.[123]

For years, the student body had been, to use a modern characterization, predominantly WASP (White Anglo-Saxon Protestant). Aside from John Brown Russwurm, Class of 1826, no Negro graduated from Bowdoin until 1910, when Samuel H. Dreer and Arthur A. Madison received their degrees.[124] As to sex, Bowdoin was an officially all-male institution, although faculty wives always played a significant part in college social functions. There is an interesting item in the *Portland Transcript* of October 7, 1872, that indicates rules were being bent a little in the more liberal post-Civil War period.

> Half a dozen young women, graduates of the Brunswick High School, have applied for admission to a select course of study and their request will no doubt be granted. It has been customary for some years for women to attend many of the lectures.[125]

Nothing more is known about this early venture into coeducation. That the students sought the company of the young ladies of the village, and in turn were welcomed by them, is a part of Bowdoin's history from the very beginning.

It is not easy to ascertain the religious preference of the student body, and this of course changed from year to year as classes graduated and new men entered. It became customary at commencement time to present statistics on the graduating class, what professions the men were going to enter, how many smoked, how many drank, and so on. In the class of 1860 there were, for example, thirty Congregationalists, ten Unitarians, eight Baptists, three Episcopalians, one Swedenborgian, one Quaker, and two who were uncertain.[126] The class of 1864 had about the same religious preference mix with the addition of one Shaker and two Mormons. Twenty years later, on the even of President Hyde's administration, the class of 1884 was made up of nine Congregationalists, two Baptists, two Episcopalians, three Unitarians, one Universalist, and two Free Thinkers. It was a small class, and as the College grew in size under President Hyde the religious diversity increased. In subsequent years Roman Catholics and Jews, although few in number, became regular members of the College. How many there were it is difficult to assess. In his annual report in 1904 President Hyde mentions a religious census of October 1903 which indicated that there were twelve Catholic students and one Hebrew in a student body of 206.[127] When, at the beginning of the twentieth century, the college records were transferred from the old cumbersome book records to a card system, religious preference was not among the items noted. From 1905 to 1910 the registrar presented, as part of the president's report, detailed statistics on the student body, but there was no mention of religious preference. Nor was this noted when the dean's report replaced the registrar's statistics in the *President's Report* of 1910-1911. It was not until 1920-1921, under President Sills, that the religious preferences of the students were regularly given as part of the president's report.[128] The biggest change was the increased number of Roman Catholics and Jews in the student body. In 1920-1921 Congregationalists still led the list with 127, followed by Roman Catholics 69, Baptists 38, Methodists 31, Episcopalians 27, Universalists 23, Hebrews 13, Unitarians 9, Christian Scientists 5, Friends 3, Presbyterians 2, Lutheran 1, and those with no preference 55 out of a total of 403.[129] The increasing diversity of the student body, particularly the increase in the number of non-Protestants and those with no religious preference, was to enhance the difficulties of continuing the college chapel services and the program of the Y.M.C.A. Many Catholics and Jews did not feel at home participating in these programs and usually gave only half-hearted support when they did join. New social problems also arose in respect to the fraternities. It was some years before Roman Catholics were freely accepted into their membership,[130] and it was not until after World War II that Jews were routinely accepted as members.

IX.

The Sills Era

IN ITS 1910 REPORT, the Visiting Committee stated: "It has been proposed to establish in the College a new office, not one that requires a new man, or that deals with new work. For some years such work as keeping the rank of the students and looking after the correspondence, interviewing students, and giving them good counsel, has been distributed among different members of the faculty who have been called, respectively Recorder, Registrar, and Secretary. The proposition is to gather up these different functions and place them in the hands of one man, giving him the title of Dean as is done in other institutions. This seems to us an excellent suggestion, especially as the man abundantly qualified for the office is at hand. We refer to Professor Sills, the head of the Latin department."[1] The Boards accepted the recommendation at their meeting in June. Bowdoin at long last had a dean,[2] and the Henry Winkley Professor of the Latin Language and Literature, Kenneth Charles Morton Sills, who had been serving as faculty secretary since 1906, was given further administrative responsibilities.[3]

Sills had received his A.B. from Bowdoin in 1901, done graduate work at Harvard and Columbia, and returned to the College in 1906 as a teacher. As dean, Sills became closely associated with President Hyde in running the College. In charge of keeping attendance records, he had the opportunity to know well the problems of conducting daily chapel services. From his days as an undergraduate and then as a member of the Alumni Advisory Committee of the Y.M.C.A., he knew the ins and outs of student-led religious activities. He was truly experienced in the ways of Bowdoin when he was suddenly called upon to take charge of the College as acting president on the death of President Hyde on June 29, 1917. The country was at war, and the College was caught up with a multitude of problems. At a special meeting in May 1918, the Boards elected Sills president, and in June named as dean Paul Nixon, Sill's colleague in the Department of Latin, who had been acting as assistant dean since October 1917. These two long-time associates, both thoroughly acquainted with the Hyde-administered College, were to shape the course of Bowdoin for more than three decades.

All previous Bowdoin presidents had been ordained Congregational ministers, with the exception of Chamberlain, who, however, had studied for the ministry although he had never been ordained. Sills, the son of a prominent Episcopalian rector, was a devoted member of the Episcopal church and deeply interested in religious and church affairs. Instead of occupying the accustomed pew in the Church on the Hill, the Bowdoin president now attended St. Paul's Episcopal Church on Pleasant Street; the dean, instead of attending the Episcopal church, now attended the Church on the Hill. This was about the only difference that the change of administration made in religious practices and customs at the College. Like past presidents of Bowdoin, Sills was not narrowly denominational, but strongly ecumenical in thought and leadership. Hyde, as president of Bowdoin, had become one of the leaders of the Congregational churches; Sills was to become one of the outstanding lay leaders among the Episcopalians.[4] Both were intent on furthering the welfare of Bowdoin as a Christian college.

In his inaugural address, a strong and succinct affirmation of liberal education, the new president did not have as much to say about religion as had his predecessors. But he did not neglect it and pledged himself to remain true to Bowdoin's traditions and heritage—which surely involved, in the words of the 1794 charter, the promotion of "virtue and piety."

> Our aim is not vocational; our goal is not efficiency. We hold that the real object of education is to make men free intellectually and spiritually, to develop the resourceful mind in a strong Christian character. Education concerns itself primarily with the individual. It strives to make him not only a more useful, but a happier, more tolerant man.... The things of the spirit are the eternal things: they live on and endure when war and lust of conquest have passed.
>
> Changes in administration and in detail there will of course be, some temporary such as are already contemplated to suit war conditions, others more lasting to adapt our course to an ever-changing world. But we shall be true to the ancient traditions, the ancient heritage of this institution: the spirit of the College will live on
> When years have clothed the lines in moss
> That tell our names and day
> and we shall be true to these principles not only for ourselves, but for our beloved country.[5]

In his first baccalaureate address, delivered three days before his inaugural, he was even more explicit in reference to the Christian character of Bowdoin.

> I am speaking today for the College and not for the church. But an institution like ours, founded on Christian principles and interpreting those principles for more than a century, cannot send forth

from her walls a group of her sons without reminding them that she expects them to be in all the relations of life Christian gentlemen. She has tried to teach through art and literature and science and philosophy not only the duty of self-development, but the no less important duty of considering the rights of others. In the complex modern world the proper interpretation of the Golden Rule calls not only for a kind heart but for a sound mind. Consideration for others, whether individuals, classes or nations we must exercise, else Christian civilization will surely fail....Wherever you [members of the graduating class] go amid the changes and chances of this mortal life, may you not forget some of the lessons which your Christian education here has taught.[6]

One of the first steps the new president took in respect to religious activity on the campus was to appoint a faculty committee on the Y.M.C.A. This committee was short-lived, for although listed in the college catalogue of 1918-1919, it gives way the next year to the Committee on Religious Activities.[7] The latter was to remain one of the regular faculty committees until 1960 when, in a general overhaul of the committees at the College, it was abolished.[8] Never one of the more active and important faculty committees, it nevertheless served a most useful purpose. It was above all a means of contact between the students and the faculty and lent its support to the Bowdoin Christian Association.

In the spring of 1918 the national Y.M.C.A. had made a drive to organize Bible classes at colleges. Bowdoin undertook to cooperate, and Rev. Thompson E. Ashby of First Parish agreed to train student leaders who would then lead discussion groups. Thirty-one such small groups were organized, which were scheduled to meet for an hour before vesper services on Sunday afternoons.[9] It was too much of a good thing, and the program was not picked up again in the fall. With military units on the campus, the Y had shifted more and more to the type of work it was carrying on in military camps everywhere. On November 6, 1918, a Y hut was formally opened in the Moulton Union, and Professor L. D. McLean was assigned to direct affairs there.[10]

With the end of the war and the return "to normalcy," the College did not again appoint a paid secretary for the Y.M.C.A. Henceforth the Y, like other campus organizations, was to have a faculty adviser. The Y had been operating with the help of an alumni advisory committee since the spring of 1910. The *Bugle* for 1923 still carries the names of this committee, but in 1924 the *Bugle* write-up of the Y lists Austin H. MacCormick '15, then Bowdoin's alumni secretary, as faculty adviser. These unsung advisers, usually recruited by the students or the college administration, are never mentioned in the college records, and it is impossible to compile a complete list of the faculty who served in this capacity. They were not only to give advice and support but were supposed to exercise a certain amount of supervision, especially in regard to financial expenditures; payment of bills required their signatures.

Although the names Christian Association and Y.M.C.A. were used interchangeably, the use of the latter gradually ended. In October 1925 the cabinet of the Y voted to change the name of the organization officially to Christian Association, the name by which it was becoming known in most of the leading colleges.[11] This did not mean any separation from the national Y.M.C.A. committee, and their travelling secretaries still visited the campus. Nor did it end the privileges which membership in the Bowdoin Y entitled the students at other Y.M.C.A.s, often reduced room charges. Yet it was not until 1927 that the *Bugle* listed the Bowdoin Christian Association among the college activities with the note "Formerly the Bowdoin Y.M.C.A." By then the Y had become the subject of a college ballad, always sung with great gusto and hilarity. When it came into being and who was responsible are unknown, but it was popular in the early 1920s. Campus wits added verse on verse, some properly best passed over. However, the anchor verse seems to indicate that it dates from the Sills era.

> The Bowdoin Y.M.C.A.
> I wish I had a barrel of rum
>   And sugar 300 pounds
> The chapel bell to mix it in,
>   And the clapper to stir it 'round.
> We'd sit on the steps of Hubbard Hall
>   So happy and so gay,
> And we'd sing to Hell with Casey Sills
>   [drink to the health of Casey Sills]
> And the Bowdoin Y.M.C.A.
> Chorus:
> Oh, we are, we are, we are, we are
>   The Bowdoin Y.M.C.A.
> We are, we are, we are, we are
>   The Bowdoin Y.M.C.A.
> So what the Hell do we care
>   What the people say
> For we are, we are, we are, we are
>   The Bowdoin Y.M.C.A.
>
> And if I had a daughter
>   I'd dress her up in green
> And send her up to the U of M
>   To coach the football team
> And if I had a son
>   He'd go to Bowdoin too
> And yell to Hell with the U of M
>   As his daddy used to do.[12]

President Sills was a strong supporter of having one nondenominational student religious association, whether called Y.M.C.A. or B.C.A., open to membership of all students who cared to join in its activities and supported, in part at least, by student activity (Blanket Tax) funds. He was adamantly against denominational clubs obtaining college funds or using college buildings; the proper place for them was in connection with their respective churches.[13] He was anxious to bring the students into relationship with their churches, and to this end the religious affiliation was listed on their college records.[14] Pastors of local churches or visiting representatives of denominations which had no church in the community but wanted to keep in touch with their student members could always get lists of their students at the college office.[14] At times, at least, the faculty Religious Activities Committee furnished these lists to pastors of the local churches, often at a meeting in the fall when the pastors were invited to meet with the committee.

Entirely student-led, the Christian Association managed to keep going, but it was by far not so active as when a professional secretary was in charge. Receptions for freshmen were held each fall, and the freshman Bible (handbook) distributed. Usually this was put together by the students but with considerable help from Massachusetts Hall. Meetings were held, various social service activities sponsored, and some deputation work (taking over church services) carried on. Special Lenten meetings were held in 1923 in one of the fraternity houses, which were led by a member of the faculty. Religious questions were discussed, and the president in his annual report stated that these meetings aroused a good deal of interest.[15] The press noted that at Bowdoin the Y was more active than it had been for many years previous. In December 1926 a meeting of the B.C.A. was held in the Zeta Psi House for "the purpose of finding out just what was wanted in a society of this sort."[16] Nothing was decided except that the college Christian Association needed reorganization. This apparently was accomplished, and in November 1927 the *Orient* stated: "The Christian Association has started out in a much more businesslike manner this year."[17] It organized a series of smokers held at different fraternity houses, where faculty members spoke and then led discussion. In general, however, the B.C.A. languished in the 1920s in comparison to the preceding or succeeding decades.

Two major gifts in the first years of President Sills helped to enrich the religious program. In 1923 a set of chimes was installed in the south tower of the Chapel. There were eight bells tuned so that many pieces in the key of C and D can also be played. On the largest bell, weighing 1,500 pounds, there is the following inscription:

Given to Bowdoin College by Edward Payson Payson of the Class of 1869 and William Martin Payson of the Class of 1874 in Memory of

Their Payson and Martin Ancestors Who Were Trustees or Graduates of the College.

There was a program of inaugural recitals on October 20 and 21, 1923.[18]

In 1926 Mr. Cyrus Hermann Kotzschmar Curtis of Philadelphia gave to the College, along with a swimming pool, a new chapel organ. In the opinion of Professor Edmund H. Wass, associate professor of music, it was the finest and best organ both instrumentally and tonally that could be obtained for the Chapel.[19] Whereas the former organ had been placed in the loft at the front entrance, this new organ was installed at the other end of the Chapel, in a room over Banister Hall which formerly had been used as a classroom for surveying and mechanical drawing. The large displayed pipes as well as the three-manual console, which was placed directly behind the pulpit, were an ornament to that part of the Chapel. The organ was dedicated at Commencement 1927 with a recital by Professor Wass and Mr. Charles R. Cronham, the municipal organist of Portland. After the dedicatory concert was over, Mr. Curtis tried out the organ and "played several selections before a small but honored audience," pronouncing himself well pleased with the instrument.[20]

The format of chapel services was well established when President Sills took over, and he was resolved to carry them forward. The end of the program of special college preachers, while regrettable, was not of major consequence. By 1914 the number had declined to four a year, hardly enough to make or break a program. But efforts to get able and distinguished speakers for the vesper services were never relaxed and were on the whole successful year after year.[21] Not as dynamic a speaker as President Hyde, President Sills was nevertheless an extremely able chapel speaker. Students always felt that he had something worthwhile to say, and his sincerity was manifest to all.

In his report for 1920-1921, President Sills resumed the practice of President Hyde of referring to religious matters at the College. If there were any ruffled feathers among the alumni over an Episcopalian being at the head of Bowdoin, his words should have brought some assurance.

> Bowdoin College is definitely a Christian institution of learning. Founded by men of deep piety and strong religious conviction, it has remained true to this early standard and has in all religious matters faithfully observed that tolerance of spirit which is reflected in the charter of the college that placed no religious or denominational tests on either professor or student. For many years Bowdoin was in close relation to the Congregational Church; and that relation has been altered rather than obliterated by the passage of time. Today the First Parish of Brunswick is still the College Church; and every Tuesday morning the minister of that church conducts the chapel service of the College.... Attendance at church is encouraged but not made

obligatory. There has been, I think, in the past ten years a great improvement both in the conduct and the attitude of students at Chapel.²²

Reading the *Orient* of that day and other college records confirms Sills's judgment of the status of the chapel services. But there was no room to rest on past laurels, and Sills constantly strove to improve the chapel services. They had been going well partly because of the generous number of cuts allowed. In January 1919 the *Orient*, in noting the small number of seniors in chapel, and that there were no monitors present to check those who were present, editorialized: "Compulsory chapel is not as compulsory as its name would indicate. If the system is not to be fully carried out, why not abolish it entirely?"²³ A year later, accepting chapel as "an established institution," the *Orient* pleaded that it should be observed "with the dignity and decorum which should be its due." Students should not drop their hymn books on the seats with a thud, nor should they show approval by banging their feet against the radiator pipes. It would be better to clap hands or show no approval at all.²⁴ Apparently the custom of snapping fingers had not yet been inaugurated, but the remarks do indicate that the students were attentive at least at times.

There had always been some opposition to compulsory chapel at Bowdoin, but this was never serious. To assure the attendance of some faculty at daily chapels, the president resorted to writing each member in the fall requesting him, if it was convenient, to attend chapel on a certain day; if this was not convenient the day could be shifted to another. The designation of a certain "chapel day" worked very well and was observed by most of the faculty, although a few never deigned to attend at all, while others attended far oftener than on their special day. In February 1928 Dean Nixon spoke on the beneficial effects of chapel, which led the *Orient* to remark: "The attitude of the student body has been, on the whole, and rather unfortunately, intolerant towards its daily required devotional exercises, and this attitude seems to be growing stronger rather than weaker, with the passing years. The daily chapel service, sorry to say, has been an evil to be endured by the students with a touch of the resignation to the inevitable." But the *Orient* questioned if the criticism of chapel meant much; it was simply a matter of blowing off steam. It came out for continuing the chapel services. "Undergraduates at Bowdoin," the editor wrote, "have long boasted of the famous old Bowdoin spirit. Abolish your daily gathering at chapel and you will see the spirit of unity and this common pride crumble gradually into nothing."²⁵

In the fall of 1925 President Sills appointed a committee of seniors as well as committees of the faculty and alumni to investigate the needs of the College for the next ten years.²⁶ Aside from expressing the need for a new chapel organ and mentioning the possibility of enlarging the Chapel, nothing was said in the faculty or alumni reports in respect to the chapel services.[27] The seniors took their assignment seriously and drew up a questionnaire of some eighty-odd questions dealing with all aspects of college life.[28] They raised the question of voluntary or compulsory chapel, and the students voted in favor of continuing the daily compulsory chapel services sixty-five to fifty-four. To the question how often chapel services should be held "...which was inserted for the men who did not want services to be compulsory," out of 110 men who submitted answers to this question, "80 wished it to be daily, 4 men wanted services to be held anywhere from two to four times a week." While opinion was divided on compulsory attendance, the committee concluded "that a very large majority of students desire that the present system of daily chapel be retained," and it so recommended. The committee found that the men who wanted attendance voluntary were at a loss to find a way to answer the question: "How would you secure attendance if voluntary?"[29] The committee nevertheless felt that a more liberal system should be established. Instead of a flat quota of twenty-three excused absences for all upperclassmen, it recommended that freshmen should be allowed twenty, sophomores twenty-five, juniors thirty, and seniors forty cuts a semester.[30] They also recommended that the double cut system (before and after holidays) be abolished for chapel, and that services not be held during examination periods when "the undergraduate should be allowed absolute freedom in planning his work."[31]

As to Sunday vesper services, the committee felt the College should provide a substantial sum to secure outside speakers who would be selected by a faculty committee. "Until this ideal can be accomplished we strongly recommend that the President speak as often as he is able at the service as we feel that he imparts more inspiration than any other man under the present system."[32]

There can be no doubt that the students did an outstanding job in their report, and the president paid high tribute to them in speaking to the Boston alumni and again in his *President's Report* for 1925-1926.[33] In that report he took occasion to give his views in regard to the chapel services, views that he held and furthered throughout his administration. They merit quotation at length.

> From one end of the country to the other during this past year the question of compulsory chapel in college has been discussed. No general rules can be laid down covering all institutions. Each college should settle the problem on its own account. At Bowdoin it is interesting to note that in the undergraduate questionnaire a decisive majority voted for the maintenance of compulsory chapel. We feel that there are the following good reasons for maintaining the traditional service. In the first place it is an advantage in a small college like ours for the college community to begin its work at the same time, and chapel attendance is of value on that side. Furthermore, it

enhances the feeling of unity in the College. The College is a corporate community. The very word itself implies that, and in maintaining the proper morale it is of decided benefit to have the college meet as a body daily. In addition to these prudential reasons there are what may be called literary reasons. In these days when there is so little acquaintance with the Bible, it helps somewhat for the undergraduates to take part in responsive readings, to hear the more familiar passages of scripture read and re-read, and to become acquainted with the great and popular hymns of the church. Finally, the chapel service recognizes that religion has its place in the development of the well rounded man. No denominational tenets are set forth or crammed down the throats of unwilling undergraduates; but the service which is simple and dignified, and distinctly not secular, can do no harm so far as proper religious feelings are concerned, and may do much good. I am more and more convinced year by year that the daily and Sunday chapel exercises are among the most helpful agencies that we have in our college life. We realize that to have them effectively conducted we must have the good-will and cooperation of the undergraduates; and I think at the present time we have that in large measure.[34]

In answer to the question on the student questionnaire "as to the new course most needed in college," 22 men wished a course in biblical history and literature; and 5 men wished a course in pedagogy and methods of teaching."[35] The other wants were so diverse that no one obtained more than four votes apiece. A course in biblical literature had undergone a rather checkered career at Bowdoin. In September 1913 the faculty had considered establishing such a course, but "it was considered inadvisable."[36] Such a course was, however, given in the spring semester of 1915. When it was dropped at the departure of Professor McConaughy, the students in June 1916, in their annual Y report, recommended that it be restored to the curriculum.[37] In February 1917 the faculty voted that the course be reinserted in the catalogue and bracketed, it being expected that Austin H. MacCormick, instructor in English, would give it in 1918-1919.[38] But the United States entered the war; Mr. MacCormick enlisted in the navy, and the course never made it into the catalogue. In his report in 1925 President Sills wrote that "the college may well consider the possibility sometime in the near future of giving instruction in the history of religion and in biblical literature."[39] Nothing was done immediately, but the year after the students submitted their report on the needs of the College, the Committee on Religious Activities, under the chairmanship of Professor Burnett, "recommended that increased opportunity for education in religion be offered the students...through the curriculum, and that there be obtained the services of a full time instructor in the history of religion and in Biblical Literature."[40] To meet this suggestion, the president sought to obtain a Tallman Professor in this field "as an experiment."

He was successful, and in 1928-1929 Professor Alban Gregory Widgery of Cambridge, as the first Visiting Professor on the Tallman Foundation, gave two semester courses on "Biblical Literature in the Light of the Philosophy of Religion."[41]

The "experiment" did not lead directly to establishment of a position for an instructor in biblical literature, although the Committee on Religious Activities again recommended that this be done in January 1930.[42] That year President Sills again dealt in more detail with the problem of religion on the campus. Referring to his report of 1921, which is quoted in part above, he wrote:

> It should always be kept in mind that the College is not primarily a religious institution; on the other hand, religion has a very definite place in all education. It is a matter for debate and discussion as to whether that place should be formal by means of courses in biblical literature, in the history of religion, in the philosophy of religion, and the like, or whether it should be informal by providing services of a religious nature in chapel and through small group opportunities for bible study and religious discussion. But whether judged by the rules of formality or of informality the College is not doing all that it should to promote the religious interests of undergraduates. We do believe that some demand for such instruction should come from the undergraduates themselves; we do not think that it would do much good to impose such instruction or such direction from above; but we should be ready when the demand comes. Personally, I believe everything depends upon finding the right man, whether he is to be professor of biblical literature, or college chaplain, or christian association secretary, would be a mere detail.[43]

In the following years the question of adding courses in religion rested for some time, while attention was focused on other issues. But the question of compulsory chapel attendance continued to be discussed. Recently the *Orient* had carried articles on chapel at Williams and Wesleyan and attempts at these colleges to change the system of compulsory daily chapels.[44] The *Orient* on December 12, 1928, carried a particularly sharp protest against chapel at Bowdoin. Yet these were rather isolated instances of opposition, and the *Orient* approved President Sills's talk in chapel in October 1929, when he defended compulsory chapel.[45] In the spring of 1930 the students became excited over the World War memorial the College planned to erect on campus. A flag pole had finally been decided upon, and it was to be placed in the center of the campus where lines drawn from the entrances of Hubbard Hall and the art museum bisect. The students not only thought that a more utilitarian memorial than a flagstaff might have been chosen, but above all they did not want it at the center of the campus, since many other sites were available. On a Saturday night some "200 lusty protestors" carried the flagpole, which was ready to be set in place, into the Chapel and celebrated by kindling a large bonfire.[46] It took until Sunday noon for the college grounds crew to get the flagpole out of the Chapel. There was a flurry of letters in the *Orient*, and President Sills spoke in chapel on the work of the committee which had been appointed to erect a war memorial. A senior wrote in the *Orient* that the flagpole affair was not a college prank, not spring fever, but a serious student protest—the students had not been given a chance to express their views. The *Orient* conducted a poll on proposed sites, and over 300 votes were cast.[47] The faculty also were in favor of another site, and finally the present location on a diagonal line between the corners of the Walker Art Building and Hubbard Hall was chosen. The flagpole was dedicated on Alumni Day, November 8, 1930.

Amid this turmoil over the flagpole, the president appointed a committee composed of undergraduates and faculty to investigate chapel programs and recommend any changes which seemed advisable. They were not asked to consider whether attendance was to be compulsory or voluntary or how often chapel should be held. The committee came up with some suggestions, and as a result minor alterations were made. Henceforth each Saturday the schedule for the next week was to be posted on the college bulletin board near the Chapel. Services were to vary more, faculty were to continue to speak, and their subjects were to be listed. There were also to be some musical programs.[48] The *Orient* was quick to note that the reforms did not touch the basic chapel problem and announced they would conduct a referendum among the students and faculty. The next week a clearly stated ballot was printed in the *Orient*. These ballots would be collected at the fraternity houses; non-fraternity men and faculty could deposit their ballots in boxes set up in the union and library. A long editorial against compulsory chapel appeared in the same issue. There were 382 votes cast out of a total of 617 students and faculty, a higher percentage than in most polls. There were 87 for continuation of compulsory chapel, 295 against. The votes were tabulated by houses, and only Delta Upsilon voted twenty-three to seventeen for continuance of compulsory chapel; of the seven non-fraternity men voting, 4 were against compulsory services, 3 for continuing them. In the long editorial in the issue announcing the results of the poll, the editors answered the points the president had been making: (1) that daily chapel was a tradition, (2) that it was good for the college to get together, (3) that it was well to use the beautiful chapel building, (4) that students came into contact with great literature and hymns, and (5) that the requirement was stated clearly in the catalogue. The *Orient* felt a large majority was opposed to compulsory chapel and quoted the remark made by a student, "that we had failed on the flagpole question and that the strong walls of the chapel and the no less strong conservatism of the administration would withstand any assault the

Orient was capable of delivering." In answer to this lament, the editors stated that they did not feel that they had failed on the flagpole issue: "We helped to keep it off the middle of the campus and almost succeeded in getting it out of the way altogether."[49]

The question of compulsory or voluntary chapel remained a campus issue throughout the year. The faculty discussed it at their meeting on February 16, 1931, but as the sparse minutes state "no conclusion was arrived at."[50] They considered it again at their next meeting, when it came to a vote on a rather roundabout resolution, "that no sufficient reasons now appear for altering the current requirement of the college concerning attendance at chapel." The motion lost twenty-two to eighteen, with three members in attendance not voting.[51] Well might President Sills write in his annual report: "Both among undergraduates and faculty members, there has been much discussion during the past year about required attendance at chapel. Probably there is a growing feeling that the time is not far distant when such requirements should be radically altered or abolished."[52] He went on to point out that the college by-laws provide that "all undergraduates shall attend daily prayers in the chapel." This by-law was made by the Boards and could only be changed by them. From his contact with board members and with alumni he was convinced that there was no immediate possibility of doing away with required chapel attendance. However, the size of the Chapel did not permit daily attendance of all undergraduates, and it would be wise to change the by-laws to be consistent with the facts. He reiterated his belief "that here at Bowdoin the Chapel has still an important part to play in college life, and that it would be a great misfortune to remove the sentiments and traditions, the kind of training and the influence that are associated with it." The Boards agreed with the president and amended the by-laws to read:

> All undergraduates shall, unless excused by authority of the Dean, attend daily prayers in the chapel under such regulations as the Dean may formulate.[53]

Although students had been granted excuses if they missed chapel from the very beginning of the College, the dean now finally had official authority to do so. The maintenance of the status quo received affirmation in answers to an elaborate questionnaire that Dean Nixon sent out the next year to members of a recently graduated class. Only eight men did not reply, one hundred did. To the question, Should compulsory morning chapel be abolished? 73 percent answered no, 18 percent yes, 1 percent yes if the students so wish, 4 percent wanted it radically altered, 2 percent were doubtful, 2 percent did not answer. If it should be changed? Forty-seven percent said no, 23 percent yes, 2 percent were doubtful, 18 percent wanted it abolished, and 10 percent did not answer. To the question,

"Changed, How?" there were many suggestions such as changing the chapel hour, increasing the number of cuts, making it optional for upperclassmen, and so on. The dean apparently was unable to come up with any tabulations in regard to them.[54]

Amid the agitation about compulsory chapel, other events related to religion were taking place. At the end of October 1930, the Chapel began to be used for Sunday morning masses for the English-speaking Roman Catholics in Brunswick. It was to be a temporary arrangement until a new Catholic church could be built; the site finally selected being on Maine Street almost directly opposite the First Parish Church. The *Orient* considered this gesture on the part of the College a manifestation of the toleration which existed at Bowdoin.[55] At this time the Christian Association also underwent one of its periodic revitalization efforts.[56] Rev. Chauncey W. Goodrich, who had been minister at First Parish from 1913 to 1917 and had now retired in Brunswick, lent his support and undertook to lead weekly Sunday noon discussion groups in the B.C.A. room in the union. Warren Palmer '32 was elected president of the B.C.A., which received a new constitution the following February. Meanwhile, a new student club was organized at the Episcopal church[57] under the leadership of Gordon E. Gillett '34. He was also active in the B.C.A. In the spring of 1932, under the leadership of Gillett and Palmer, the Religious Forum of Modern Religious Thought was organized at Bowdoin, an annual event which was to last until 1961. Gillett was directly in charge, and under the auspices of the B.C.A. twelve clergymen representing various denominations were invited to the campus to spend three days in the different fraternities.[58] One of the guests conducted morning chapel, and in the evening they each led a discussion group in one of the various houses. These discussions centered on "The Social Aspects of Christianity" and "The Personal Aspects of Christianity." In later years there was also a leader for the non-fraternity men. The clergy regularly arranged "office hours" for private individual consultation by students. There was some skepticism on the part of the faculty whether the students would take to the forum,[59] but the Committee on Religious Activities lent its support, and the chairman of that committee quietly approached selected faculty members for modest contributions to augment the limited funds available to the students. President and Mrs. Sills, with their usual hospitality, gave a tea for the visiting clergy and the faculty and student committees.

Each morning the clergy gathered, with a few faculty members present, to discuss their experiences. It was immediately evident that the students were cooperating and the forum was going to be a success. But it was equally clear that there was a very startling lack of knowledge of the Bible, of the principles of Christianity, and of religious and church history. The clergy, in their report to the president on their experiences, respectfully suggested "that the problems of many students might be better met if the curriculum should include certain constructive courses in religion and that a resident director or counselor of religion would be of great value in promoting religious life on the campus."[60]

The introduction of religion courses into the curriculum had been hanging fire, but now the president stated in his annual report that he believed "courses on Biblical Literature or the History of Religion should be added to the curriculum as soon as practicable."[61] He again emphasized that the College was "not primarily a religious institution" but that from its foundation it had been glad to be "regarded as an ally of religion." As such, some religious training was proper, but much of this "must be informal in character." In this, Sills was in accord with Bowdoin's past. He also stated clearly his position in respect to another proposal when he wrote: "Some people feel that we ought to have a chaplain for the College but I have personally not yet come to that point of view." And he never did change his views on this issue as long as he was president.[62]

The next year the forum, when the general topic was "The Place of the Church in Social, Economic and Political Construction," went even better. More students participated in the discussion groups. The *Orient* called it a success and commented:

> From discussions in the fraternity houses the clergymen discovered that the greater part of the undergraduate body is ignorant in matters pertaining to religious theory or the Bible. Because of this, it was recommended to the President and Dean that some course in religion should be added to the curriculum.[63]

It was the same proposal that the clergymen had made before. With the faculty and other officers of the College who received salaries in excess of $2,000 contributing, at the request of the Boards, 10 percent of their salaries to the Alumni Fund,[64] it was not a simple matter to add courses to the curriculum and appoint a new member of the faculty to teach them. Nothing was done. The third religious forum, in January 1934, was again most successful, and the *Orient* wrote:

> The chance to discuss "How can I find God" was a welcome one for a majority of Bowdoin Men. And the enthusiasm with which they participated in the fireside group proves for the third time—that there remains a fertile field for the incorporation of a chair of religion at Bowdoin.[65]

In May of 1934 the president announced in chapel that plans were being made to offer a course running through both semesters in biblical literature if there was enough student interest to warrant giving the course. It would be a regular literature course and would be counted towards meeting the requirements for a minor in that subject. There was sufficient interest, and the president appointed John Charles Schroeder, pastor of the State Street Congregational Church in Portland, as lecturer on biblical literature.[66] He was well-known on campus, for he had preached numerous times at vesper services, had participated in the religious forums, and had received a D.D. from Bowdoin in 1933. His appointment was important, for it was the forerunner of the appointment of a full-time member of the faculty to teach religion and of the eventual establishment of religion as a major at the College.

Able, enthusiastic, liberal in his religious thought, attuned to the needs and spiritual outlook of youth, Schroeder was most successful; for three years he gave courses to an ever-increasing enrollment. In the spring of 1937 he accepted an appointment as professor of homiletics and pastoral theology at Yale, serving at the same time as chairman of the Department of Religion and master of Calhoun College. In referring to Schroeder's departure in his annual report, President Sills wrote: "He has been of great help to the religious interests of the College; liberal and generous in his outlook, forceful and effective in the presentation of his ideas, he has left a lasting impression upon the undergraduates and upon his colleagues on the faculty."[67]

The vacancy left by Dr. Schroeder's resignation was filled for the next year by Robert H. Lightfoot of Oxford, who was appointed Visiting Professor of Biblical Literature on the Tallman Foundation. The ad hoc status of the religion courses at this time is evidenced by the fact that they were not bracketed but were simply omitted from the college catalogue for 1938-1939. In February 1939 the president appointed a special committee to report on the possibility of offering a course in biblical literature or the history of religions the next year.[68] This led to the appointment of Henry G. Russell as the first full-time instructor in biblical literature at the College. He was a graduate of Haverford with advanced work at Harvard. During the year the curriculum committee and faculty approved the addition of two more semester courses in the history of religions to the curriculum.[69] Bowdoin now offered four elective semester courses in religion: Biblical Literature, open to sophomores, juniors, and seniors; and History of Religions, open to juniors and seniors. In October 1946, a semester course in major Christian authors was added, and the next fall this was extended into a full-year course.[70] From the time Professor Russell was appointed, religion courses have regularly been part of the curriculum, except for the year 1944-1945, when he was granted leave of absence and the college catalogue carried this solemn notice: "The courses in Religion will not be given for the duration of the war."[71] But the president did not want religion to be a wartime casualty and in April 1945 asked the Committee on Religious Activities to make a study of the possibility of arranging for temporary instruction in religion and report to him. Fortunately, the end of the war brought Professor Russell back to Bowdoin that fall.[72]

The mid-1930s brought not only instruction in religion to the College, but also a renaissance in music. In the fall of 1936 Frederic E. T. Tillotson, a concert pianist and teacher of wide experience, was appointed professor of music. The next spring the president wrote in his report: "[Tillotson] has during the year inspired his department with enthusiasm and has done a remarkably fine piece of work both in the classroom and with the choir and musical clubs."[73] He soon organized from among his best singers a chapel choir which added much to the beauty and effectiveness of the vesper services. Starting in the fall of 1938, the selection the choir was to sing at vespers was regularly listed on the college calendar; week in, week out, they were of high quality, as were their choral responses. Periodically he took over morning chapels and conducted song services. He tried to acquaint the students with the great treasures of hymnody. To this end a new hymnal was adopted, which was prepared especially for use in colleges.[74]

The new hymnal was, however, not a success, for many of the hymns which the students knew and enjoyed singing were not in it. President Sills no doubt gave expression to what many thought when at this time he stated, in chapel, that he noticed that to most individuals the great hymns were the ones they were brought up on, and which they liked to sing.[75] By 1948 the number of responsive-reading books which had been "used for about twenty years" had dwindled by actual count to seventy-two.[76] The Boards in February of that year appropriated $600 for the purchase of new books, and the Committee on Religious Activities was given the task of selecting a new volume.[77] They found no book of responsive readings in print and so fell back, much to the delight of President Sills, on purchasing a new hymnal which also contained a good selection of responsive readings. It was a volume prepared by the General Assembly of the Presbyterian Church in the United States and the publisher furnished it to the College with the Bowdoin seal and the words "Bowdoin College Chapel" stamped on the dark green cover.[78] The book was dedicated at the chapel service on April 21, 1948.

Professor Tillotson not only did much to improve the music in chapel, he also acquainted the students and community with some of the great religious music of the centuries. The Glee Club and the Community Chorus, which he recruited and directed for many years, gave Handel's *Messiah* annually to capacity audiences in the First Parish Church. Likewise they presented, among other works, Fauré's *Requiem,* Mendelsohn's *Hymn of Praise,* Schubert's *Mass in G,* Mozart's *Requiem Mass,* Brahms's *Requiem,* J.S. Bach's *Mass in B Minor,* and J. S. Bach's cantata *If thou wilt suffer God to guide thee.* Singing was encouraged at the fraternities, and an annual college-wide contest in which fraternities competed was held. He coined the phrase, and for a time it prevailed, "Bowdoin is a Singing College." In 1953 Robert K. Beckwith joined Professor Tillotson in the Department of Music and shared in carrying on the music programs at the College.

The well-established religious program continued to function smoothly during World War II. Attendance at chapel was made voluntary during the summer schools, which were inaugurated in 1942, and the hour shifted to twelve o'clock noon. In respect to this change in practice the *Orient* reported:

> Freshmen attendance at voluntary chapel this summer has been practically nil. Never having been under compulsory chapel regulations, freshmen do not realize what an integral factor of Bowdoin life they are overlooking. The sizable senior attendance testifies to this. Freshmen should attend chapel in greater number or attendance should be made compulsory for them.[79]

When college opened for the first semester in the fall, the new chapel hour was retained, classes starting at eight o'clock. Attendance was again compulsory. This practice was generally accepted, but in August 1944 the president apparently thought it necessary to come to its defense. In an address in chapel he pointed out that this was a policy set by the Boards. It was not maintained "only because of sentiment and tradition but because it is felt that daily chapel is... a symbol, a gesture if you wish, of the thought that it is also the wisdom that comes from on high." He quoted a statement from Plato that the "science of good and evil" is the most satisfying portion of human knowledge, and left the students to ponder how many of them "ever thought about a science of good and evil."[80] There were in these years, as in former times, occasional protests against required chapel attendance, but there were also articles in the *Orient* defending the practice.[81] A far more controversial question than chapel, the problem of racial discrimination at Bowdoin, was now raised by students.[82] It was brought to the fore by some students who were also active in the B.C.A.

This is not the place to go into this matter in detail, for it was largely a fraternity concern. Yet there were religious overtones involved, and so some comment is necessary. It had long been the practice of most of the fraternities not to pledge Jews or Blacks. These constituted the majority of the non-fraternity men. In order to give this group some voice and representation in student government affairs, as well as to enable them to join as a group in social affairs and intramural athletics, the Thorndike Club was organized in 1937 on the initiative of Carl F. Barron '38. This was an open-membership organization and, with very few exceptions, all the non-fraternity men belonged.[83] Although the grades of the organization were computed and listed, and the Thorndike Club usually led the pack, the club was not eligible to receive the Student Council Cup or the Peucinian Cup, a practice which rankled at times.[84]

The denunciation of racial discrimination connected with World War II policy was bound to raise the issue of discrimination on the campus. A small group, among them a returned veteran, David A. Works '42, brought the issue to the fore. Largely because of their agitation, five houses pledged Jewish men in 1944-1945, but this practice soon slacked off.[85] In January 1946 the Thorndike Club petitioned the administration for the status of a local fraternity. In their letter they stated: "The Club feels that if it were recognized as a local fraternity with a Greek letter name, it will be more capable of pursuing the democratic policy of the organization. We have pledged ourselves to exclude no man from our membership because of color or religious ideologies."[86] As an earnest of this pledge they had chosen the name of Alpha Rho Upsilon; ARU could also be said to stand for "All Races United." The *Orient* vehemently opposed the move:

> Let's review the facts. The fraternities here have refused to come out with a definite stand on where Bowdoin's Jews belong. They just refuse to take the men in. So, a group of members of the predominantly Jewish Thorndike Club started with a small provision to change their constitution to form a non-sectarian fraternity....
>
> However, if the new fraternity is formed, we see only one possibility: It will be the place where every Jewish boy will be pledged. It will solve the conscience of the Christians here on campus. It will take the Hebrews out of the "socially imposed" exclusiveness of the dorms and put them into a house with a Greek letter name. Some of the alumni will sigh and the rest won't care.... The student body of Gentiles will dust off their signs of "Juden Verboten" and hang them on their beautiful fraternity houses. And at long last the dreams of democracy which have been breeding in the hearts of the Jewish students — who are really children of God too — will be abolished and smashed. Joe Bowdoin says: "They are Jews and we glory in the title of Christian Gentlemen".....
>
> Several of the houses are extremely anxious to pledge Jews, but the national charter or the "Democratic" black-ball, whereby one or two members can stop a majority, has hindered their pledging. Hitler and Goebbels have at last invaded that stronghold of American education — Bowdoin College. We have won the physical war, but we are losing the spiritual peace.
>
> The *Orient* is opposed to the idea of the new fraternity. We do not believe it is the only alternative; it is the easy way out and we refuse to throw in the towel. We shall continue to work for the day when prejudice, selfishness, complacency, and ignorance will give way to democracy on our campus.[87]

It was a hard-hitting editorial which, along with the Thorndike Club petition, did much to bring the problem of racial discrimination out into the open. James B. Longley '48, later to become the first independent governor of Maine, in the first student-led chapel of the second semester, scorned racial prejudice on the campus.[88] Several faculty members joined the chorus in their chapel talks. The faculty committee appointed to consider the Thorndike Club petition, after consultation with representatives of the club, recommended to the faculty that the club be permitted to change its name to Alpha Rho Upsilon if it so desired, that the request to be known as a local fraternity be laid on the table for the time being, and that the college provide suitable clubrooms for the organization.[89] A temporary recreation room for ARU was arranged in Moore Hall, and in December 1946 the ARU Club, having given renewed assurances that it would not resort to any discriminatory policy, was given recognition as a local fraternity.[90] Most of the members came to live in Hyde Hall, and they ate in the Moulton Union. In April 1948 they bought the Campus Lodge at 204 Maine Street and in 1952, when the Sigma Nus purchased the Baxter House on College Street, the ARUs purchased the former Sigma Nu property on Maine Street, selling their former house.[91]

The general status of fraternities on the campus became a hotly discussed subject on campus at this time. The *Orient* issued a special edition in which, among other reforms, it called for:

> A rule, enforced by the College, that all national fraternities represented at Bowdoin eliminate from their constitutions any undemocratic stipulations which forbid pledging and initiation for reasons of race, color, or creed, with the alternative of the withdrawal of their Bowdoin chapters.[92]

This was a bold program and, considering past policy of the College towards fraternity autonomy, not one to be implemented overnight. Yet it was a goal, and there were those on campus who kept pushing to achieve it. It is difficult to recall how deep-seated prejudices and attitudes were. In January 1947 the B.C.A., Political Forum, and Student Council jointly sponsored a poll to determine student opinion on discrimination. Questions were asked which no one would think of asking in 1981. Out of 963 students 537 participated. They opposed a quota system for admission of Jews (60.7 percent), Negroes (70.4 percent), Catholics (90.9 percent), and Orientals (74.2 percent). The fraternity practice of restricting pledging of students on account of race, color, or creed was condemned by 64.4 percent. Only 69.7 percent favored employment of properly qualified Negro faculty members. As to completely unsegregated housing for members of all races in their home towns, 55.8 percent were opposed to it, but 76.3 percent endorsed it for the campus.[93] With such a constituency it is not surprising that the campaign against racial discrimination moved slowly.

In April 1947 the B.C.A. asked the administration for aid in fighting racial discrimination in the fraternities. They were advised that the first step was to have each fraternity report on such discriminatory restrictions to the faculty Committee on Fraternities headed by Professor Stanley P.

Chase, which would then collate the material.[94] This was a special, not a regular, faculty committee and is not listed in the catalogue. It ultimately was successful in getting the faculty to adopt a policy that no new fraternity would be permitted to be established on campus whose membership was restricted by race, color, or creed.[95]

The B.C.A. was particularly active at this time. It had broadened its participation and had even chosen a Jewish student as its president. It had committees to head up its various activities, and its Fraternity Policy Committee submitted to the president a petition signed by 171 students including five fraternity presidents and nine student council representatives.[96] The president passed the petition to the faculty Committee on Fraternity Policy for its consideration. This committee approved of the requests mentioned in the petition, and its report was overwhelmingly accepted by the faculty.[97] Two of the proposals were to go into effect immediately. The president at an opportune time would affirm the position of the College as disapproving discrimination in Bowdoin fraternities through membership restrictions. Henceforth the Dean's Office would also no longer supply information on the religious affiliation of incoming students for purposes of fraternity rushing. The faculty committee also had drawn up a statement on fraternity policy in regard to election of members that included the College's position in respect to discriminatory practices, and which they recommended be included in the college catalogue, along with a brief statement as to fraternity dues and expenses. This proposal was referred to the Governing Boards. The Examining Committee of the Boards objected to such a statement,[98] and it never made its way into the college catalogue.

While in the beginning the problem of racial discrimination involved the status of Jewish students, it soon embraced the admission of Blacks to the fraternities. This first came to the fore when a member of the class of 1949 was pledged to two fraternities, which were forced to cancel his pledge due to alumni pressure and restricting clauses in their charters.[99] He finally was accepted as a member by Delta Upsilon, but when that fraternity pledged a second Black, over the opposition of some alumni but with the strong support of others, the local D.U. members chose to drop their national affiliation and become Delta Sigma, a local fraternity. In this dispute with the national headquarters and with some alumni, the students had the warm and unfailing support of President Sills. The number of local fraternities had now grown to two; the numbers were to increase before the issue of racial discrimination was settled. But the path had been charted; diversity of race and religion in the fraternities slowly but surely became a reality.

During these years when the issue of racial discrimination held the spotlight, the chapel program functioned smoothly. In September 1948, when the College went on a unique program of rotating class hours from year to year, the chapel hour was shifted from ten minutes after twelve to ten minutes after ten.[100] Attendance increased. In the spring of 1951, Dean Nathaniel C. Kendrick changed the attendance requirement for daily chapel as he had done earlier for the vesper services. Instead of a student being marked absent, he was asked to attend a certain number of times each semester. The new system proved popular with the students, and it received warm commendation from President Sills.[101] As always there was some discussion of required chapel attendance. A faculty committee was appointed in 1950 to study various complaints about chapel services.[102] They suggested that the acoustical properties of the Chapel—a matter of complaint ever since the Chapel was built—should be remedied as soon as possible. It was thought that installing a tiled ceiling would help, but this, the president pointed out in his annual report, would cost about $15,000, and the money was not available. At times students with an eye on the faculty would make reference to the phrase in President Hyde's famous "Offer of the College," "to form character under professors who are Christians." In his annual report in 1951, Sills referred to this statement and wrote:

> Anyone who knew Dr. Hyde at all well is sure that he would use this term in no narrow or restrictive sense. He meant, I think, that the members of the faculty should be aware of the fact that Bowdoin is a Christian college; that they should keep in mind the role which religion plays in education; that they should recognize the importance of the spiritual, and set forth the essential characteristics of the Christian attitude.[103]

In short, as President Sills once told the writer, the College could not expect all members of the faculty to be members of a church, or to be active in church affairs. It could, however, expect of them not to scoff at religion and the churches. The faculty at Bowdoin had changed from the time when many of them were ordained clergymen, but how about their religious affiliation? Sills made an informal census of the ninety-five men whose names appeared in the current catalogue under the title Officers of Instruction and Government, and he found "of these, some fifty-five could well be listed as having active associations with some church, twenty-eight as having nominal membership, and twelve as having neither status, although in this latter group several had in their families active church membership." He was the last person to claim accuracy for such an evaluation, but he felt it was "worth recording as a protest against the common idea that our colleges are hotbeds of irreligion and atheism."[104]

Sills was constant in his reiteration that Bowdoin is a Christian college, as was demonstrated by its history, tradition, and teaching. In March 1952 there was a sharp letter in the *Orient* attacking the Blanket Tax allotment of $1,500 to the B.C.A., which was using the money to sponsor the religious forum. The forum, which was to stimulate religious thinking among undergraduates, was all right, but the means by which the B.C.A. was able to do this was reprehensible. "According to the College Catalogue Bowdoin has been non-sectarian since 1908. There is therefore no justification in its continued support of a Christian Association....Why... does the College compel Atheists, Agnostics and non-Christians to support an organization which opposes their beliefs?"[105] The president was not slow in answering the letter in a chapel address, in which he pointed out the difference between non-sectarian and non-Christian, terms which the student had misused. He termed the opinion of the student callow and asserted that "as long as I am President this will be a Christian College."[106] That June, at the last commencement over which he presided, the class of 1942 placed a brass cross on the wall back of the pulpit and dedicated this age-old symbol of Christianity to the memory of eight classmates who had lost their lives in World War II.[107]

Just what is a Christian college was a question which was being raised in academic circles at this time. In February 1952 the President appointed a special committee to study this question.[108] In the summer of that year a conference centering on that topic was held at Cedar Crest College in Pennsylvania. Representatives from many colleges, including Bowdoin, attended.[109] Hard and fast criteria or guidelines were not drawn up at the meeting—nor were they expected. It was clear, however, that Bowdoin in the best sense of that term was a Christian college.[110] It was the kind of a college President Sills had received from the hands of President Hyde, and the kind he handed over to James Stacy Coles in October 1952.

X.

The Recent Decades

THE COLLEGE CELEBRATED the one-hundred-and-fiftieth anniversary of its opening at Commencement in June 1952, a fitting opportunity to honor the many years of service by President and Mrs. Sills. It was not until after the next academic year had begun that President Coles took office on October 1. In his inaugural address two weeks later, he affirmed his support of the liberal arts and the values which the College had upheld throughout its past.

> Our colleges must not allow the lack of specific goals which is customarily associated with the liberal arts program to be translated in its graduates into vagueness of achievement in their life work. Nor can we allow our emphasis on freedom from restraint to be extrapolated into freedom from responsibility. We must educate for responsibility.... We must not only educate for responsibility, but we must be sure our education includes responsibility beyond that to our own freedom. It must include responsibility to our community, our nation, our society, and our God. This responsibility has ancient tradition. That it is more blessed to give than it is to receive is a Christian concept compatible with Bowdoin's tradition as a Christian college. This tradition has grown from the needs of the community rather than from fiat of charter. The Christian heritage and mores of the larger community in these United States is so great that there will always be need for Bowdoin as a Christian college. She will remain so, and will, with the help and guidance of God, continue to educate in knowledge and in virtue and in piety.[1]

In the 1945-1946 college catalogue there had been inserted, after the traditional historical sketch, an attractive page giving a quotation from the college charter stating the purpose of the College, and also Hyde's "Offer of the College." To these statements in 1960-1961, the closing words of President Coles's inaugural address on the need for Bowdoin as a Christian college were added under the rubric "Knowledge, Virtue and Piety."

An Episcopalian layman, active in church affairs, Coles did not have the ministerial background or training of his predecessors as president of the College. But he lent his full and active support to the chapel program and to other religious activities on the campus. He took his share of daily and Sunday chapel services but did not speak as often and regularly as did President Sills.[2] His activity in the capital fund campaign often took him away from the campus. Educated as a chemist and with a broad interest in scientific matters, he undertook to improve the acoustics in the Chapel. In the spring of 1953, flags of the first thirteen colonies and Maine were hung in the Chapel in an effort to improve speaking conditions.[3] This was followed the next year by placing acoustic tiles upon the wall above the gallery over the entrance and by laying full carpeting to replace the tile flooring.[4] A public address system was installed, and tape recordings were made of chapel addresses. A faculty committee was appointed to collect these talks with a view towards possible future publication.[5] It never did come to this, but it was a stimulus for a time to better preparation of chapel talks by members of the faculty. The improvements helped but did not entirely solve the acoustic problems in the Chapel.

It did not take long for a discordant letter to appear in the *Orient*. In April 1953 the same student who had attacked granting Blanket Tax money to the B.C.A. the year before, drawing a sharp answer from President Sills, wrote another letter. This time he complained about the cross which had been added to the decor of the chapel. He had been eyeing it for a semester and a half; it emphasized the religious nature of the chapel services and reminded you that you were compelled to attend them.[6] The next week brought a forceful answer in the *Orient* by another student, and the issue subsided. A year later, in March 1954, this same student crusader again attacked the chapel program because it was a religious service; the Sunday vespers were even more religious than the daily ones.[7] No one should be compelled to attend religious services. His letter is of some interest because he stresses the religious nature of the chapels, whereas the most often heard criticism was that they were secular, worldly, and not proper chapel services.

A Newman Club had been organized at Bowdoin, but under the longtime Bowdoin policy, strongly maintained by President Sills, it was centered off campus and received no student activity funds. In May 1954 this group requested permission to form the Newman Club of Bowdoin College and to affiliate with the National Organization of Newman Clubs. They also asked for the privilege of using college buildings, that the notice of the Newman Club continue to be carried in the college handbook; and that the club be given the privilege of using college bulletin boards. The dean referred their letter to the Religious Activities Committee for their advice. The committee was split, three to two: three members were willing to grant them all their requests; the other two members held back on some points. The latter preferred the Newman Club at Bowdoin College to the Newman Club of Bowdoin, a slight but nevertheless significant difference. While willing to grant the club the privilege of using some college facilities for occasional lectures, they wanted no regular use of college buildings. The headquarters should be off campus; there were no differences on the use of bulletin boards.[8] No clear-cut decision was reached by the dean as to future policy in regard to such denominational clubs. For the time being the old policy of supporting one non-denominational religious organization was maintained.

The B.C.A. had for some time been contemplating a change of names so as to broaden its membership and make it more acceptable to Catholics and non-Christian students.[9] In the fall of 1954, at a special meeting with nine members present, they decided henceforth to be known as the Bowdoin Interfaith Forum (B.I.F.), deriving their name from the popular religious forums conducted by the B.C.A. since 1932.[10] The new name, except perhaps at the very beginning, failed to win the support of those students who had always stood aloof. In May 1956 the editor of the *Orient* levied a sharp attack on the organization, opposing its grant of Blanket Tax funds.

> A sizeable group of undergraduates at Bowdoin are Roman Catholics. If they are good Catholics they cannot support the BIF in any way whatsoever. Should Roman Catholics, who do not wish to affiliate with the BIF be compelled to support it? We think not.
>
> Likewise, there is a portion of undergraduates who simply lack any formal religion. Why should they be required to support a religious group? They certainly won't have to once they graduate.
>
> Thirdly, there is a goodly number of students attending churches or synagogues who simply find enough religious fellowship without belonging to the BIF. Why should they be required to support it?
>
> In our estimation the BIF organization puts the cart before the horse anyway. There should be religious groups, supported by the various sects, before an interfaith forum is formed. These groups, through their own volition, could form an interfaith forum if they felt that the exchange of ideas on religious matters was valuable.[11]

It is doubtful if this blast truly mirrored the views of most Catholics on campus, but it was in line with the teaching of Bishop Daniel J. Feeney of the Portland diocese at this time. He was not ecumenically minded and two years later forbade Catholic parents and students to attend high school baccalaureate services. The bishop pointed out in his letter to parish priests "that Roman Catholics must not attend religious services of another faith. The format of baccalaureate rites is always that of New England Congregationalism and therefore violates the consciences of those who are not products of this tradition."[12] The bishop's edict was generally interpreted as applying to colleges as well. President Coles met the challenge head-on and stated that the College would in no way alter its traditional services, which were held in the First Parish Church, the president giving the address and the pastor of the church usually giving the invocation and benediction. Attendance had always been voluntary, but he took occasion to point out "that every man who elects to attend Bowdoin College is fully advised of compulsory chapel attendance requirements during the academic year."[13]

During 1954-1955 the College undertook an elaborate self-study project under a grant from the Ford Foundation. There were few topics covering the College which were not investigated by the committee in charge and by numerous sub-committees, although the project primarily dealt with curricular matters. The one aspect of college life which seems to have been studiously avoided in the lengthy report of the committee was the matter of chapel. This omission is all the more remarkable inasmuch as the questionnaire sent to the alumni asked them to check five extracurricular activities which seemed the most worthwhile to them and among those listed was "Chapel."[14] In this list of extracurricular activities, no mention was made of the B.C.A., certainly the activity with the longest history at the College. Nor is the B.C.A. referred to in the section on Extra-Curricular Activities.[15] Even in the reference to the Tallman Professors made in the report, no mention is made of the professors who taught religion courses, although there had been three of them.[16] It is as if the Chapel and religion were no longer part of what was called "The Conservative Tradition in Education at Bowdoin College." But obviously this was not the case; it was an omission in the self-study report which has generally gone unnoticed.

The committee did cover the problem of racial discrimination. It came out for the retention of fraternities, but "since admission to Bowdoin is free from discrimination for reasons of race, color, or creed, the admissions practice of Bowdoin fraternities [should] be equally freed from discrimination for reasons of race, color, or creed." To this end, no new fraternity which had a discriminatory clause would be admitted to the campus, and each fraternity that had discriminatory clauses on race, color, or creed was to "report annually to the Faculty on its efforts to ease or eliminate discriminatory clauses and practices at both the local and the national level."[17] The College would review these efforts and if they were found to "lack sincerity, consistency, or results, it will consider taking drastic action." What "consider taking drastic action" meant was not spelled out. It was good to have these statements put into writing and formally adopted; they were, however, but a formulation of the policies worked out during the last years of Sills's administration.[18]

Self-study or not, the chapel programs and the Bowdoin Interfaith Forum activities went their accustomed ways. Students were able to get representatives of the Jewish and Catholic faiths to join with others in carrying on the annual religious forums, which regularly were successful. But there also were periodic protests against compulsory attendance at chapel services. In December 1961 a member of the faculty joined the fray.[19] He centered his remarks on the provision of the by-laws stating that undergraduates should attend daily prayers under such regulations as the dean may formulate. Prayer was no longer the important thing about chapel services; in fact at times it was omitted altogether. The chapel talk was now the important part of the service, and why should students be required to listen to it? There might well be occasional college assemblies and also daily religious services for those who desired them; at neither should attendance be required.

President Coles immediately took steps to clarify what the position of the College was in regard to chapel. In a note to the college editor on January 3, 1962, he suggested that the statement in the college catalogue that attendance at religious exercises "is governed by regulations laid down by the College" be changed to read "is required according to regulations of the College."[20] This was done. He also requested the director of admissions to include a statement regarding chapel attendance requirements on forms supplied applicants for admission. In a chapel talk a week later he warmly defended the chapel services and concluded: "I find it difficult to deny the view that in a broad sense chapel is a useful and viable instrument, and a symbol of collegiate concern... a token, at least, of a desirable interest in a common good."[21] Other members of the faculty came out in support of the daily chapel services, and there were editorials pro and con in the *Orient*.[22] There were also public manifestations against chapel attendance. At times some students refused to stand when the hymns were sung. The cross was surreptitiously removed from behind the lectern and hidden in the custodian's closet. The attacks against compulsory attendance at the chapel services kept growing in intensity in the next few years until vespers and daily chapel services were ended.

The fall of 1962 brought the multiplication of deanships at the college. Dean Kendrick now took over as dean of the College and Assistant Professor Arthur LeRoy Greason became dean of students. The new dean, who believed that if you had regulations they should be obeyed and enforced,[23] sent out letters at the end of the semester reminding a good number of students that they were delinquent in attendance at chapel. This resulted in a protest demonstration when on January 9, 1963, the chapel was jammed (filled past capacity), and the United Press International carried it as a news item.[24] The *Orient* marked the event with a long editorial opposing compulsory attendance, and in return the next issue brought a letter expressing a contrary opinion.[25] The issue was kept alive in the *Orient* and in May reached a climax. The ARU fraternity passed a resolution calling for the dean to suspend the chapel requirement.[26] It asked the other fraternities and independents to discuss such a resolution and then unite in a petition to the dean, who would be asked to present the matter to the Governing Boards. It was felt that previous attempts by individuals to change requirements had not been successful and the administration had done nothing; concerted action by the fraternities could not be so easily ignored.

The B.C.A. voted to support the ARU resolution as did the Student Council, which appointed a committee to study the problem over the summer.[27] At the end of May the petition signed by nine fraternities was presented to the president. The *Orient* commented that the students did not want to abolish chapel completely, "for as the President had indicated in his May 10 chapel address there are many significant reasons to maintain the chapel on the Bowdoin Campus."[28] The students felt that changes must be made in order to increase the significance of chapel, but they did not discuss or give thought to how the abolition of compulsory attendance would accomplish this end.

The Student Council informed the president of its appointment of a committee to study the chapel program over the summer but requested no action on the part of the administration. In answer to the petition from the fraternities, President Coles expressed his willingness to appoint a faculty committee which would consult with the student council committee. Robert S. Frank '64, who was the leading spirit in the whole protest movement, expressed his wish for a joint faculty-student committee, and that Dean Greason and Mr. Philip Wilder, assistant to the president, be on the committee so as to give it standing and to represent the administration.[29] On October 14, 1963, President Coles appointed a Committee on Consideration of the Chapel Program consisting of Dean Greason as chairman, Professors Geoghegan (Religion), Taylor (Sociology), Chittim (Mathematics), and Leith (Romance Languages), with Dean Kendrick and Mr. Wilder as ex-officio members.[30] In a letter to the committee, the president stated:

> It shall be the duty of this committee to consider the Chapel program at Bowdoin College, relative to its contribution to the development of the individual student, and his interests and his attitudes toward those affairs which may not be immediately concerned with an individual's own academic program. The many factors to be considered are so numerous that they could not be fully delineated here. Neither could the various influences which the Chapel program has had on the subject, the student body, the alumni, and the College over the years be fully detailed.
>
> The Chapel program has changed both in form and in substance over the years since the founding of the college. It is appropriate, therefore, to make a formal assessment of the means by which it might be made as fully consistent as possible with the present needs of the students and of the college, and of the society in which Bowdoin graduates will live.[31]

This was a broad assignment, and the committee worked diligently.[32] Its report was placed on file at the faculty meeting on February 5, 1964, and was debated and adopted on March ninth.[33] Henceforth there were to be two forums, secular in nature, each week, and one religious chapel. The specific days were to remain flexible to accommodate special visitors to the campus and to recognize special occasions. On Saturdays the normal break between classes would be omitted, along with forums and chapels, and the ten-thirty and eleven-thirty classes would be moved forward to ten and eleven o'clock. Previously seniors had been required to attend fifteen daily chapels a semester, juniors and sophomores twenty, and freshmen twenty-five. Now juniors, sophomores, and freshmen were to attend ten forums or chapels, or any combination totaling ten each semester; attendance of seniors was to be on a voluntary basis. A motion in faculty meeting to make all attendance voluntary was defeated. As to Sunday vespers, the committee recommended that they should be continued as at present, attempts should be made to obtain distinguished speakers of various denominations, and all students should be required to attend four services each semester. By a vote of thirty-five to thirty-two the faculty voted to make attendance at Sunday service entirely voluntary. This vote was sent to the Boards, who refused to go along with it.[34] The Boards, however, did recognize the new forums when they amended by-law 65, which required attendance at daily prayers, to read:

> All undergraduates shall attend such exercises as may constitute the Chapel Program, under such regulations as the Dean of the College may formulate.[35]

The program of two forums and one chapel a week went into effect in September 1964. The opening college exercises in the First Parish Church were still announced in the college calendar as "Convocation and First Chapel Service," with the note that students were expected to attend. The following year the calendar simply referred to convocation, and there was no longer reference to a chapel service. Actually, there was no great change in the format of the exercises. It had become customary to read the parable of the sower, and this continued to be done.[36]

A regular committee of the faculty on the "Chapel and Forum Program" was now appointed, with the dean of students as chairman.[37] For a time they worked out a schedule of concerted programs on current topics of interest, but these soon ended. The *Orient*, in an editorial against compulsory chapel and forums in March 1966, charged: "With a few exceptions, the forum program this year has been bad."[38] When the faculty committee made its annual report in April, it stated there would probably be increasing resistance to Sunday chapel as this was a widespread trend at colleges, but it recommended no changes. The faculty, however, passed a motion that the committee make further study regarding the efficacy of Sunday chapel.[39] The committee did so and made a report to the faculty on June 6, 1966, which aroused sharp debate. If the report were adopted, one member charged that the Chapel, with its spires, which had been meaningful symbols, would become a mere museum. Nevertheless the report was adopted.[40] Henceforth there were to be no Sunday vespers, ending a practice which was established in 1870. Funds which had normally been budgeted for Sunday vespers would henceforth be used by the committee for a program of lectures, symposia, conferences, or discussions on appropriate religious and moral issues. Considering how students usually absented themselves from public lectures at the College, some faculty members viewed the probable success of this proposal with skepticism. There were to be forums twice a week, and attendance at ten of these was required for juniors, sophomores, freshmen, and seniors who had been delinquent in meeting their attendance requirements. Attendance at the chapel services on Wednesdays was to be completely voluntary, and attendance at chapel was not to count towards the ten attendances required at forums each semester. A motion to change this last provision, which would have given support for attendance at chapel by making it possible for chapel attenders to avoid going to the forums, was defeated.

The changes adopted by the faculty obviously required some approval by the Boards, for they ended Sunday vespers. The Boards not only approved but went even further. In a thorough revision of the by-laws adopted in June 1966, they eliminated any mention of chapel services and omitted the long-standing requirement that the first college exercises of the academic year "shall be morning prayers." The only reference to religious matters left in the by-laws was the statement:

> No test with respect to race, color, or creed shall be imposed in the choice of Trustees, Overseers, officers, members of the Faculty, any other employees, or in the admission of students; nor shall distinctly denominational tenets or doctrines be taught to the students.[41]

Once the Boards had abandoned the chapel program and all prayers, it did not take long for the faculty to follow suit.

The new program was to be reviewed by the faculty committee in December 1966, and their report at that time was promptly disposed of by placing it on file.[42] The forums had not been going well, and the *Orient* denounced them as meaningless and serving no purpose.[43] When the committee made its annual report in May 1967, it recommended that the forum program be abolished and that the Department of Music be invited to provide the College with a series of Sunday vesper services composed primarily of appropriate religious music.[44] It was hoped that interested faculty members would assist by providing readings and prayers. Furthermore, appropriate speakers on religious topics should be invited to the campus on the same basis as other lecturers. The president was also authorized to establish appropriate machinery to ensure the possibility of ad hoc forums at appropriate places and times, attendance at these occasions to be voluntary. With this report the Committee on Chapel Forums was discharged and the long-established college-sponsored program of chapel services ended. What had happened at Bowdoin was not unlike what was going on at colleges elsewhere. It was a period of unrest among students in protest against the United States's participation in the Vietnam War. It was also a time when curricular requirements were being, one by one, cancelled. Attendance at forums, the last bit of the old chapel requirements to go, vanished along with compulsory class attendance, required gymnasium classes, foreign language study, science, literature, and social science prescriptions, and, not least of all, the comprehensive examinations. Henceforth, more than ever before, students were to be free to chart their own educational program.

In these years when chapel services were gradually being abandoned, there were a few changes made in the Chapel itself. In 1961 new front entrance lights were installed through a gift of Mrs. Paul Tiemer of Cundy's Harbor in memory of Mr. William Stark Newell h'40.[45] In 1969 the class of 1929 paid for automation of the chimes so that they would function much like a player piano. Rolls with Bowdoin songs, Christmas carols, or whatnot, can be inserted and the chimes played without the use of the old manuals.[46] But even with this ease of operation, or perhaps because of it, the ringing of a chime program in the late afternoon has ceased; and afternoons in the community are more drab without it. The chimes were also equipped to mark the hours of the day, sparing those of the night. With the subsequent disappearance of the "chapel hour" on Tuesdays and Thursdays and the inauguration of 1½-hour as well as 1-hour classes, the ringing of the chapel bell, which for years had marked the beginning and end of classes, was ended. No longer is there at Bowdoin a student bell ringer who slips out of his classes early in order to liberate his classmates a few minutes later.

Aside from the abandonment of the chapel program, there were other changes in these years in practices touching on religion. In the spring of 1962 the Bowdoin Interfaith Forum decided to resume its old name of the Bowdoin Christian Association.[47] The B.I.F. had been unsuccessful in bringing into its activities a broader spectrum of the student body, and in justifying the change of names, the president of the B.C.A. stated "that many of us felt that in order to have a dynamic organization, one had to take his personal stand somewhere."[48] The old B.I.F. was a "conglomeration of nothingness." The B.C.A. would be open to all who wished to participate.

At this time the B.C.A., along with conducting a traditional annual Sunday service at the First Parish Church and the annual religious forum, was regularly conducting the chapel services on Thursday as one of its activities. Usually the students asked neighboring members of the clergy to speak, and a member of the B.C.A. presided. It was a welcome aid to the assistant to the president, Philip S. Wilder, who was in charge of getting chapel speakers and too often had to resort to a measure of arm twisting in persuading faculty members to speak in chapel.

In February 1963 a Catholic student sharply criticized these B.C.A.-sponsored services. He called them sterile and religiously biased, and said that through the B.C.A. monopoly of the Thursday chapel hour the religious expression on campus had "become stiflingly sectarian."[49] The charge was unjustified and not difficult to refute. The B.C.A. president, in reply to the attack, pointed out that it was not the fault of the B.C.A. that there were no Catholic or Jewish organizations on campus. He urged that his critic attempt to get the Newman Club accepted as a campus organization.[50] He probably did not realize how contrary to established practice this was and what a departure it would be to permit college-sponsored denominational groups on campus. This, however, was what was to happen and in the end to lead to the demise of the Christian Association, an organization which traced back directly to the founding of the Praying Society in 1815.

A major step towards recognition of college-supported denominational organizations on campus was taken on May 6, 1963, when the Student Council adopted a proposal made to them by two students that a Bowdoin Interfaith Council be formed.[51] The council was to conduct religious activities on campus and was to take the place of the B.C.A., which would now become a member organization of the council. The function of the council was to be administrative and serve "both continuous and non-continuous religious organizations." What that meant exactly is not clear, but it probably covered well-established societies and also ad hoc groups that wanted to put on a special program. Since 1963-1964 denominationally centered religious organizations have received appropriations from the activity fees paid by students.[52]

The formation of the Interfaith Council coincided with the ending of the Blanket Tax and the institution of student activities fees.[53] Half of the fifty-dollar activities fee paid by each student was now reserved to supplement the "operating appropriations made by the Governing Boards for Athletics, Masque and Gown, Debating, Glee Club, Music Club and White Key"; the other half was to go to "support such student activities as the Faculty may recommend." According to a vote by the faculty, all organizations receiving money from student activities fees are to be open to participation by all students.[54] The students were now granted more say in determining how much each activity was to receive, although the faculty had to approve of these allotments. For a time the Interfaith Council received the entire appropriation for religious groups and parceled it out to its member organizations.

In the spring of 1964 the Bowdoin Student Religious Liberals Club was formed, which was affiliated with the Continental Religious Liberals, and these in turn were tied to the Unitarian-Universalist Association.[55] It was active for a time and along with the B.C.A., the Episcopal Students Association, and the Newman Club was allotted money from the student activities fees. It was the Newman Club which soon was receiving by far the largest amount. This was largely the result of a project sponsored by the Newman Apostolate for conducting social service work at the Catholic Mission station at the Indian reservations at Dana Point and later at Pleasant Point. In spring vacation of 1968, twelve students went to Dana Point, and, since many Bowdoin students were flying south to Bermuda at that time, their project of going to the Indian reservations became known as Bermuda North. At the reservation the students instructed the children in "weaving, woodworking, leathercraft, silk-screening, candlemaking" and other similar handicrafts. Tutoring in reading, mathematics, and other academic subjects soon came to play an important part in the program. It was the practice to work with the school children in the afternoons and in the evenings with adults and young people. The latter group received training mainly in the arts and music. By the fourth year the project expanded to nine weeks and in 1972 to twelve weeks. A historical article in the *Orient* in 1975 stated that some sixty students were involved in the project and that they would miss a total of 720 hours of classes, travel over 10,000 miles, and use 650 gallons of gasoline.[56]

While the project was no doubt a worthy one, it seemed to some members of the faculty that to support it from student activities fees was using student funds to further an essentially Catholic mission project. In October 1971 the Student Activities Committee reported no allotment to the Interfaith Council but only one directly to the Newman Apostolate. A motion was made in a faculty meeting to delete the appropriation of $1,500 to the Newman Apostolate of which $1,200 was to go to Bermuda North.[57] Not only was the Newman Club supporting the work at the Catholic Indian missions and various activities on campus, but it also sponsored a weekly folk mass, first held in the union on October 19, 1967.[58] The masses were shifted to the Chapel from December 1973 to February 1976, when they were again held in the union. It was felt by some members of the faculty that common student monies should not go to further denominational or sectarian interests. The motion was defeated forty-eight to twenty-three, striking evidence of the change which had taken place in college policy with respect to denominationalism since the Sills administration.[59] Henceforth allotments were usually made directly to various religious groups, but now and then the Interfaith Council is still granted funds. This is, however, of no significance, for the account numbers of the Interfaith Council and the Newman Apostolate are one and the same in the Business Office. Whether funds are technically appropriated to the Newman Apostolate or to the Interfaith Council, they go to the Newman association.[60] The Interfaith Council no longer performs its original function of allotting funds to different religious organizations; in fact the Interfaith Council no longer exists.

The Jewish students at Bowdoin for many years never formed their own religion-oriented organization. It was unusual, perhaps, but some Jewish students did share in the B.C.A. activities, and the B.C.A. had one of its most successful years when it had an ecumenically minded Jewish student, Shepard Lee '47, as president. The College invited Jewish rabbis to speak in chapel and participate in the religious forums. Excused absences from classes were always willingly granted on Jewish holidays. Unless there were strenuous objections, in which case Jewish students could be excused, they were supposed to attend chapel. Most of them did not object to this college requirement, which existed when they enrolled. There is no synagogue in Brunswick, and consequently the Jewish students are in a different position from most of the others in respect to attending religious services. In the early 1960s there was a student interested in organizing a ritual Sabbath evening meal and service. He was granted permission to use a room at the Moulton Union and to have wine at the meal. This decision set aside for this group the strict rule which prevailed at that time of no liquor at any time in the union. When the student interested in leading the service left college, these Jewish services soon ended.

The report of the Student Activities Fees Committee in 1970-1971 indicates that the Interfaith Council at that time was allotting funds to a Bowdoin Jewish Association[61] along with the Newman Apostolate and Student Religious Liberals. Since 1973 the Jewish Association has regularly received an appropriation from the student activities fees separate from any sum which may have been voted to the Interfaith Council. It has never sought ties with the Hillel Foundation, an international Jewish college organization. The activity of the Jewish Association varies greatly from year to year. At times it sponsors lectures and discussions, invites a neighboring rabbi to meet with students, makes it possible for groups to attend services at synagogues in Portland or Lewiston, and arranges for the observance of the high holidays on campus. While the meetings of the Jewish Association are open to all students, it nevertheless is, as the name implies, a religious denominational group.

Along with the change of policy towards supporting denominational organizations with student activities fees, another quite different policy was inaugurated. Ever since a full-time member of the faculty was appointed to teach religion in 1939, the Department of Religion has grown. This growth accelerated in the late 1950s. When Professor William D.

Geoghegan went on sabbatical leave in 1964-1965, Dr. Jerry W. Brown was brought in to take over the religion courses, and stayed on. With two men in the department, one of the basic requirements for offering a major in religion was met. On April 18, 1966, the faculty approved offering a major program in religion, contingent upon the arrival of an additional instructor.[62] Dr. Brown was on temporary appointment, and apparently the Educational Policy Committee wanted to be sure there would be a two-man department to handle the majors. This reservation was met when Dr. Brown was retained and was appointed dean of students. The College now had three deans, a proliferation of deanships which aroused some merriment on campus. The offering in religion was augmented in April 1965 when the faculty approved three new courses: Problems in the Development of Religion in America, Biblical Theology, and Old Testament Prophetic Literature.[63] Since then the Department of Religion has expanded into a three-man department offering some eighteen different courses plus a program of independent study and honors work.[64] Opportunity is provided not only for the study of various aspects of Christianity, but also of different world religions.

The College had changed in many ways from the time President Coles assumed office in 1952 to December 1967, when he resigned while on sabbatical leave. The changes in the vesper and chapel programs, which had taken place in spite of his real efforts to prevent them, have been mentioned; there can be no attempt here to evaluate the many other programs he successfully inaugurated and furthered. Professor Athern P. Daggett '25, who was serving as acting president, continued to do so until January 1969, when Roger Howell, Jr., a graduate of the College in 1958, became president. He had been a Rhodes Scholar and completed his work for a doctorate at St. John's College. He returned to the College in 1964 to teach history, and in February 1968 had been appointed acting dean of the College. He was the third successive Episcopalian to be appointed president. Contrary to the practices of his nine predecessors he said nothing directly about religion in his inaugural address on "A New Humanism." The long historic progress towards secularization of the College was to continue during his administration. By the time he was elected president the page in the college catalogue which had carried the quotation of the charter on teaching virtue and piety, Hyde's "Offer of the College," and President Coles's reference to Bowdoin as a Christian college had been dropped.[65]

When the forum-chapel program was ended in May 1967, the faculty committee had proposed that the Department of Music be invited to provide the College with a series of Sunday vesper services composed primarily of appropriate religious music. Acting President Daggett did this, and the Department of Music agreed to arrange fifteen such services for the following year.[66] On the initiative of Gary R. Roberts '68, a self-constituted committee on weekday chapel was formed, and Roberts was recognized as moderator.[67] Under his leadership two to three chapels and forums were scheduled weekly through the greater part of the academic year 1967-1968. On November 13, 1967, a Prayer for Peace in Vietnam was held, modeled on the liturgy of the Confessing Church of Germany at the time of the Sudeten Crisis in 1938. In February 1968 appropriate forums were held in recognition of Negro History Week. There were also several memorial services for alumni killed in Vietnam, arranged by the acting president. Attendance on the whole was small and irregular. Some members of the student committee were still on hand after Roberts's graduation, and largely through the efforts of Bernard C. Ruffin III '69, the program of a limited number of weekday chapels and forums was continued in the following year. The students made an honest effort to keep the program going, but the last chapel in this two-year effort was held on April 22, 1969. Both years the student committee, with the help of Professor John E. Sheats of the Department of Chemistry, carried on a weekly evening hour of Bible study, which touched a very small number of students.[68] Such study groups had long been sponsored by the B.C.A., but by this time that organization had ceased to exist.[69]

The chapel choir, although it did not sing at the weekday meetings, continued briefly to exist as a separate musical organization. It made a successful tour to France during the spring vacation of 1969 under the direction of Rodney J. Rothlisberger, but it was disbanded later that year.[70] At Christmas 1968 the custom that was followed for some years of having the annual carol service in the Walker Art Building was inaugurated. A combination of Bible readings and carols, with the setting of candlelight and biblical paintings in the festively decorated rotunda of the gallery, made it a very effective and memorable service. Except for an occasional concert, the musical vespers which the faculty committee had proposed in 1967 came to an end in the spring semester of 1969. On March 15, 1970, the "Episcopal Undergraduate Committee" undertook to sponsor regular Sunday vesper services. Their last vesper service was on February 7, 1971, and was followed by four services of Holy Communion held at the traditional vesper hour of five o'clock.[71] With these, the Episcopal effort to bring vespers back to Bowdoin ended.

During the following years there were repeated attempts to revive weekday chapel services. In 1972-1973, largely due to the efforts of Richard D. Barr '70, who was serving as student intern minister at the First Parish Church, a student chapel-forum committee initiated two chapel services a week throughout the year.[72] The next year, under Barr's successor at First Parish, Ronald Staley, the chapel program was continued. It was a matter of the faithful few maintaining the services. In the fall of 1974 the Bowdoin Christian Fellowship, a rather small ecumenically oriented group of students, organized a series of meetings in Terrace Under of the Moulton Union for Bible study, study of Christian teaching, and music. A few chapel-forum meetings were held at the regular chapel hour, but no sustained program was carried through. The Bowdoin Chapel Committee, under the leadership of Jeffrey Wilson '76, continued to exist and in March 1976, sponsored a special Lenten vesper service where Rev. Kristen Stendahl, dean of the Harvard Divinity School, spoke. Later that year an Easter service was held, but no regular vespers were scheduled. Again, in April 1978, some midweek ecumenical prayer services were begun during the chapel hour, but they soon ended. These attempts to bring back a limited number of weekday chapels never enjoyed widespread support among students, faculty, or administration. Those people in the past who maintained that without a limited compulsory attendance requirement it would be impossible to maintain a chapel or vesper program at Bowdoin were apparently right. Yet they still may be shown to be wrong, for there always apparently are some students who want to give it a try. In the spring semester of 1980 a small number of students made a serious effort to conduct a program of "Ecumenical Vesper Services." They recruited faculty and student speakers and worked hard on publicity. Attendance hovered around the seventy-five mark.

The disappearance of a regular daily chapel-forum program brought an end to other observances at the College. Formerly there had been services on Armistice Day, when for years President Sills read the list of men who had been killed in World War II; on United Nations Day, when Professor Daggett always spoke on the work of that organization; and on St. Patrick's Day, when Dr. Daniel Hanley customarily presided, wearing a green tie, and there were appropriate tenor solos of Irish favorites. There were also observances of the festivals of the church year. The chapel or forum hour, call it what you will, also provided an opportunity for the presentation of student awards, which added some distinction and acclaim to the recipients. The chapel gatherings regularly gave an opportunity for memorial services on the deaths of faculty members, students, and other Bowdoin notables. While there are still a few memorial services, they are no longer held as a matter of course, ending a long tradition at Bowdoin. "Seniors' Last Chapel" was last held on May 21, 1964. Baccalaureate services continue, although they are no longer held in the First Parish Church but in the college Chapel, and the graduating class does not attend in gowns or enter as a group. The services are no longer an integral part of commencement but are held about a month earlier.

When President Howell resigned in June 1978, what so many in the pre-Civil War period feared might happen, did happen. Willard F. Enteman, a Unitarian, was elected president of the College. In his inaugural address he made "an open, honest, and blunt defense of liberal arts education" but made no specific reference to religion.[73] In line with the climate of opinion of the present day, but in contrast to the days when the College was established, religion as training in virtue and piety was no longer considered of vital significance in the educational process. By this time religious matters at the College had been relegated to the Department of Religion, as well as to other courses to which it was relevant and to what initiative the students might take in making it a part of extracurricular affairs. The Newman association with its weekly folk mass, under the professional leadership supplied by the Roman Catholic church, is the most active religious organization on the campus. The project Bermuda North, having been terminated in 1976, has been replaced by Project BABE.[74] In this program Bowdoin students assist the staff at Bancroft School in Owl's Head, Maine, working with children with learning disabilities. While the Newman Association sponsors the project, participation in it is open to all qualified students. Currently Jewish and Christian Science Associations also are present on campus; tomorrow there may well be others. There no longer is a non-denominational, religiously oriented organization in the tradition of the historic college-sponsored and -supported Y.M.C.A. or B.C.A., although the ecumenical Bowdoin Christian Fellowship still exists. There are students who participate in the activities of the various churches in the community, and the students still conduct an annual service at First Parish. The College has given up sponsoring religious services, although there are still invocations and benedictions at convocations and at commencement exercises. Grace is still customarily said at Alumni Day and Commencement Day dinners.

On the resignation of President Enteman effective January 1, 1981, the Boards appointed former Dean Arthur LeRoy Greason, a member of First Parish, acting president. He was elected president on July 24 and formally inaugurated in October 1981.

Although the status of religion at Bowdoin has changed over the years, practices once abandoned may be restored or new ones instituted. Since its founding the College has gradually shifted to the acceptance of the pronouncement of the German Socialists at the Erfurt Congress of 1891 that "Religion is a Private Matter," one which is not the concern of the College as a corporate entity. If there are those who regret these changes, they may find solace in President Appleton's dying statement, resplendent in faith and conviction: "God has taken care of the college and God will take care of it."[75]

Notes

Chapter I

1. Olmstead, *Religion in the U.S.*, pp. 218-21; Brauer, *Protestantism in America*, pp. 92-93; Atkins and Fagley, *American Congregationalism*, p. 136; Smyth, *Three Discourses*, p. 5.
2. Joseph Williamson, "Conditions of the Religious Denominations of Maine at the Close of the Revolution," *Collections of the Maine Historical Society*, 7 (1876): 217-29.
3. This act was printed in the *Cumberland Gazette*, February 7, 1788; a copy is in Sp. Col., Bowdoin College Records, 1788-1794.
4. Isaac Weston, "History of the Association of Ministers of Cumberland County, Maine from 1788 to 1867," *Congregational Quarterly*, 9 (1867): 336, 345.
5. Records of the Association of Ministers as quoted, ibid., p. 343.
6. Sp. Col., Bowdoin College Records, 1788-1794; Alfred Johnson to Alpheus C. Packard, January 19, 1835, Sp. Col., Documentary History, I, misc. dates, 1806-1902, p. 1, loose papers.
7. Photostats of the petitions, Sp. Col., Bowdoin College Records, 1788-1794.
8. Little, *Historical Sketch*, pp. x-xiii.
9. Johnson to Packard, January 19, 1835, Sp. Col., Documentary History, I, misc. dates, 1806-1902, p. 1, loose papers.
10. James Bowdoin to the Overseers and Corporation of Bowdoin College, June 27, 1794, Sp. Col., Bowdoin College Records, 1788-1794. The gift was formally accepted and the letter answered on December 27, 1794.
11. The charter has often been reprinted, usually in connection with printing the by-laws. It has been amended twice. "In 1891, limitations on the amount of property which could be taken and held by the College and on the amount of income which could be received were eliminated. In 1973, changes were made (1) to enable the Trustees and the Overseers to establish terms of office for their members in lieu of life tenure and (2) to permit officers of the College other than the Treasurer to execute deeds." *The Charter of Bowdoin College (Effective January 25, 1974)*, foreword by Wolcott Anders Hokanson.
12. Little, *Historical Sketch*, p. xvi.
13. See the early college charters and other pertinent documents collected in Cohen, *Education in the U.S.*, 2:641-713.
14. Hatch, *History of Bowdoin*, p. 5.
15. Sills, *Joseph McKeen*, p. 8.
16. *Encyclopedia Britannica*, 11th ed., s.v. "Edwards, Jonathan (1763-1758)."

17. John Locke, "Some Thoughts Concerning Education" in Axtell, *The Educational Writings of John Locke,* pp. 240-42, being paragraphs 134-36 of Locke's essay. Locke goes on to write in paragraph 139: "Having laid the Foundations of Vertue in a true Notion of a God, such as the Creed wisely teaches, as far as his Age is capable, and by accustoming him to pray to him...." (p. 244).
18. Morison, *Founding of Harvard College,* pp. 250-51.

Chapter II

1. Little, *Historical Sketch,* pp. xvi-xviii; Hatch, *History of Bowdoin,* pp. 8-10.
2. Woods, *An Address Delivered on the Opening of the New Hall of the Medical School,* pp. 7-8.
3. Cleaveland and Packard, *History of Bowdoin,* pp. 7-8; Hatch, *History of Bowdoin,* pp. 10-14.
4. For biographical material on President McKeen see Cleaveland and Packard, *History of Bowdoin,* pp. 111-13; Jenks, *Eulogy;* Sills, *Joseph McKeen.*
5. Hatch, *History of Bowdoin,* p. 13.
6. Ibid.; the Trustees voted on May 19, 1802, to give McKeen 1,000 acres of average quality in Township 6 (Trustee Records, 1794-1853, p. 34).
7. Cleaveland and Packard, *History of Bowdoin,* p. 112. The Reverend William Jenks, in his eulogy at the funeral of President McKeen, stated, "that his peculiar excellency seemed to be a sound discriminating Judgment" (Jenks, *Eulogy,* p. 34).
8. Cleaveland and Packard, *History of Bowdoin,* p. 113.
9. Packard, *Our Alma Mater,* p. 39.
10. Trustee Records, 1794-1853, pp. 37-38.
11. *Inaugural Address Delivered by the Rev. Joseph McKeen,* pp. 7-8.
12. Ibid., pp. 4, 6.
13. Ibid., pp. 6-7.
14. Ibid., p. 8.
15. Ibid., p. 13.
16. Trustee Records, 1794-1853, May 20, 1801, p. 31; May 20, 1802, p. 35.
17. For laws at Harvard and Yale see Cohen, *Education in the U.S.,* 2:657-60, 675-79; Morison, *Founding of Harvard College,* pp. 333-39, 433-34.
18. Jenks, *Eulogy,* p. 29.
19. Trustee Records, 1794-1853, Sept. 1, 2, 1802, pp. 37-38; Nov. 3, 1802, p. 42.
20. Ibid., May 17, 1808, p. 63; Sept. 6, 1808, p. 64; Sept. 1, 1812, pp. 81-82.
21. Ibid., May 19, 1813, p. 85.
22. Ibid., May 19, 1813, p. 85; June 6, 1814, p. 91; Sept. 6, 1814, p. 93; May 16, 1815, p. 98.
23. There were printed editions of the *Laws of Bowdoin College* published in 1817, 1824, 1825, 1832, 1837, 1844, and 1855; amendments in 1858, 1863, 1868, and 1873 with a new section pp. 20-22 entitled "Regulations Regulating the New Merit System" in 1875; Regulations of Bowdoin College, in 1883, 1884, 1887, 1890, 1895, 1898, and 1905; from then on various editions of the charter and by-laws of Bowdoin College, some printed, others mimeographed.
24. Jenks, *Eulogy,* p. 29. Whether Jenks is quoting directly from the laws is not clear. Anyway, his list of requirements contrasts with the more detailed statement in the 1817 *College Laws,* Chapter I: "No person shall be admitted a member of the College, unless, upon examination by the President, or, under his direction, by some other Instructor, he shall be found acquainted

with the fundamental rules of Arithmetic, be able to read, construe, and parse Cicero's select orations, the Bucolics, Georgics, and Aeneid of Virgil, the Greek Testament, and the Collectanea Graeca Minora of Dalzel, and to write Latin grammatically; and shall also produce satisfactory credentials of his good moral character." Submission of letters attesting to good moral character continued to be a requirement for admission until 1943, when the wording was changed to: "Satisfactory testimonials of sound character and personality must be presented by all candidates...." (*Bowdoin College Catalogue*, 1943-1944, p. 35).
25. "Of the exact course of study pursued ... no definite statement seems to be extant" (Little, *Historical Sketch*, p. xxxii; statement repeated in Hatch, *History of Bowdoin*, p. 23).
26. *Laws of Bowdoin College*, 1817, p. 7.
27. Hatch, *History of Bowdoin*, p. 24.
28. Woods, *An Address Delivered on the Opening of the New Hall of the Medical School*, pp. 11-13.
29. John McKeen's account of the Thorndike Oak as reprinted ibid., pp. 11-12. Mr. McKeen was an eyewitness of the planting of the acorn.
30. *Laws of Bowdoin College*, 1817, p. 8.
31. Ibid., pp. 4-5.

Chapter III

1. Ashby, *First Parish Church*, pp. 22, 36.
2. Ibid., pp. 26-33.
3. Ibid., pp. 46-47.
4. Ibid., pp. 66, 71.
5. Ibid., p. 73.
6. Ibid., pp. 78-79; Wheeler, *History of Brunswick, Topsham, and Harpswell*, pp. 377-380.
7. As quoted in Ashby, *First Parish Church*, p. 79.
8. Ibid., p. 101.
9. Trustee Records, 1794-1853, p. 49; Sp. Col., Votes of the Boards, May 1805, in Bowdoin College Board Votes, 1794-1815.
10. Sp. Col., Samuel Melcher's Ledger, 1803, p. 35.
11. On Sept. 4, 1833, the Trustees voted to put up a stove in the Chapel at an expense not exceeding forty dollars. The Overseers, however, refused to concur (Trustee Records, 1794-1853, p. 232). For churches and chapels to be unheated was not uncommon at this time, and the second meeting house erected by the First Parish had no heating at first.
12. Article by J.A. Peters on the old chapel in *Orient*, March 5, 1884, pp. 212-14. The seniors were privileged to leave the chapel first, the freshmen were to leave last.
13. Trustee Records, 1794-1853, p. 51.
14. Sp. Col., Bowdoin College Board Votes, 1794-1815. The votes of the Trustees were not acted upon by the Overseers until December 18, 1805.
15. Ibid.
16. Sp. Col., Samuel Melcher's Day Book, 1803, no page numbers.
17. Sp. Col., Samuel Melcher's Ledger, 1803, pp. 35-36. Hatch is clearly wrong when he writes: "He [Melcher] appears to have been also a good business man, for his papers recently examined by his grandson show that his contract price was twelve hundred dollars and the actual cost of the chapel eight hundred" (*History of Bowdoin*, p. 414).

18. Trustee Records, 1794-1853, Sept. 2, 1817, p. 108; May 19, 1818, p. 109; J.A. Peters in *Orient*, March 5, 1884; Hatch, *History of Bowdoin*, p. 415. There is a picture in the Cram Alumni House at Bowdoin of the College in 1821, which shows both Massachusetts Hall and the chapel with belfries.
19. Not only was the old meeting house inconveniently located, but it was sadly in need of repair. After the erection of the second meeting house, Town Meetings continued to be held in it for some time. It gradually fell into rack and ruin, all the windows were broken, and there were great holes in the floor. It burned down on Sunday evening, October 26, 1834, and it was generally held that it had been set on fire by the students (Ashby, *First Parish Church*, pp. 87-89, 160-62; Hamlin, *My Life and Times*, p. 143).
20. Trustee Records, 1794-1853, Sept. 3, 1805, p. 50.
21. Ibid., p. 110. The Visiting Committee in its 1827 report listed eight shares in the meeting house as unproductive property but states it was "valuable for purpose of Commencement." The reports of the Visiting Committee in 1829 and 1830 list the eight shares in the meeting house and assign them a value of $808 (Visiting Committee, 1826-33, pp. 37, 81, 102).
22. Ashby, *First Parish Church*, p. 91.
23. Trustee Records, 1794-1853, Oct. 23, 1805, p. 52. The vote was not concurred in by the Overseers until December 18, 1805.
24. *General Catalogue of Bowdoin College, 1794-1950*, p. 45.
25. For the agreement, see Ashby, *First Parish Church*, pp. 96-97.
26. Ibid., p. 96.
27. In 1845 Rev. George E. Adams, in writing about the necessity of erecting a new meeting house, states: "After having a cart-load of boards and joists brought into our House every year for forty years for a Commencement stage, we are weary of the system ...." (ibid., p. 188).
28. Ibid., p. 97.
29. Folder, "Deeds and Plans II" in Bowdoin College Business Office files; registered in Office of Brunswick Town Clerk, vol. 3, p. 64.
30. Trustee Records, 1794-1853, pp. 110, 115.
31. Cumberland County Registry of Deeds, book 117, p. 390; also in Folder, "Deeds and Plans II" in Bowdoin College Business Office files; see Ashby, *First Parish Church*, pp. 268-271; Barrett Potter, *Report to the Treasurer Describing Land of the College*. The Boards accepted the indenture on September 4, 1821 (Trustee Records, 1794-1853, p. 132).
32. That is the $800 paid for the eight shares subscribed to the venture of erecting the meeting house.
33. Wheeler, *History of Brunswick, Topsham, and Harpswell*, pp. 145, 371; Ashby, *First Parish Church*, p. 146.
34. The belfry on Massachusetts Hall was probably removed in the fall of 1830. At least the Visiting Committee in the summer of 1830 stated: "Last Visiting Committee reported cupola should be removed from Massachusetts Hall and roof reshingled. This should be done without delay" (Visiting Committee, 1826-1833, Report of 1830, p. 93).
35. Visiting Committee, 1840-1844, letter appended to the Report of 1844.
36. Ibid.; the vote as given in Ashby, *First Parish Church*, p. 147, has a few minor textual variations.
37. Ashby, *First Parish Church*, p. 147.
38. Trustee Records, 1794-1853, Aug. 31, 1830, p. 128.
39. Sp. Col., Records of Executive Government, 1831-1875, p. 77.
40. Trustee Records, 1794-1853, Sept. 2, 1835, p. 245.

41. The College held that it owned the north gallery and was not obligated to pay on it, a position disputed by the First Parish (Ashby, *First Parish Church*, pp. 268-73).
42. Ibid., p. 147.
43. Trustee Records, 1794-1853, Oct. 27, 1843, p. 319.
44. The commodious vestry on School Street, formerly known as the Second Baptist Meeting House, was sold to the Congregational church (not the parish) in 1841 for $500. In 1891 it was sold for $1,000 to the Pejepscot Historical Society, which still owns the building (Ashby, *First Parish Church*, pp. 174, 364; John Furbish, "Notes Read at the Dedication of the Historical Society Building" in Louise R. Helmreich, ed., *Our Town*, pp. 5-16).
45. See the letter from Rev. George E. Adams to the Boston *Recorder* in Ashby, *First Parish Church*, p. 188.
46. Sp. Col., Diary of Charles P. Roberts, Class of 1845, April 18, 1845. The dove subsequently found its way to the Pejepscot Historical Society.
47. Ashby, *First Parish Church*, p. 210.
48. Commencements are now held either on the steps of the Walker Art Building or in the Morrell Gymnasium.
49. Trustee Records, 1794-1853, pp. 342, 344-45.
50. Ashby, *First Parish Church*, pp. 212-13.
51. Ibid., p. 213. Gas lighting was introduced in the meeting house in 1871 (ibid., p. 328).
52. Ibid., p. 205.
53. Ibid., pp. 103-09.
54. Trustee Records, 1794-1853, Sept. 6, 1814, p. 94.
55. Ashby, *First Parish Church*, p. 132.
56. Ibid. President Allen was apparently not fond of preaching without compensation. In August 1822 he submitted a bill to the College for preaching to the students during the present term, six times at five dollars—$30.00. The Trustees agreed to pay, but the Overseers did not concur (Trustee Records, 1794-1853, Aug. 20, 1822, p. 132).
57. Ashby, *First Parish Church*, p. 132; Sp. Col., Records of Executive Government, 1821-1831, Sept. 7, 1821, p. 19.
58. Sp. Col., Records of Executive Government, 1821-1831, p. 64.
59. Trustee Records, 1794,1853, pp. 136, 151, 160, 165. Votes of the faculty to pay Rev. Keep and then Rev. Mead $200 for instructing the seniors in moral philosophy four hours a week are to be found in Sp. Col., Records of Executive Government, 1821-1831, pp. 19, 64.
60. Trustee Records, 1794-1853, Sept. 5-6, 1826, p. 171. Perhaps the vote was not sent down to the Overseers in order to spare Rev. Mead embarrassment. He was a member of the Board of Overseers from 1826 to 1831.
61. Sp. Col., Bowdoin College Records, 1823-1826. The letter was signed by Jacob Abbot, Charles Packard, Class of 1817, and Noah Hinckley.
62. Mary Ann Kendrick, "Some Vague Reminiscences of Olden Times in Brunswick, Commencing in the Early Twenties," in Louise R. Helmreich, ed., *Our Town*, pp. 24-25; Ashby, *First Parish Church*, pp. 137-38.
63. Sp. Col., Records of Executive Government, 1821-1831, p. 74.
64. Rev. Adams was a member of the Board of Overseers from 1830 to 1872; vice president of the Board from 1865 to 1871. He was awarded a D.D. in 1849.
65. Writing about Bowdoin in 1825, Hatch states: "All the Faculty were orthodox Congregationalists, although for a time Professor Newman was believed to lean towards the Unitarians" *(History of Bowdoin,* p. 73). Professor Henry

W. Longfellow, Class of 1825, was on the list of First Parish members, but when the Unitarian Society was formed in Brunswick he identified himself with it (Ashby, *First Parish Church*, p. 349).
66. Burnett, *Hyde*, p. 199.

Chapter IV

1. In the *General Catalogue of Bowdoin College, 1794-1894*, pp. 3-14, the names of all the Trustees and Overseers are listed with their terms of service. The ministers are all designated by Rev. and the others generally receive the title Hon.
2. *Memorial Catalogue of Bowdoin College, 1794-1894*, pp. 44-45.
3. Trustee Records, 1794-1853, p. 59.
4. In September 1827 the Boards voted: "That Professor Upham be authorized to instruct such students as may desire it in the Hebrew language" (Trustee Records, 1794-1853, p. 176); *Bowdoin College Catalogue*, 1828, p. 15; Little, *Historical Sketch*, p. xlviii.
5. Olmstead, *Religion in the U.S.*, p. 285.
6. These figures are based on data in *General Catalogue of Bowdoin College, 1794-1950;* they no doubt are reasonably complete although the professions of some graduates are not given. In addition, of the Bowdoin graduates from 1806 to 1831, fourteen went on to study at Andover and a scattering at other theological seminaries without ever being ordained. Until the early 1830s Bangor Seminary was attended largely by graduates of three-year classical academies, and it was only then that it began to enlist college graduates (Hamlin, *My Life and Times*, p. 143); Smyth, *Three Discourses*, p. 80.
7. Sp. Col., Scrap Book Hyde, vol. 1, p. 8.
8. Faculty Records, 1876-1884, p. 172.
9. Paley, *A View of the Evidences of Christianity*.
10. Paley, *Natural Theology*, 1855 ed., p. 4 of the preface.
11. Visiting Committee, 1845-1850, Report of 1847, p. 20.
12. See below, pp. 90-93.
13. Little, *Historical Sketch*, p. xlii.
14. *Addresses of Rev. Jesse Appleton*, pp. 11-12.
15. Visiting Committee, 1834-1839, Report of 1836.
16. Visiting Committee, 1845-1850, Report of 1850.
17. *Addresses of Rev. Jesse Appleton*, p. 7.
18. *Laws of Bowdoin College*, 1817, p. 28. This provision was incorporated directly in the 1824 edition of the laws, p. 6, law 4. In Special Collections there are various editions of the laws issued to students.
19. Burnett, *Hyde*, p. 159.
20. *Laws of Bowdoin College*, 1817, chap. 3, pp. 6-8.
21. Ibid., chap. 4, pp. 10-15.
22. This particular law was adopted September 6, 1814 (Trustee Records, 1794-1853, p. 92).
23. *Laws of Bowdoin College*, 1824, p. 7.
24. Ibid., 1817, chap. 4, p. 12.
25. Ibid., p. 15.
26. Ibid.
27. Trustee Records, 1794-1853, Aug. 31, 1841, p. 294; *Laws of Bowdoin College*, 1844, law 5.
28. *Laws of Bowdoin College*, 1824, p. 19.

29. Trustee Records, 1794-1853, Aug. 31, 1847, p. 350.
30. Sp. Col., Records of Executive Government, 1821-1831, p. 56.
31. *Laws of Bowdoin College,* 1825, p. 18.
32. Trustee Records, 1794-1853, Aug. 31, 1830, pp. 197-98. The prohibition of smoking is omitted in *Laws of Bowdoin College,* 1832, law 34, pp. 18-19. Professor Smyth, in his lectures on the religious history of Bowdoin, pleads for action against the use of tobacco *(Three Discourses,* p. 74).
33. Item from the *Lewiston Journal* in Sp. Col., Documentary History, 1884-1888, p. 112.
34. Sp. Col., Records of Executive Government, 1805-1820, Jan. 4, 1808, pp. 65-66.
35. *Laws of Bowdoin College,* 1825, pp. 17-18.
36. Sp. Col., Records of Executive Government, 1805-1820, p. 34.
37. Ibid.
38. Ibid., p. 63.
39. Ibid., pp. 92, 94.
40. Ibid., p. 95.
41. Ibid., p. 99.
42. Ibid., p. 103.
43. Ibid., pp. 106, 114, 124.
44. Ibid., pp. 98, 112, 114, 121, 123, 124, 129, 130, 140.
45. Ibid., 1825-1848, pp. 27, 47. The First Baptist Church in Brunswick was organized in 1803. The Universalists were organized in 1812 and their first church building erected in 1829. The Unitarian Society was formed in January 1830, but they never had a settled minister, and an agreement was subsequently reached that they would maintain preaching in Topsham; the Universalists would do the same in Brunswick. Methodist activity in the community began in 1821, and in 1835 there were seven college students among the forty members of the society. The Methodist Episcopal Society was formally organized the following year, and they acquired a church property on Federal Street. Asabel Moore, Class of 1835, who was licensed to preach before he entered Bowdoin, preached at times and later served the Methodists as pastor in 1842-1843. The Methodist church on Pleasant Street was erected in 1866. The first Episcopal service in Brunswick was held in the college chapel in 1842; the parish was organized in 1842 and St. Paul's Church on Pleasant Street erected in 1845. Professor D.R. Goodwin was one of the leading organizers of the parish. Although there were visits by a Roman Catholic priest from Bath starting about 1860, the first Catholic church in Brunswick dates from 1866 (Wheeler, *History of Brunswick, Topsham, and Harpswell,* pp. 381, 392-405; Everett Nason et al., *History of the United Methodist Church in Brunswick,* 1821-1973, pp. 9-10; Herring, *Berean Baptist Church,* pp. 5-14; Lincoln, *St. Paul's Episcopal Church,* pp. 8-12; *Souvenir of St. John the Baptist Parish,* brief historical accounts in French and English.
46. Sp. Col., Diary of Charles P. Roberts, Oct. 16, 1842.
47. Ibid., Dec. 28, 1843. Roberts also notes errors in the faculty records, all to his advantage, in his entry on May 25, 1845. The faculty were well aware that the monitors were not exact in their reports (Sp. Col., Records of Executive Government, 1848-1868 misc., pp. 77, 95, 100.
48. Sp. Col., Diary of Charles P. Roberts, March 21, 1848.
49. Ibid., Oct. 22, 1841.
50. Ibid., Oct. 30, 31, 1841. In October 1873 the Bible was "stolen" from the chapel and not returned for over a month (*Orient,* Oct. 29, 1873, p. 114; Dec. 3, 1873, p. 141).

51. Sp. Col., Records of Executive Government, 1821-1831, April 5, 1827, p. 155. The letters of the parents to President Allen in which they agreed to pay their share of the cost are to be found in Sp. Col., College Records, 1827-1829, Folder, Loss of Chapel Bell. Both students who were caught were firm in refusing to implicate others that were involved in the "frolic."
52. Article by J.A. Peters in the *Orient*, March 5, 1884, pp. 212-14.
53. Sp. Col., Diary of Charles P. Roberts, March 20, 1842.
54. Ibid., Oct. 9, 18, 1844. Although there is mention of many misdemeanors in the Records of the Executive Government, there is no mention of these events.
55. Ibid., July 28, 1842; Foster, *Down East Diary*, July 24, 1852, p. 345.
56. Sp. Col., Records of Executive Government, 1849-1868, misc., Oct. 10, 1854, pp. 63-64. On October 27, 1860, four members of the sophomore class were detected attempting to dislodge the chapel bell. They were immediately sent home (ibid., p. 120).
57. Ibid., Oct. 19, 1863, p. 126.
58. Minot and Snow, *Tales of Bowdoin*, p. 229. This tale is confirmed in a slightly different version by an article on the chapel bell in the *Orient* which stated that about 1862 the bell had been filled with coal ashes and water and left to the severity of a winter night *(Orient*, March 13, 1889, p. 212). "On cold winter mornings the clapper of the Chapel bell was so often missing that the college had learned to keep on hand a supply of tongues so that voice could be summarily restored to the bell" *(Tales of Bowdoin*, p. 229).
59. *Orient*, Nov. 27, 1878, p. 102.
60. Sp. Col., Diary of Charles P. Roberts, Oct. 12, 18, 1844.
61. Visiting Committee, 1845-1850, Report of 1845, p. 4.
62. Ibid., Report of 1847, p. 26. The lowest cost for destruction of property charged to students in a year was $141.22 in 1831, the highest $505.58 in 1845, the average for the years 1831 to 1847, $304.57.
63. Foster, *Down East Diary*, p. 337.
64. *Laws of Bowdoin College*, 1825, p. 9. The punishment as detailed in Articles 13-17 of the 1825 edition of the laws are a reformulation of Section 10 of Chapter 4 of the 1817 edition, and of laws 12-16 of the 1824 edition.
65. *Laws of Bowdoin College*, 1825, p. 13.
66. Sp. Col., Records of Executive Government, 1805-1820, April 2, 1805, p. 4.
67. *Laws of Bowdoin College*, 1825, law 15, p. 10. Rustication—"to dismiss or 'send down' from a university for a specified time as a punishment"—was a practice derived from England and was also used at Harvard and Yale at this time *(The Oxford English Dictionary*, 8:928).
68. Sp. Col., Diary of Peleg Whitman Chandler, Class of 1832, Oct. 26, 1832.
69. As quoted in Handy, *A Christian America*, pp. 23-24.

Chapter V

1. Smyth, *Three Discourses*, pp. 12-13; Little, *Historical Sketch*, pp. xlviii-xlix.
2. Hamlin, *My Life and Times*, p. 97.
3. Smyth, *Three Discourses*, p. 13.
4. Ibid., p. 14.
5. Sp. Col., Theological Society Records, 1836-1846, p. 14.
6. Ibid., art. 4.
7. Ibid., 1846-1850, p. 12.
8. Ibid., p. 20.

9. Ibid.; Little, *Historical Sketch,* p. xlix; Sp. Col., Bowdoin College, Soc. and Clubs, Folder, Theological Society, 1847. The library in 1847 numbe. 722 volumes, an increase of 48 over the previous year. In Special Collection there are six volumes of the Theological Society Librarian's Records, 1820-1850, giving names of students and the books and periodicals they charged out. The library contained many religious books, but also some dealing with secular subjects. More books were charged out in the earlier years of the society than in the later. According to the Constitution of 1836 the library was open from twelve to one P.M. each Saturday; each member could take out three books and retain them three weeks, periodicals one week. A fine of ten cents a week was imposed on books or periodicals kept overtime (Sp. Col., Theological Society Records, 1836-1846, p. 4.)
10. Ibid., pp. 14, 18, 20, 26, 29, 32, 34, 35, 36, 47, 58, 69, 71, 75; ibid., 1846-1850, pp. 11, 16, 17, 18.
11. For an account of the founding and activities of the Peucinian and Athenaean societies, see Hatch, *History of Bowdoin,* pp. 304-13; Little, *Historical Sketch,* pp. 87-88.
12. Smyth, *Three Discourses,* p. 14. On the influence of Southgate and Cargill, see ibid., pp. 14-20; A.S. Packard, "Historical Sketch of Bowdoin College," *The Quarterly Register,* 8 (Nov. 1835): 115-16.
13. Sp. Col., Records of the Praying Society, 1815-1832, pp. 8, 18, 163. There are five volumes of the records of the society (and later the circle) available in Special Collections. There is an article on the history of the Praying Circle by C.C. Torrey in the *Orient,* Feb. 6, 1884, p. 184.
14. Hamlin, *My Life and Times,* p. 97.
15. Sp. Col., Records of the Praying Society, 1815-1832, p. 9.
16. Ibid., art. 10.
17. Ibid., pp. 52, 84, 90, 98, 135.
18. Ibid., p. 10.
19. Ibid., p. 69.
20. Atkins and Fagley, *American Congregationalism,* pp. 158-163; Ashby, *First Parish Church,* p. 120. Anderson among others joined the First Parish Church as a result of a revival in 1816.
21. *Orient,* Feb. 18, 1910.
22. Smyth discusses the revivals of 1815-1816, 1826, 1830-1831, 1834 *(Three Discourses,* pp. 20-26, 43-48, 63-68); A.S. Packard, "Historical Sketch of Bowdoin College," *The Quarterly Register,* 8 (Nov. 1835): 117.
23. "The Annual Concert of Prayers for Colleges" was established in about 1822 (Smyth, *Three Discourses,* p. 43).
24. Sp. Col., Records of the Praying Circle, 1832-1847, p. 10.
25. Hall, *College Words and Customs,* p. 33.
26. Sp. Col., Diary of Charles P. Roberts, April 6, 1842. Professor Smyth was an old hand at trying to stop bonfires. We have a record that on April 13, 1832, he caught Peleg Whitman Chandler, Class of 1832, who had taken refuge in a Temple (Sp. Col., Diary of Peleg Whitman Chandler, April 13, 1832).
27. Sp. Col., Diary of Charles P. Roberts, April 7, 8, 9, 11, May 4, 1842; Sp. Col., Records of Executive Government, 1831-1855, pp. 123-24.
28. Foster, *Down East Diary,* pp. 337-38.
29. Sp. Col., Records of the Praying Society, 1815-1832, pp. 12, 135.
30. Ibid., pp. 141, 146-47; ibid., 1832-1847, p. 2.
31. Ibid., arts. 10, 16, 17, 18, pp. 2-6.
32. For the dismissal of two members see ibid., 1855-1867, pp. 65, 68.
33. Ibid., p. 87; see also pp. 78-79.

34. Ibid., 1832-1847, p. 61.
35. Ibid., 1845-1855, p. 24.
36. Ibid., p. 55.
37. Ibid., 1855-1867, pp. 1-5, 13.
38. Ibid., p. 30.
39. Ibid., pp. 57-58.
40. Ibid., p. 80.
41. A copy of the constitution is to be found ibid., 1867-1882, pp. 1-5.
42. Ibid., 1855-67, p. 118.
43. Ibid., 1867-1882, pp. 5, 32, 72, 79, 81.
44. Meeting of Oct. 27, 1881, ibid., p. 110.
45. Ibid., p. 111.
46. Sp. Col., Records of the Bowdoin Y.M.C.A., vol. 1, Oct. 18, 26, 1882.
47. Trustee Records, 1794-1853, Sept. 2, 1832, p. 120; Cleaveland and Packard, *History of Bowdoin,* p. 130.
48. Hamlin, *My Life and Times,* p. 111. Smyth also states: "Several societies of inquiry, having special reference to the wants of the heathen world, were also sustained" *(Three Discourses,* p. 62).
49. As quoted in Hatch, *History of Bowdoin,* p. 289.
50. Sp. Col., Bowdoin College, Societies—Clubs, Folder, Bowdoin Unitarian Society.
51. Sp. Col., Diary of Charles P. Roberts, April 5, 1845.
52. Sp. Col., Bowdoin College, Societies—Clubs, contains three folders on the Benevolent Society. There are also four bound volumes, including some accounts. None of the records go beyond 1827.
53. On July 13, 1869, the Boards voted: "That the President be authorized to remit sixty dollars a year from the term bills of needy and worthy young men, not exceeding five in number, in each class as it enters college; and such assistance to be continued through the college course if required." On July 8, 1873, the Boards rescinded this vote on the recommendation of the Finance Committee (Trustee Records, 1854-1905, pp. 164, 219).
54. *Bowdoin College Catalogue,* 1930-1931, p. 118. The first State of Maine Scholarships were awarded for the academic year 1931-1932.
55. Sp. Col., Bowdoin College, Societies—Clubs, Folder, Benevolent Society, 1814-1827, Constitution of 1814.
56. Sp. Col., Bowdoin College, Societies—Clubs, Folder, Benevolent Society, 1814-1827.
57. Sp. Col., Records of the Benevolent Society of Bowdoin College, Incorporated January 24, 1826, p. 1.
58. Ibid., pp. 3-4.
59. Ibid., pp. 5-6; Sp. Col., Bowdoin College, Societies—Clubs, Folder, Benevolent Society, 1814-1827; also Folder, Benevolent Society, 1826-1827. Cleaveland and Packard state that the Benevolent Society did not long survive its public incorporation *(History of Bowdoin,* p. 29).
60. Smyth, *Three Discourses,* app. A, p. 73.
61. Sp. Col., Records of the Temperance Society of the Maine Medical School at Bowdoin College.
62. Sp. Col., Bowdoin College Temperance Society, 1854-1855, p. 60; Bowdoin College, Societies—Clubs, Folder, Temperance Society, notice.
63. Sp. Col., Bowdoin College, Societies—Clubs, Folder, Enigma Society.
64. Sp. Col., Records of Executive Government, 1821-1831, p. 181. This surveillance of societies was enjoined on the faculty by a vote of the Boards on September 1, 1812 (Sp. Col., Bowdoin College Board Votes, 1794-1815).

65. Sp. Col., Diary of Charles P. Roberts, April 10, 1842.
66. Sp. Col., Record Book of the Bowdoin Dole of the Raxian. Many pages of the record book have been torn out.
67. As quoted in Smyth, *Three Discourses,* pp. 79-80.
68. On this complicated question of the removal of President Allen from office see Cleaveland and Packard, *History of Bowdoin,* pp. 14-15; for the opinion of Justice Story, pp. 103-107; Hatch, *History of Bowdoin,* pp. 74-82; Little, *Historical Sketch,* pp. lxix-lxx.
69. Sp. Col., Records of Executive Government, 1831-1875, p. 4.
70. Ibid., p. 40.
71. Trustee Records, 1794-1853, p. 222. The accepted distribution of duties was suspended a year later when President Allen was restored to his office (ibid., p. 229).
72. However, the attitude of some Bowdoin students is no doubt mirrored when Hawthorne writes in *Fanshawe:* "At Harland College there prevailed a deep and awful sense of religion" (p. 336).

Chapter VI

1. Trustee Records, 1794-1853, p. 161.
2. Ibid., pp. 163-64.
3. Ibid., p. 164.
4. Sp. Col., William Allen Correspondence, Allen to R. Williams, Feb. 10, 1825, Jan. 5, 1827. The petitions to the legislature are undated.
5. Trustee Records, Sept. 1827, p. 179.
6. Sp. Col., Bowdoin College Buildings: Chapel, Folder, 1828-1839. The report is signed by Prentiss Mellen, per order, but is not dated.
7. Sp. Col., William Allen Correspondence, Allen to R. Williams, Feb. 10, 1825, Jan. 5, 1827.
8. Cleaveland and Packard, *History of Bowdoin,* pp. 14-15, 103-06; Hatch, *History of Bowdoin,* pp. 74-82.
9. Visiting Committee, 1834-1839, Report of 1834, pp. 2-3.
10. Sp. Col., Bowdoin College Buildings: Chapel, Folder, 1828-1839.
11. Trustee Records, 1794-1853, Sept. 7, 1836, p. 254.
12. Ibid., Sept. 4, 1833, p. 232.
13. Visiting Committee, 1834-1839, Librarian's Report for 1838.
14. Sp. Col., Bowdoin College Buildings: Chapel, Folder, 1828-1839. The minutes of the meeting are signed by Asa Cummings.
15. Ibid. There are other letters in this folder.
16. Ibid.; Sp. Col., Robert H. Gardiner, 1782-1864, Folder, Correspondence.
17. Visiting Committee, 1840-1844, Report of 1841, p. 14.
18. Trustee Records, 1794-1853, Aug. 31, 1841, p. 296.
19. Visiting Committee, 1840-1844, Report of Aug. 1842; Sp. Col., Contributors to Bowdoin College from 1846 to 1852 including the subscriptions of 1842, p. 2.
20. Visiting Committee, 1840-1844, Report of Aug. 1842.
21. Ibid., Report of 1843.
22. On the settlement of the Bowdoin estate see Cleaveland and Packard, *History of Bowdoin,* pp. 108-110; Park, *Leonard Woods,* p. 35.
23. Trustee Records, 1794-1853, pp. 305-06, 314.
24. The agreement was reached on September 28, 1843, and gave the College 3/10 of the proceedings of certain lands which were to be sold; a long sum-

mary account of these proceedings is given in the Trustee Records, 1794-1853, pp. 321-25.
25. President Woods to R. H. Gardiner, Feb. 15, 1844 (Sp. Col., Leonard Woods Papers, Correspondence, 1840-1844). President Woods was in New York for a month at this time. Mr. Gardiner was acquainted with Upjohn since he had designed Gardiner's house in Gardiner, Maine. Gardiner also wrote directly to Upjohn on Jan. 8, 1844 (Upjohn Papers, Box 1, N.Y. Public Library. Manuscripts and Archives Div.; copy of letter courtesy of Prof. W.H. Pierson of Williams College).
26. Sp. Col., Robert H. Gardiner, 1782-1864, Folder, Correspondence. On February 15, 1844, President Woods wrote to Mr. Gardiner: "Mr. McKeen has given you such full information of the results of our interview with him [Upjohn] that I need add nothing (Sp. Col., Leonard Woods Papers, Correspondence, 1840-1844).
27. Sp. Col., Leonard Woods Papers, Correspondence, 1844-1845.
28. Sp. Col., Bowdoin College Buildings: Chapel, Folder, Correspondence, 1844-1845, Gardiner to Woods, July 1, 1844; Upjohn to Woods, July 8, 1844.
29. Ashby, *First Parish Church,* p. 180; see above, p. 28.
30. N. Appleton to A. Lawrence, Lawrence to Woods, A.S. Packard to Woods, Woods to General King (Sp. Col., Records, Folder, 1844; Bowdoin College Buildings: Chapel, Folder, Correspondence, 1844-1845. The letters of Packard to Woods, Lawrence to Woods, and Woods to King were numbered VI, VII, and VIII by someone, probably President Woods.
31. This letter is undated but on the back of it is a notation in President Woods's handwriting: "Original Letter to Gen. King for name of Chapel, Summer of 1844" (Sp. Col., Bowdoin College Buildings: Chapel, Folder, Correspondence 1844-1845).
32. Sp. Col., Leonard Woods Papers, Correspondence, 1840-1844.
33. Visiting Committee, 1840-1844, Report of 1844, pp. 3-4.
34. Ibid., p. 5.
35. Trustee Records, 1794-1853, Sept. 3, 1844, pp. 325, 327.
36. J. McKeen to R.H. Gardiner, Nov. 7, 1844 (Sp. Col., Robert H. Gardiner, 1782-1864); Woods to Gardiner, Nov. 11, 1844 (Sp. Col., Leonard Woods Papers, Correspondence, 1840-1844).
37. Sp. Col., Leonard Woods Papers, Correspondence, 1840-1844.
38. Woods to Daveis. The letter is undated but is postmarked June 8, 1845 (Sp. Col., C.S. Daveis Papers, Correspondence, 1844-1845).
39. Ibid., Address at the Laying of the Corner Stone of King Chapel, p. 44.
40. Sp. Col., Bowdoin College Buildings: Chapel, Folder, Correspondence, 1844-1845; Trustee Records, 1794-1853, pp. 332-33.
41. Trustee Records, 1794-1853, p. 333.
42. Abstract from the records of the United Lodge, June 28, 1845; Woods to Daveis, July 5, 1845. Woods wrote: "Our views agree exactly with yours as to the propriety of having Gov. Dunlap perform the masonic part of the ceremonies and this has been definitely arranged (Bowdoin College Buildings: Chapel, Folder, Correspondence, 1844-1845.
43. Sp. Col., Diary of Charles P. Roberts, July 15, 1845.
44. Ibid., July 16, 1845.
45. *Maine Democrat,* July 29, 1845. There is a copy of the article in Sp. Col., C.S. Daveis Papers, Correspondence, 1840-1864, Folder, 1844-1845.
46. Ibid. The Latin inscriptions are in the Folder, Miscellaneous. In Sp. Col., Bowdoin College Buildings: Chapel, Folder, Correspondence, 1844-1845,

there is an engraved silver plaque 2½ by 4 inches stating: "This foundation stone of King Chapel was laid by the Most Worshipful Grand Lodge of the State of Maine, July 16 A.D. 1845." The cornerstone is not clearly marked and it is impossible to say exactly where it is.

47. There are a preliminary draft and two handwritten copies of the address in Sp. Col., C.S. Daveis Papers, Correspondence, 1840-1864, Folder, July 16, 1845, Address at Laying of Cornerstone of King Chapel. The address is forty-seven pages long on copybook size paper.
48. Sp. Col., Diary of Charles P. Roberts, July 16, 1845.
49. Visiting Committee, 1845-1850, Report of 1846, pp. 44, 46.
50. Trustee Records, 1794-1853, Sept. 1, 1846, p. 340.
51. Ibid., Sept. 2, 1846, pp. 345-46.
52. Thomas C. Upham to Woods, Aug. 1, 1846 (Sp. Col., Leonard Woods Papers, Correspondence, August-December 1846). This letter is part of a collection of letters dealing with the Declaration. See also Professor Packard's recollection (Packard, *Upham*, pp. 15-16).
53. R.H. Gardiner to Prof. Wm. Smyth, Nov. 30, 1857; Smyth to Gardiner, Dec. 3, 1857, quoting Professor Upham (Sp. Col., Robert H. Gardiner, 1782-1864, Correspondence); Gardiner to Daveis, Dec. 29, 1846 (Sp. Col., Leonard Woods Papers, Correspondence, August-December 1846).
54. Cleaveland and Packard, *History of Bowdoin,* p. 21. Here there is this statement in a footnote: "The original of this Declaration is left in the keeping of Prof. Smyth." Today it is not to be found, nor is the original draft, which was revised by Mr. Evans and Mr. Gardiner, at hand. The text of the Declaration as given here is from ibid., pp. 21-22.
55. Leonard Woods to R.H. Gardiner, Nov. 29, 1846 (Sp. Col., Leonard Woods Papers, Correspondence, August-December 1846).
56. Sp. Col., Contributors to Bowdoin College from 1846 to 1852, including the subscriptions of 1842.
57. The building of a new dormitory was voted by the Boards on September 7, 1842, and a loan not exceeding $5,000 was authorized. The building was ready for use in the fall of 1843. It was named Appleton Hall on August 31, 1847 (Trustee Records, 1794-1853, pp. 305, 347; Visiting Committee, 1840-1844, Report of 1843, p. 5). The statements in Little, *Historical Sketch*, p. lxxix and Hatch, *History of Bowdoin,* p. 409, are misleading.
58. Professor Wm. Smyth also strongly maintained this position (Smyth to Gardiner, Dec. 3, 1857, Sp. Col., Robert H. Gardiner, 1782-1864, Correspondence).
59. Cleaveland and Packard, *History of Bowdoin,* p. 23; see also Gardiner to Woods, Nov. 14, 1846; Gardiner to Daveis, Dec. 29, 1846; A.D. Wheeler to E. Peabody, Nov. 4, 1846; Peabody to Wheeler, Dec. 7, 1846, in Sp. Col., Leonard Woods Papers, Correspondence, August-December 1846.
60. Trustee Records, 1854-1905, p. 29; Nathan Weston to Gardiner, Sp. Col., Robert H. Gardiner, 1782-1864, Correspondence.
61. Cleaveland and Packard, *History of Bowdoin,* p. 23; Little, *Historical Sketch,* pp. lxxxi-lxxxii; Hatch, *History of Bowdoin,* pp. 113-15.
62. Visiting Committee, 1845-1850, Report of 1847, p. 2.
63. Ibid., pp. 8-9; Trustee Records, 1794-1853, p. 349.
64. Visiting Committee, 1845-1850, Report of 1848, p. 3. The old chapel was removed during the winter vacation of 1847-1848 (A.S. Packard in the *Orient,* Feb. 3, 1873, p. 181).
65. Trustee Records, 1794-1853, p. 357; Visiting Committee, 1845-1850, Report of 1848, p. 8; Report of 1849.

66. Trustee Records, 1794-1853, p. 376.
67. Ibid., p. 377.
68. Visiting Committee, 1850-1855, Reports of 1850, 1852, 1855. There have been five successful attempts of students to climb the chapel spires. In the fall of 1887, Jonathan P. Cilley, Class of 1891, placed the class banner on the top of the spire; a day later, George B. Chandler, Class of 1890, removed it and left the 1890 class flag. In November 1894 Charles D. Moulton, Class of 1898, fastened the 1898 class banner on a spire, only to have it replaced the next night by Donald B. MacMillan, Class of 1897, who raised the 1897 flag. (MacMillan graduated out of course and is carried as a member of the class of 1898 in the *General Catalogue*.) On June 7, 1900, four members of the class of 1903 put the class banner on the spire. They were Clement F. Robinson, Philip T. Harris, Daniel I. Gould, and Leon J. Emerson. Credit is usually given to Gould or Emerson for actually climbing to the top. In the spring of 1914 the flag of 1917 was hoisted to the top of the spire, an accomplishment usually attributed to Frank E. Noyes '17 of Topsham. The college authorities now removed the lightning rods from the spires by means of which the ascent had been accomplished. In October 1948, on their third attempt, Julian Holmes, Independent, and six ATO pledges, Brian A. Poynton, George C. Maling, Jr., Linwood A. Morrell, Donald M. Russell, T. Peter Sylvan, and John V.W. Young, all freshmen, succeeded in getting a freshman cap on the top of the spire by means of a balloon and guide lines. Getting a freshman cap or other insignia on the top of the chapel spire brought, by campus tradition, the suspension of all freshman rules, notably the wearing of freshman caps. Sp. Col., Documentary History, 1894-1895, p. 13; June-December 1909, p. 103; May 1914-December 1914, pp. 42, 46; September 1919-June 1920, p. 100; *Orient*, October 27, November 3, 1948; Clement F. Robinson, "Banner and Spire," *Bowdoin Alumnus*, 4 (May 1930), 92-97.
69. Correspondence with Mr. Wheeler can be found in Sp. Col., Bowdoin College Buildings: Chapel, Folders, Correspondence January 1848-May 1848, May 1848-October 1848, 1850-1851 and Miscellaneous. On differences between Upjohn and Wheeler see particularly letters of Upjohn to Woods, July 15, 1851 and August 2, 1851. On the carving see letters of Upjohn to Woods, April 2, 1852, May 14, 1852, June 19, 1852, June 23, 1852, July 10, 1852, ibid., Folders, January-May, 1852, June-August 1852.
70. Ellingwood to Daveis, July 10, 1847, Sp. Col., C.S. Daveis Papers, Correspondence, 1840-1864, Folder, 1847. On King's declining health see Smith, *General William King*, pp. 134-36.
71. Letter of President Woods, July 15, 1850, Sp. Col., Leonard Woods Papers, Correspondence, 1845-1857.
72. On August 19, 1851, C.R. Porter wrote to President Woods: "I have been requested to appear before the College Committee at Brunswick in relation to their claim against Gov. King. Will you do me the favor to inform me when the Comt. will have a meeting" (Sp. Col., Bowdoin College Buildings: Chapel, Correspondence, 1850-1855).
73. Woods to Upjohn, April 10, 1852, ibid., Correspondence, January 1852-May 1852. At this time Upjohn was asking for the last $100 payment on his original fee of $750, and also for 5 percent on the expenditures made since the resumption of building in 1851. The long delay in completing the structure had caused Upjohn more work, and he felt entitled to further remuneration. He did not, however, press the matter, and since he had clearly agreed on a total compensation of $750 the College did not feel

obligated to pay him more. See particularly letters of Upjohn to Woods, May 14, 1852; Woods to Upjohn, May 15, 1852; Upjohn to Woods, May 18, 1852, May 29, 1852, ibid., Correspondence, January 1852-May 1852; Woods to Upjohn, June 23, 1852; Upjohn to Woods, July 5, 1852, August 18, 1852, ibid., Correspondence, June 1852-August 1852.

74. Ibid., Correspondence, January 1852-May 1852.
75. E. Everett to Daveis, June 19, 1852, Sp. Col., C.S. Daveis Papers, Correspondence, 1850-1854; Smith, *General William King*, pp. 136-41.
76. Ibid.; Woods to Upjohn, April 10, 1852, Sp. Col., Bowdoin College Buildings: Chapel, Correspondence, January 1852-May 1852.
77. Visiting Committee, 1850-1855, Report of 1852 where the letter is appended and marked as C. Hatch states that "the meaning of the last clause in the letter is obscure" *(History of Bowdoin*, p. 417). Four thousand dollars was the amount Professor Upham was confident could be raised if another name could be given to the Chapel. When it was apparent that work on the Chapel would be "indefinitely suspended" if funds were not provided, Professor Upham signed a note in September 1852, obligating himself to pay $1,500 towards completing the Chapel. It was understood that when he raised this amount by solicitation the note would be cancelled. He was successful, and in 1855 the Boards voted that the note should be cancelled (Trustee Records, 1854-1905, pp. 4, 13; see also Visiting Committee, 1850-1855, Reports of 1852, 1854).
78. Visiting Committee, 1850-1855, Report of 1852; Trustee Records, 1794-1853, p. 403; Smith, *General William King*, p. 134, is in error on the name being retained.
79. Gideon L. Soule to Daveis, Sept. 17, 1854; Woods to Daveis, Sept. 21, 1854, Feb. 26, 1855, May 11, 1855, Sp. Col., C.S. Daveis Papers, Correspondence, 1850-1854.
80. *Brunswick Telegraph,* June 9, 1855, in Sp. Col., Bowdoin College Buildings: Chapel, Folder, Dedication of Chapel 1855. There are also other clippings and pertinent material in this folder as well as in the Folder, Correspondence, 1853-1862. See also Sp. Col., Documentary History, 1860-1865, p. 11.
81. Sp. Col., Bowdoin College Buildings: Chapel, Folder, Finance, 1839-1855.
82. Trustee Records, 1854-1905, July 31, 1855, p. 13.
83. Ibid., p. 19; Visiting Committee, Report of 1856, p. 4.
84. Visiting Committee, 1856-1860, Report of 1860; Trustee Records, 1854-1905, p. 52. This room was later used as an art gallery (Little, *Historical Sketch,* p. lxxvii).
85. Visiting Committee, Report of 1858, p. 2, Report of 1861, p. 7; Trustee Records, 1854-1905, p. 63.
86. Trustee Records, 1854-1905, p. 94.
87. Ibid., pp. 155, 174.
88. Visiting Committee, 1856-1860, Report of 1857, p. 1; Report of 1860; Visiting Committee, 1861-1864, Report of 1861, p. 2; Report of 1862, p. 2.
89. Ibid., 1861-1864, Report of 1863; Report of 1869, p. 10; Trustee Records, 1854-1905, pp. 82, 106.
90. See above, p. 79.
91. Trustee Records, 1794-1853, pp. 347, 374, 377, 404.
92. Visiting Committee, 1851-1855, Report of 1852, see also detailed expense of cleaning in appended account marked M; Visiting Committee, 1856-1860, Report of 1857, p. 1.
93. Ibid., Report of 1884, p. 4, Report of 1885, p. 5.

94. Ibid., 1856-1860, Report of 1856, p. 4, Report of 1860; Visiting Committee, 1861-1864, Report of 1861, pp. 2-3, Report of 1862, p. 2. While the new library quarters were a great improvement over the old ones, they left much to be desired. As a Visiting Committee later reported: "The library rooms are ill adapted to the purpose for which they are used." They were dark and cold, and the committee considered the main room a "blunder of the architect." To improve the lighting, the Boards in 1884 authorized the removal of the stained glass from the body of the windows and the insertion therein of clear glass; the stained glass in the borders was to be retained (Ibid., Reports of 1882, 1883, 1885; Trustee Records, 1854-1905, p. 403).
95. Visiting Committee, 1856-1860, Report of 1858, p. 15.
96. Ibid., Report of 1856.
97. Ibid., Report of 1858, p. 15.
98. Eckert, *Peter Cornelius,* pp. 88, 91. See letters of H.O. Apthorp, Class of 1829, to John McKeen of July 5, 1856, and July 31, 1857 (Sp. Col., Bowdoin College Buildings: Chapel, Correspondence, 1853-1867). Hatch writes that the anonymous donor is "now known to be Timothy Walker of Boston, a cousin of President Woods...." *(History of Bowdoin,* p. 422). Walker is also stated to be the donor in the brochure "The Chapel of Bowdoin College" (Sp. Col., Folder, Chapel). Hatch does not state where he obtained his information, and I have not come across a reference to Walker in the archives. Hatch must be in error here, for Walker was not a graduate of the College, and the Visiting Committee in 1858 states definitely that the gift was by a graduate of the College.
99. Mr. Cummings sold the *Danae* to George Hall, a New York artist *(Orient,* March 1876, p. 198).
100. Sp. Col., Documentary History, 1875-1879, p. 55; 1884-1888, p. 12; *Orient,* March 29, 1876, p. 198.
101. Sp. Col., Documentary History, Dec. 1907-June 1908, pp. 103, 132.
102. *Descriptive Catalogue of the Art Collections of Bowdoin College,* p. 111; *Orient,* September 30, 1913, p. 95; Sp. Col., Documentary History, Dec. 1915-July 1916, p. 20; *President's Report,* 1915-1916, p. 57 (report of the Director of the Museum of Fine Arts, Henry Johnson). Hatch, *History of Bowdoin,* p. 423 is clearly in error here when he attributes the gift of the reproduction of the *Isaiah* panel to Lucien Howe, Class of 1870, in memory of his brother Albion Howe, Class of 1861, and seems to indicate it was painted after the Delphic Sibyl panel. Moreover, clippings in the folders of Lucien Howe, 1848-1928, or Albion Howe, 1840-1873, in Sp. Col. do not refer to any gift of a mural, although there is mention of the other benefactions by Lucien Howe.
103. *Descriptive Catalogue of the Art Collections of Bowdoin College,* p. 111.
104. Little, *Historical Sketch,* p. lxxvi. This statement apparently goes back to Woods himself (see Park, *Leonard Woods,* p. 14).
105. In 1878 Professor Alpheus S. Packard, in his report as Collins Professor to the Visiting Committee, complained about the bad acoustics. "It is a serious hindrance in all efforts for the moral and religious influence of the college....I cannot refrain from repeating that the college has suffered material loss in its moral religious influence from this single cause and to urge the attention of the Boards to what I deem an urgent necessity for its very best interests. It is very desirable at times to address the students, as occasion sometimes arises in college life, in a familiar way, but we are absolutely prevented, I have reason to know, from such attempts by the bad acoustic properties of the prayer room" (Visiting Committee, Report of 1878).

106. Visiting Committee, 1850-1855, Report of 1855, p. 2.
107. *Orient,* March 26, 1903, p. 267.

Chapter VII

1. Trustee Records, 1794-1853, p. 358. There are numerous inaccuracies in the account of the founding of the Collins Professorship in *Named Professorships at Bowdoin College,* p. 1.
2. Minot and Snow, *Tales of Bowdoin,* Introduction. On Woods as a disciplinarian see also Park, *Leonard Woods,* pp. 35-36; Everett, *Leonard Woods,* pp. 26-28.
3. Visiting Committee, 1845-1850, Report of 1845, p. 5.
4. Ibid., Report of 1847, p. 26.
5. Ibid., p. 22.
6. Ibid., Report of 1848, Paper marked MI; Trustee Records, 1794-1853, p. 364; Board votes and terms of the Collins Fund are given in Sp. Col., Potter, Titles and Donations of Funds, 1794-1898.
7. Trustee Records, 1794-1853, p. 358.
8. Ibid., pp. 358, 368.
9. Sp. Col., Contributors to Bowdoin College from 1846 to 1852 including the subscriptions of 1842; Packard, *Upham,* p. 16.
10. Trustee Records, 1794-1853, pp. 363, 370.
11. Visiting Committee, 1845-1850, Report of President Woods, 1850.
12. Trustee Records, 1794-1853, p. 373. The $400 did not cover the cost of moving, and the Boards later raised the sum to $500. This was refunded to the College by Phillips Academy (ibid., p. 400).
13. Ibid., p. 385.
14. Visiting Committee, Report of 1853.
15. Ibid., Report of 1854, appended report of Professor Hitchcock.
16. Ibid., Report of 1855.
17. Ibid., 1856-1860, Report of 1859.
18. On holders of the Collins Professorship see *Named Professorships at Bowdoin College,* pp. 1-4.
19. See below, p. 100.
20. Trustee Records, 1854-1905, p. 250; see also ibid., 1794-1853, p. 365.
21. Ibid., 1854-1905, p. 46.
22. Ibid., July 18, 1874, p. 250.
23. Susan Collins to the President and Trustees, Sept. 27, 1875; William P. Putnam to George R. Swasey, April 13, 1896, Business Office, 33108-1434, Collins.
24. Trustee Records, 1854-1905, p. 279; Visiting Committee, Report of 1877, p. 8.
25. Statement of Ira P. Booker, Business Office, 33108-1434, Collins.
26. Trustee Records, 1854-1905, p. 291; Sp. Col., Potter, Titles and Donations of Funds, 1794-1898, pp. 5-8; Statement of Ira P. Booker and letters of Putnam to Bradbury, Jan. 25, 1896, Putnam to Swasey, April 13, 1896, Business Office, 33108-1434, Collins.
27. Putnam to Swasey, June 20, 1896, Business Office, 33108-1434, Collins. Mrs. Collins died in 1890, and her will was allowed January 19, 1891. The bond definitely states "without interest," but the College made some claim to interest. In regard to such payment, a letter to W.S. Hutchinson (sender's signature illegible) of January 25, 1896, states: "There may be some question whether there should not be some interest, but in view of all cir-

cumstances, I do not think the college would claim it or ought to claim it." On the other hand, William P. Putnam, in a letter to Mr. Swasey of April 13, 1896, claimed interest payments. He wrote: "Probably, by the terms of this bond, the college had no right to demand anything of her [Mrs. Collins] during her lifetime. At any rate it did not, so that no part of the interest of the seventy-five hundred dollars has been paid, for a period of now over twenty years." Later in the letter he, however, asks Mr. Swasey, a lawyer in Boston, "to ascertain the rights of the College as to interest under the bond" (Business Office, 33108-1434, Collins).

28. As quoted in Hatch, *History of Bowdoin,* p. 299.
29. Visiting Committee, Report of 1897. At this time the Boards undertook to review the College's lands and funds, and Barrett Potter, Class of 1878, a local lawyer and secretary of the Trustees, submitted two reports (Business Office, 33108-1434, Collins).
30. Burnett, *Hyde,* p. 172.
31. Copy of the decree, Business Office, 33108-1434, Collins.
32. Ibid.; Trustee Records, 1906-1929, p. 376.
33. Business Office, 33108-1434, Collins.
34. Trustee Records, 1854-1905, pp. 101-03.
35. Ibid., p. 103.
36. Ibid., p. 110.
37. Ibid., pp. 169-70. In July 1877 Boody asked to be relieved of his debt to the College in order to avoid bankruptcy, as he had just lost a suit for $200,000. In July 1878 the Boards granted this release (ibid., pp. 292, 308).
38. *Whig and Courier,* July 17, 1869, in Sp. Col., Documentary History, 3:153.
39. Trustee Records, 1854-1905, pp. 316, 330, 348. The letters exchanged by Mr. Winkley and President Chamberlain are to be found, Business Office, 33101-414, Winkley. Mr. Winkley was also one of the largest benefactors of Bangor Theological Seminary (Clark, *Bangor Theological Seminary,* p. 291).
40. Business Office, 33104-414, Winkley; Trustee Records, 1906-1929, p. 52; *Named Professorships at Bowdoin College,* pp. 25-30.
41. Trustee Records, 1854-1905, pp. 349, 352-53, 360; Sp. Col., Potter, Titles and Donations of Funds, 1794-1898; *Named Professorships at Bowdoin College,* pp. 22-24.
42. Trustee Records, 1906-1929, p. 49; Business Office, Stone Professorship (Account Closed). Other correspondence relative to the Stone Professorship can be found in this folder in the Business Office.
43. Trustee Records, 1854-1905, p. 174; 1906-1929, pp. 7, 46, 49; see also the statement of General Thomas H. Hubbard of February 1908 in Sp. Col., Documentary History, December 1907-June 1908, p. 49.
44. Sp. Col., Documentary History, December 1907-June 1908, p. 49; see also *President's Report,* 1907-1908, pp. 23-34.
45. On the founding of these scholarships see Trustee Records, 1854-1905, pp. 182, 200, 266, 291; Sp. Col., Potter, Titles and Donation of Funds, 1794-1898, pp. 19-20, 31-32. Mr. Delano also bequeathed to the College $500 to be added to the Collins Professorship fund.
46. Trustee Records, 1854-1905, p. 410; Sp. Col., Potter, Titles and Donations of Funds, 1794-1898, p. 55. The current college catalogue does not carry these preference restrictions.
47. Preference statements as listed in *Bowdoin College Catalogue,* 1979-1980.
48. Trustee Records, 1854-1905, pp. 358-59, 374-76, 446, 512-13; Sp. Col., Potter, Titles and Donations of Funds, 1794-1898, pp. 40, 50.

49. Hatch, *History of Bowdoin*, p. 90; Deems, *Maine—First of Conferences*, pp. 14-17.
50. Deems, *Maine—First of Conferences*, pp. 18-19.
51. Ibid., pp. 19-20.
52. Sp. Col., Documentary History, January-June 1907, p. 101.
53. Trustee Records, 1854-1905, January 14, 1874, p. 232.
54. Copy of the letter in Sp. Col., Documentary History, 3:87.
55. Little, *Historical Sketch*, p. xciv.
56. Ibid., pp. lxxxiii-lxxxiv; Hatch, *History of Bowdoin*, p. 123; Wallace, *Soul of the Lion*, pp. 30-31.
57. President Harris in his inaugural address mentions the denominational character of colleges but never refers to Congregationalism in connection with Bowdoin; this was no doubt taken for granted (Harris, *Inaugural Address*, pp. 18-19).
58. *Addresses at the Inauguration of the Rev. William DeWitt Hyde*, pp. 38-39.
59. Sp. Col., Documentary History, 1884-1888, p. 82.
60. Ibid., letter of July 12, 1886, p. 60.
61. Rev. M. Ellis, "The Legal Situation of the Congregational Colleges with Reference to the Denomination," *The Pacific: San Francisco, Cal.* (Sp. Col., Documentary History, July 1888 to June 1891, p. 121, clipping).
62. See newspaper clippings on the proposed transfer in Sp. Col., Documentary History, 1899-1900, pp. 35, 53, 85, 99, 105. The seminary had very few students at this time, 23 in 1899, 17 in 1900, 23 in 1901-1903 (Clark, *Bangor Theological Seminary*, pp. 285-86). There had long been a friendly relationship between Bowdoin and the seminary. Professor Henry L. Chapman of Bowdoin was a member of the Seminary Board of Trustees from 1885 to 1913 and president of the board from 1887 to 1911 (ibid., p. 351).
63. Trustee Records, 1854-1905, June 1900, p. 630. The faculty followed the lead of the Boards and adopted a resolution welcoming the Bangor Seminary to Brunswick (Faculty Records, 1894-1900, June 30, 1900, p. 380).
64. Sp. Col., Documentary History, May-September 1911, p. 59.
65. Ashby, *First Parish Church*, p. 270.
66. Letter of First Parish Assessors Danl. Elliot and Wm. Smyth to the College Visiting Committee in Visiting Committee, 1861-1864, Report of 1863.
67. Ashby, *First Parish Church*, p. 271.
68. Trustee Records, 1854-1905, p. 155; Visiting Committee, Report of 1869, p. 22, Report of 1876-1877, appended report of Finance Committee of 1876.
69. Ibid., Report of July 19, 1877, p. 16.
70. Trustee Records, 1854-1905, July 11, 1877, p. 297; the life of the committee was extended in 1878, p. 308.
71. Ashby, *First Parish Church*, p. 337.
72. Trustee Records, 1854-1905, July 8, 1879, pp. 316-18.
73. Ibid., June 1894, p. 542.
74. *Orient*, October 16, 1889, p. 129.
75. The *Orient* stated in 1889 that the Church on the Hill "is the official college church, and the one which the professors of the college attend and support" (*Orient*, October 16, 1889, p. 130).
76. Ashby, *First Parish Church*, pp. 367-70.

Chapter VIII

1. Harris, *Inaugural Address*, pp. 16-19.
2. Sp. Col., Records of Executive Government, 1849-1868, misc., p. 121.

3. Visiting Committee, 1861-1864, Report of 1862, appended report of Professor Egbert C. Smyth.
4. Ibid., Report of 1864, p. 25.
5. Ibid., Report of 1866; Trustee Records, 1854-1905, p. 125.
6. Visiting Committee, Report of 1867, appended report of A.S. Packard.
7. Sp. Col., Records of Executive Government, 1831-1875, April 18, 1870, p. 216.
8. Faculty Records, 1956-1968, p. 348.
9. Ashby, *First Parish Church,* pp. 338-39. The installation of gas lighting in the church building was completed on July 3, 1871 (ibid., p. 328).
10. Sp. Col., Records of Executive Government, 1831-1875, July 1, 1871, p. 236.
11. Visiting Committee, Report of 1870, appended report of President Harris.
12. Little, *Historical Sketch,* p. xc; see also Wallace, *Soul of the Lion,* p. 229.
13. Sp. Col., Chamberlain, *The New Education,* typescript, pp. 3-4.
14. Ibid., p. 9. Chamberlain expressed much the same views in his speech at the Wycliff Semi-Millennial Celebration, December 2, 1880, when he said: "Sad and dire would be the day...which God grant may never dawn or darken on the land... when the American people should cease to study and know the word of God" (Sp. Col., Cross, "Joshua Lawrence Chamberlain," pp. 68-69).
15. These changes can be traced in Sp. Col., Cross, "Joshua Lawrence Chamberlain," pp. 55-75; Hatch, *History of Bowdoin,* pp. 156-80; Wallace, *Soul of the Lion,* pp. 229-47.
16. Faculty Records, 1871-1876, September 2, 1871, p. 2.
17. Visiting Committee, Report of 1872, appended report of President Chamberlain.
18. Faculty Records, 1871-1876, June 24, 1872, p. 34.
19. Ibid., August 29, 1872, p. 35. There apparently had been some omissions of evening prayers earlier, related to the introduction of the program of military training, for the college catalogue of 1872, p. 34, states: "Evening Prayers or Roll Calls are held at six o'clock or at sunset." This statement also appears in the 1873 catalogue, p. 34, but then disappears in later editions.
20. Sp. Col., Records of Executive Government, 1876-1884, p. 102.
21. Visiting Committee, Report of 1878; appended report of Professor Alpheus S. Packard; *Bowdoin College Catalogue,* 1878-1879, p. 27.
22. Visiting Committee, Report of 1874, appended report of President Chamberlain, July 1, 1874.
23. Sp. Col., Records of Executive Government, 1831-1875, p. 243.
24. Faculty Records, 1871-1876, January 27, 1873, p. 49.
25. Ibid., pp. 140-41.
26. *Orient,* March 10, 1875.
27. Sp. Col., Records of Executive Government, 1876-1884, December 12, 1881, p. 309.
28. Visiting Committee, 1861-1864, Report of 1862, appended report of Professor Egbert C. Smyth, April 22, 1862.
29. *Orient,* March 24, 1873, p. 246.
30. Ibid., March 13, 1878, p. 187.
31. Sp. Col., Records of Executive Government, 1876-1884, February 5, 1877, p. 50; Faculty Records, 1884-1894, p. 183.
32. *Orient,* March 30, 1887, p. 257.
33. Ibid., May 12, 1897.
34. *First Annual Reunion of the Bowdoin Alumni Association of New York,* p. 64.
35. Ashby, *First Parish Church,* p. 271.

36. Ibid.; Minot and Snow, *Tales of Bowdoin,* p. 91; *Orient,* March 25, 1874.
37. *Orient,* October 16, 1878, p. 70.
38. For articles or communications against compulsory attendance see *Orient,* May 1, 1871, p. 22; June 26, 1871, p. 89; November 29, 1876, p. 112; November 13, 1878, p. 86; January 12, 1881, p. 149; October 19, 1881, pp. 83-84; April 30, 1884, pp. 6-7; October 30, 1889, pp. 149-50; May 12, 1897, p. 21; January 16, 1917, p. 231.
39. For articles or communications defending compulsory attendance see *Orient,* November 2, 1881, pp. 96-98; November 16, 1881, pp. 104-05; November 13, 1889, p. 162; February 4, 1891, p. 227; March 18, 1891, p. 266; March 21, 1901, p. 247; January 16, 1917, p. 231.
40. Sp. Col., Records of Executive Government, 1876-1884, May 28, 1880, pp. 239-41.
41. Ibid., January 28, 1881, p. 270.
42. Ibid., April 30, 1883, p. 370; Faculty Records, 1884-1894, January 17, 1887, p. 83.
43. Faculty Records, 1884-1894, September 12, 1885, p. 34.
44. Ibid., September 16, 1889, p. 176; September 30, 1889, pp. 178-79; October 7, 1889, pp. 180-81; October 21, 1889, p. 183; October 28, 1889, p. 184; December 16, 1889, p. 190.
45. *Orient,* December 18, 1889, p. 202.
46. Ibid., February 4, 1891, p. 227; see also March 18, 1891, p. 266.
47. Sp. Col., Records of Executive Government, 1876-1884, December 10, 1877, p. 103; *Orient,* February 12, 1890, p. 245.
48. Faculty Records, 1884-1894, pp. 268-69, 359.
49. Ibid., 1894-1900, March 16, 1896, p. 98. The committee consisted of Professors Little, Chapman, and MacDonald.
50. Ibid., April 27, 1896, pp. 105-06.
51. Ibid., p. 341.
52. Ibid., p. 348.
53. Visiting Committee, Report of 1910, p. 10; Trustee Records, 1854-1905, June 1900, p. 633.
54. *Orient,* October 11, 1900, November 8, 1900.
55. *President's Report,* 1902-1903, p. 13.
56. *Orient,* February 24, 1905, p. 278.
57. Faculty Records, 1900-1907, March 13, 1905, p. 351; November 13, 1905, p. 385.
58. *Orient,* March 20, 1902, pp. 243-44.
59. Visiting Committee, Report of 1902, p. 11.
60. Faculty Records, 1900-1907, March 24, 1902, p. 172.
61. Ibid., June 27, 1902, p. 193. No record of what the committee of two proposed is at hand, but the faculty apparently did not mend its ways much, for President Hyde soon reminded them again of the desirability of their attendance at chapel (ibid., 1907-1915, p. 230). In 1908 the Visiting Committee was "happy to observe more of the faculty present" at chapel, and that there were more quiet and reverence among the students (Visiting Committee, Report of 1908, p. 6).
62. Trustee Records, 1854-1905, p. 703.
63. Faculty Records, 1900-1907, February 13, 1905; September 25, 1906, p. 436.
64. Before the semester system was adopted in 1904-1905 there had been fifteen cuts for each term, making it forty-five for the year; the students gained one cut under the new system (*Orient,* January 27, 1905, p. 249; February 17, 1905, p. 267; see also October 12, 1887, p. 107).

65. Cleaveland and Packard, *History of Bowdoin,* p. 30.
66. Sp. Col., Records of Executive Government, 1821-1831, September 2, 1831, p. 181.
67. Article by Josiah Crosby, Class of 1835, on the old chapel organ, *Orient,* June 27, 1888, p. 75.
68. Ashby, *First Parish Church,* pp. 162-65.
69. *Orient,* March 14, 1877, p. 184.
70. Ibid., March 11, 1872, p. 246; see also February 10, 1873, p. 200.
71. Ibid., March 24, 1875, p. 189; May 21, 1879, p. 27; June 23, 1880, p. 162.
72. Sp. Col., Records of Executive Government, 1876-1884, May 28, 1880, pp. 239-41.
73. Visiting Committee, Report of 1881, appended report.
74. *Orient,* November 2, 1881, p. 99; Sp. Col., Records of Executive Government, 1876-1884, December 17, 1883, p. 402.
75. Visiting Committee, Report of 1884, p. 7; also appended report of Professor Packard.
76. *Orient,* September 29, 1886, p. 106.
77. Faculty Records, 1884-1894, June 25, 1887, p. 106.
78. *Orient,* May 30, 1888, p. 29. The Crockers were wealthy merchants of New Bedford, Massachusetts.
79. Trustee Records, 1854-1905, June 26, 1888, p. 459; see also *Orient,* May 30, 1888, p. 29.
80. *Orient,* May 30, 1888, p. 29; Faculty Records, 1884-1894, p. 131. The program of the recital and concert are to be found in Sp. Col., Folder, Oliver Crocker Stevens, 1876.
81. Faculty Records, 1884-1894, p. 167; Trustee Records, 1854-1905, pp. 461, 470, 530; Visiting Committee, Report of 1888, p. 10; Report of 1889, appended president's report.
82. Sp. Col., Documentary History, 1888-1891, p. 43, clipping from *Boston Journal,* January 30, 1890.
83. Faculty Records, 1888-1894, March 9, 1891, p. 248, ibid., 1894-1900, p. 75; ibid., 1900-1907, p. 30.
84. *President's Report,* 1900-1901, p. 18.
85. *Orient,* May 9, 1901, p. 17; October 24, 1901, p. 111. The *Bugle* of 1913 listed twenty members of the chapel choir along with the members of a quartet and a double quartet.
86. Faculty Records, 1907-1915, November 11, 1907, pp. 77, 82; Sp. Col., Documentary History, June-December 1907, p. 151, clipping, November 15, 1907.
87. Sp. Col., Documentary History, September 1912-May 1914, p. 21; Faculty Records, 1907-1915, pp. 198, 261, 312, 323; ibid., 1915-1919, p. 112.
88. *Bowdoin College Catalogue,* 1912-1913, pp. 91-92. Five semester courses were offered.
89. Burnett, *Hyde,* p. 113.
90. Olmstead, *Religion in the U.S.,* pp. 489-94; Hudson, *Religion in America,* p. 310.
91. Hyde, *College Man and College Woman,* p. 127.
92. *President's Report,* 1902-1903, p. 13; ibid., 1903-1904, pp. 20-21.
93. *Songs of Bowdoin,* p. 26; *Orient,* June 11, 1873, p. 42; June 21, 1876, p. 21; June 13, 1888, p. 55; June 5, 1914, p. 69.
94. Faculty Records, 1894-1900, December 4, 1899, p. 331; see also January 27, 1890, p. 194; *Orient,* February 2, 1906, p. 250; Hopkins, *History of the Y.M.C.A.,* pp. 284-85.
95. *President's Report,* 1892-1893, pp. 24-25; ibid., 1893-1894, p. 10.

96. Ibid., 1906-1907, pp. 9-10. The *Orient* regularly covered many other Sunday and weekly chapel services as well, so that the chapel messages reached more students than those who were actually present.
97. Dr. Ashby states that the program continued for a score of years *(First Parish Church,* p. 386). Since there is no list of college preachers in the 1918-1919 college catalogue, it can be assumed that the program ended before the death of Professor Files on April 23, 1919. He had been making annual gifts for the program (Burnett, *Hyde,* p. 176).
98. Sp. Col., Records of the Bowdoin Y.M.C.A., 1882-1893, p. 1; the volume does not have page numbers. This volume of records was lost but found in 1899 and placed in the college library. Another volume (labelled Vol. 2) covers the period April 13, 1898 to November 5, 1908. There must have been a volume containing the records from 1893 to 1898 (which is referred to in Vol. 2 as Vol. 1) which is lost, as are the records for the years after 1908.
99. Sp. Col., Records of the Bowdoin Y.M.C.A., 1898-1908, p. 55. Mention of the adoption of the constitution is made here, and it is stated that it is given in Vol. 1, p. 169. This volume of the records has been lost.
100. Ibid., pp. 74-75, 77, 82, 95, 105.
101. Visiting Committee, Report of 1909; appended report of the Christian Association.
102. *Orient,* October 12, 1906; see also October 11, 1907. On November 18, 1910, the *Orient* reported that the previous year out of 198 members only 120 paid dues.
103. Visiting Committee, Report of 1884, appended report of Professor Alpheus S. Packard.
104. *Orient,* November 9, 1887, p. 130.
105. Ibid., September 28, 1898, p. 99; *President's Report,* 1902-1903, p. 13; 1903-1904, pp. 21-24; *Orient,* October 12, 1906.
106. Whiteside, *Boston Y.M.C.A.,* p. 32.
107. At least in 1890 and 1891 the Y arranged a course of lectures which were very popular. There was a charge of $1.50 for the course, $.35 for a single ticket. The course for 1890 was as follows: January 19, J.P. Baxter, president of the Maine Historical Society on "An Historic City"; January 23, F.A. Hill, master of English High in Cambridge, "New England Pioneer Days"; February 5, Professor L.A. Lee, Bowdoin, "The Straits of Magellan (illustrated by the stereopticon)"; February 12, N.T. Whittaker, D.D., "America, Her Mission and Destiny"; February 24, Professor H.L. Chapman, Bowdoin, "Chaucer"; March 3, Dudley A. Sargent, M.D., Harvard, "Physical Culture"; March 13, Edward Stanwood, of the *Youth's Companion,* "The Spirit of the Age." On February 4, 1891 the *Orient* lamented "But 75 course tickets have been taken by students."
108. This became a regular activity of the association. In the fall of 1915 circular letters were sent to fifty representative churches within a one hundred-mile radius of Brunswick in an effort to extend the deputation work of the association (*Orient,* December 7, 1915, p. 180).
109. *Orient,* April 19, 1899, p. 18.
110. This "Freshman Bible" continued to be published until 1969 (*Orient,* April 16, 1971); Hopkins, *History of the Y.M.C.A.,* p. 284.
111. See the two excellent chapters "The Rise of the Student Movement" and "Fifty Years of the Student Y.M.C.A." in Hopkins, *History of the Y.M.C.A.,* pp. 271-308, 625-656.
112. *President's Report,* 1903-1904, pp. 20-21; 1905-1906, pp. 11-12; *Orient,* March 17, 1905.
113. *Orient,* July 31, 1908, p. 91. Money to pay part of his salary was now available

from the funds of the Collins Professorship, and the Visiting Committee in 1900 stated: "The wisdom of that arrangement [use of the Collins fund] has been amply justified by the results in the religious life and activity of the students during the year" (Visiting Committee, Report of 1909, p. 11).
114. *Orient,* October 16, 1908, p. 119. Mr. Scott reported to the Visiting Committee that during the year the Y had held twenty-two weekly meetings with an average attendance of fifty, addressed by fifteen outside speakers, three members of the faculty, and four undergraduates (Visiting Committee, Report of 1909, appended report).
115. *Orient,* January 21, 1910, p. 199; March 18, 1910, p. 241. This Alumni Advisory Committee is listed in the spread of the Y.M.C.A. for the last time in the *Bugle* of 1923.
116. *President's Report,* 1909-1910, pp. 27-32; McConaughy's report to the Visiting Committee, Visiting Committee, Report of 1910. The president failed to mention some of the Y activities. See list of the appointed committees, *Orient,* May 20, 1910, p. 55.
117. *Orient,* March 17, 1911, p. 245; October 13, 1911, p. 98.
118. *Bowdoin College Catalogue,* 1914-1915, p. 67.
119. *President's Report,* 1913-1914, p. 20; 1914-1915, p. 14. The practice of reporting on religious activities at the College was continued by President Sills but was dropped by later presidents.
120. *Bowdoin College Catalogue,* 1910-1911, p. 91; 1911-1912, p. 99; 1912-1913, p. 117.
121. *Orient,* April 9, 1912, p. 6; June 4, 1915, p. 79.
122. Sp. Col., Documentary History, October 1911-May 1912, pp. 71, 77; May-December 1912, pp. 26, 29. The Gibbons Club is listed in the *Bugle* for the years 1913 to 1916, but not thereafter. There was no English Catholic church in Brunswick at this time.
123. Sp. Col., Documentary History, October-May 1912, p. 96.
124. Ibid., January-July 1910, p. 141. For a biographical sketch of Dreer see Sp. Col., Chenault, "The Blackman at Bowdoin," pp. 11-20.
125. Sp. Col., Documentary History, August 1865-July 1875, p. 76. In 1877 and 1888 Bowdoin conducted summer sessions to which women were admitted (Sp. Col., Cross, "Joshua Lawrence Chamberlain," pp. 57-58; Wallace, *Soul of the Lion,* p. 231).
126. Sp. Col., Documentary History, 1860-1865, pp. 11, 72; 1884-1888, p. 15.
127. *President's Report,* 1903-1904, p. 21. The other denominations were: 115 Congregationalists, 32 Methodists, 29 Universalists, 19 Episcopalians, 19 Unitarians, 18 Baptists, 2 Presbyterians, 2 Swedenborgians, 1 Christian, and 16 with no preference.
128. This was the first time religious preference was entered on a student's college record. There is no mention of religious preferences in the old bound student records c. 1853-1900, nor in the loose leaf records 1840-1853. I was unable to find the student records for the years before 1840. Starting with the class of 1927, the religious preferences of students were regularly entered on their college record cards; this practice was ended with the class of 1974. There are a few scattered religious preference entries on cards of classes before 1927, probably late entries.
129. *President's Report,* 1920-1921, p. 10.
130. Conversation with President Sills when the writer was chairman of the Committee on Religious Activities at the College. On the membership of Jews in fraternities see below, pp. 147-50.

Chapter IX

1. Visiting Committee, Report of 1910, pp. 9-10; Report of 1911, p. 8.
2. Professor Henry L. Chapman had served as dean of the faculty from 1883 to 1885, but the duties of his office were quite different.
3. Brown, *Sills,* pp. 70-75, 77-78, 88-92.
4. Ibid., pp. 418-20.
5. *Addresses at the Inauguration of Kenneth Charles Morton Sills,* pp. 22-23.
6. Sills, *Baccalaureate Address, June 16, 1918,* pp. 10-11. In his baccalaureate address in 1921 on "The Virtue of Hope," Sills stated: "But the Christian College which deals eternally with the things of the spirit ought not to leave her sons ignorant as those who have no Hope [of immortality]" *(Baccalaureate Address, June 19, 1921,* p. 5).
7. *Bowdoin College Catalogue,* 1918-1919, p. 43; 1919-1920, p. 43; Faculty Records, 1915-1919, pp. 151, 198.
8. The Committee on Religious Activities is last listed in the 1959-1960 college catalogue.
9. *Orient,* March 5, 12, 19, April 30, 1918.
10. Ibid., November 12, 1918, p. 130.
11. Ibid., October 21, 1925, p. 1.
12. I am indebted to Philip S. Wilder '23, Richard G. Wignot '26, and Donovan D. Lancaster '27 for these verses.
13. Conversation with President Sills when the writer was chairman of the Committee on Religious Activities. In his report in 1951, Sills stated: "I have felt that the individual churches in Brunswick should shoulder responsibility for keeping in their particular folds those who naturally belong there" *(President's Report,* 1950-1951; see also 1931-1932, p. 12).
14. See above, p. 129.; also the longhand record, Sp. Col., Student Religious Preferences, Classes 1930-1948, Compiled by Religious Denominations. An attached sheet gives religious preferences of students from 1920-1921 to 1936-1937.
15. *President's Report,* 1922-1923, p. 10; Sp. Col., Documentary History, April 1923-January 1924, p. 71.
16. *Orient,* December 15, 1926.
17. Ibid., November 2, 1927, p. 1; November 30, 1927, p. 1; May 9, 1928, p. 2.
18. *Portland Press Herald,* August 17, 1923, clipping in Sp. Col., Documentary History, April 1923-January 1924, pp. 109-10; *Orient,* November 7, 1923, p. 2, February 19, 1930, p. 30, December 21, 1932, p. 1. The chimes were manufactured by Meneely and Company, Watervliet, New York. The College issued a souvenir programme of the inaugural recitals with descriptive notes on the chimes and how they are played (Sp. Col., College Buildings, Box 2, Folder, College Buildings: King Chapel. Hatch is in error as to when the bells were installed *(History of Bowdoin,* p. 291).
19. Sp. Col., Documentary History, June 1926-July 1927, p. 43; *Orient,* June 1, 1927, p. 1; June 23, 1927, p. 1.
20. The recital program listed the specifications of the organ (Sp. Col., College Buildings, Box 2, Folder, College Buildings: King Chapel; Sp. Col., Documentary History, June 1926-July 1927, p. 145. Mr. Curtis had studied organ with Mr. Hermann Kotzschmar of Portland, a good friend of Mr. Curtis's father.
21. See the lists of chapel speakers which President Sills regularly incorporated in his annual reports.

22. *President's Report*, 1919-1920, pp. 8-9.
23. *Orient,* January 22, 1919, p. 188.
24. Ibid., December 1, 1920, p. 250.
25. Ibid., February 18, 1925, p. 2. The editorial by John R. Aspinwall '26 seems to have aroused little interest as there were no answering or supporting comments in succeeding issues of the *Orient.*
26. Ibid., September 30, 1925, p. 2; October 7, 1925, pp. 2, 4; October 14, 1925, p. 2; February 10, 1926, p. 1.
27. *Report on the Needs of the College (Committee of the Faculty)*, p. 22; *Report on the Needs of the College (Committee of the Alumni)*, p. 19.
28. No copy of the questionnaire is available; some of the questions can be gleaned from articles in the *Orient* and from the report of the committee.
29. *Report on the Needs of the College (Committee of the Students)*, pp. 38-39; see also *Orient,* February 24, 1926.
30. Seniors came to be allowed forty cuts, juniors thirty-five, sophomores thirty, and freshmen twenty-five. Double cuts for chapel were ended (Instructions on chapel attendance, Registrar's Archives).
31. *Report on the Needs of the College (Committee of the Students)*, p. 40. Chapel services apparently had been discontinued during final examinations at the end of the second semester, but not the first *(Orient,* January 13, 1926, p. 2). Starting in 1926 chapel services were also suspended during first semester final examinations (Faculty Records, 1920-1940, p. 147).
32. *Report on the Needs of the College (Committee of the Students)*, p. 41.
33. *President's Report*, 1925-1926, p. 11; Brown, *Sills,* p. 238.
34. *President's Report*, 1925-1926, pp. 8-9.
35. *Report on the Needs of the College (Committee of the Students),* pp. 13-14.
36. Faculty Records, 1907-1915, p. 421.
37. *Orient,* June 13, 1916, p. 99.
38. Faculty Records, 1915-1919, February 21, 1911, p. 85.
39. *President's Report,* 1924-1925, p. 10.
40. Ibid., 1927-1928, p. 11.
41. *Bowdoin College Catalogue,* 1928-1929, p. 96.
42. Faculty Records, 1920-1940, January 30, 1930, p. 255.
43. *President's Report,* 1929-1930, pp. 14-15.
44. *Orient,* March 2, 1927, p. 2; October 17, 1928, p. 2.
45. Ibid., October 9, 1929, pp. 1, 3.
46. Ibid., April 16, 1930, p. 1.
47. Ibid., April 23, 1930, p. 1; April 30, 1930, p. 1; May 7, 1930, p. 1.
48. Ibid., October 8, 1930, p. 1; October 15, 1930, p. 2.
49. Ibid., October 29, 1930, p. 2.
50. Faculty Records, 1920-1940, p. 282.
51. Ibid., March 23, 1931, p. 283.
52. *President's Report,* 1930-1931, p. 19.
53. Trustee Records, 1930-1938, June 16, 1931, p. 70.
54. *President's Report,* 1931-1932, appended report of Dean Nixon, pp. 30-31.
55. *Orient,* November 5, 1930, pp. 1-2. President Woods had made the college chapel available to the Episcopalians, and during World War I, when the Milliken Regiment was stationed in Brunswick, mass was said regularly in the Chapel (ibid., December 10, 1930, p. 3).
56. Ibid., October 29, 1930, p. 3; December 5, 1930, p. 1; December 18, 1930, p. 3; February 19, 1931, p. 1.
57. Ibid., December 18, 1930, p. 1.
58. Ibid., April 13, 1932, p. 1; April 27, 1932, p. 1.

59. The writer's personal recollection. In 1937 Dean Nixon stated: "When Gordon Gillett originally proposed a Religious Forum, I was among those who doubted its success. I thought I knew more about undergraduate inertia in such matters, more about youth's indifference to things of the spirit than I did know. The student interest in the first Forum proved me a badly mistaken Dean" (ibid., February 24, 1937, p. 3).
60. *President's Report,* 1931-1932, p. 13.
61. Ibid., p. 12.
62. The writer's personal impression based on conversations with President Sills; also the impression of Philip S. Wilder '23, who for many years worked closely with President Sills on the chapel program.
63. *Orient,* February 22, 1933, p. 2.
64. *President's Report,* 1932-1933, p. 2.
65. *Orient,* January 10, 1934, pp. 1-2.
66. Faculty Records, 1920-1940, June 18, 1934, p. 353; *Bowdoin College Catalogue,* 1934-1935, p. 15; Visiting Committee, Report of June 1935, in Original Records of the Boards.
67. *President's Report,* 1936-1937, p. 10.
68. Faculty Records, 1920-1940, February 17, 1939, p. 457.
69. Ibid., October 30, 1939, p. 471; November 7, 1939, p. 472; March 11, 1940, p. 478.
70. Ibid., October 21, 1946, p. 179; September 25, 1947, p. 215.
71. *Bowdoin College Catalogue,* 1944-1945, p. 75.
72. Robert M. McNair, acting rector at the local Episcopal church, served as lecturer in religion in 1948-1949 while Mr. Russell was on leave; Carl F. Andry did the same in 1950-1951. Ronald P. Bridges '30 joined Mr. Russell in the department in the spring semester of 1954 as Visiting Professor of Religion on the Tallman Foundation. Professor Russell resigned in June 1954 to assume a position in the Finance Department of the American Friends Service Committee *(Orient,* December 16, 1953). He was followed by William D. Geoghegan as assistant professor of religion.
73. *President's Report,* 1936-1937, p. 9.
74. *Hymns for Worship.*
75. Personal recollection.
76. Van Dyke, *Responsive Readings.*
77. *Orient,* March 10, 1948. The committee consisted of Professors E.C. Helmreich (chairman), A.P. Daggett, W.C. Root, P.S. Turner, H.G. Russell, and P.S. Wilder.
78. *The Hymnal.*
79. *Orient,* July 8, 1942. The average daily attendance of students and faculty for the first term of summer school was 57, for the second term 43. There were three days when attendance was below 30 and nine when it was over 70. Musical services were particularly popular (Sp. Col., Faculty Committees, Misc. Reports, 1928-1947, Folder, 1942, Report by A.P. Daggett). The enrollment at summer school was 382 *(President's Report,* 1942-1943, p. 8).
80. *Orient,* September 6, 1944.
81. Ibid., November 15, 1944.
82. This question was raised at other colleges as well at this time. Report of the Fourth Pentagonal Conference on the Undergraduate College, held at Bowdoin February 28 to March 2, 1947, in Sp. Col., Faculty Committees, Misc. Reports, 1928-1947, Folder, 1947; Report of the Ninety-first Meeting of Association of Colleges in New England, October 11-12, 1949, p. 9, in Sp. Col., Faculty Committees, Misc. Reports, 1948-1958, Folder, 1949; also

Folder, 1950, for the meeting of the Association of Colleges in New England, 1950, p. 10.
83. *President's Report,* 1936-1937, p. 16. Throughout its existence the writer was the faculty adviser to the Thorndike Club.
84. See reports of the dean appended to the various reports of the president. In a letter to the *Orient,* October 23, 1976, Philmore Ross '43 wrote: "During the pre-World War II era at Bowdoin College, Anti-Semitism manifested itself in two ways. First, there was the obviously practiced but officially denied negative quota system in admissions. Secondly, there was the exclusion of Jews from fraternities. Both of these acts of bigotry were equally applied to Blacks. Admission was so selective that almost invariably the non-fraternity group came out on top in scholastic standing, but was deemed ineligible for the annual award which went to the top fraternity."
85. *Orient,* January 30, 1946, p. 1.
86. Ibid., letter from the Thorndike Club, January 25, 1946, Sp. Col., Bowdoin College, Societies—Clubs, Folder, Thorndike Club.
87. *Orient,* January 30, 1946.
88. Ibid., February 27, 1946, p. 1; see also March 8, 1946, Special Fraternity Issue; March 13, 27, May 15, 1946.
89. Ibid., March 13, 1946; Sp. Col., Bowdoin College, Societies—Clubs, Folder, Thorndike Club.
90. Faculty Records, 1940-1956, December 5, 1946, p. 179; letters in Sp. Col., Bowdoin College, Societies—Clubs, Folder, Thorndike Club.
91. *Orient,* April 7, 1948; April 23, 1952.
92. Ibid., March 8, 1946. Some students charged that the *Orient* misrepresented student opinion and called a meeting to which representatives of all fraternities were invited to discuss the matter (ibid., May 1, 1946). The *Orient* carried no report on this meeting if it was ever held.
93. Ibid., January 15, 1947.
94. Ibid., April 23, 1947.
95. This was the policy set by the committee, and it was recognized by the administration. See statements as to Bowdoin's position in Report of Fourth Pentagonal Conference on the Undergraduate College at Bowdoin, 1947, in Sp. Col., Faculty Committees, Misc. Reports, 1928-1947, Folder, 1947. The faculty did not formally adopt such a policy until 1956 (Faculty Records, 1940-1956, p. 492).
96. Petition with signatures, Sp. Col., Bowdoin College, Societies—Clubs, Folder, Thorndike Club, Faculty Records, 1940-1956, pp. 234-35.
97. Faculty Records, 1940-1956, pp. 236-37; S. Chase to E. C. Helmreich, March 11, 1948, Sp. Col., Bowdoin College, Societies—Clubs, Folder, Thorndike Club; *Orient,* April 7, 1948.
98. Faculty Records, 1940-1956, May 10, 1948, p. 245.
99. *Orient,* November 16, 1949; Report of the Fourth Pentagonal Conference on the Undergraduate College at Bowdoin, 1947, pp. 10-11, in Sp. Col., Faculty Committees, Misc. Reports, 1928-1947, Folder, 1947.
100. *Orient,* March 17, 1948; September 29, 1948; November 10, 1948.
101. *President's Report,* 1950-1951, p. 19.
102. Faculty Records, 1940-1956, October 24, 1950, p. 304; January 15, 1951, p. 337; *President's Report,* 1950-1951, p. 20.
103. *President's Report,* 1950-1951, p. 19.
104. Ibid.
105. *Orient,* March 26, 1952, p. 2.
106. Ibid., April 2, 1952, p. 1; see also March 26, 1952, p. 2.

107. Sp. Col., Documentary History, December 12, 1951-December 31, 1952, p. 76.
108. The members of the committee were Professors E. C. Helmreich (chairman), W.C. Root, P.S. Turner, and L. N. Barrett. In the summer of 1952, when Professor Barrett left Bowdoin, Professor E. Pols was appointed to take his place (Faculty Records, 1940-1956, p. 385). For study the committee was supplied with "Complete Progress Report of Study, What is a Christian College," *Christian Education,* 34 (December 1951), no. 4.
109. Professor Ernst C. Helmreich represented Bowdoin.
110. In its progress report in the spring of 1952 the Bowdoin committee stated: "What the latter term [Christian college] implies has perhaps never been minutely defined....Briefly, however, the term has always seemed to signify that the College recognized the importance of religion in a well-rounded and purposeful life, and supported those ethical and moral values which are an inherent part of our Christian-Judaic heritage" (Sp. Col., Faculty Committees, Misc. Reports, 1948-1958, Folder, 1952).

Chapter X

1. *Inauguration of James Stacy Coles, October 13, 1952,* p. 28.
2. For example, in the first semester of 1937 President Sills took daily chapel twenty-four times, Rev. Thompson E. Ashby eleven times, Professor Mitchell ten times, Dean Nixon five times, other faculty members eleven times, other local clergy two times, and there were musical services seven or eight times. In the first semester of 1963, President Coles took chapel four times, Dean Kendrick once, Dean Greason twice, and introduced speakers twice; there were five B.C.A.-sponsored speakers, two musical services, six outside speakers, and other faculty took the services forty times. It was difficult to recruit this large number of faculty (P.S. Wilder to President Coles, December 3, 1963, Coles Papers, Folder, Chapel, 1963-1964, Registrar's Archives).
3. *Orient,* April 22, 29, 1953.
4. Ibid., November 17, 1954.
5. Faculty Records, 1940-1956, December 13, 1954, p. 450.
6. *Orient,* April 22, 1953.
7. Ibid., March 10, 1954.
8. Committee on Religious Activities to Dean Kendrick, May 5, 1954, Sp. Col., Interfaith Forum, Folder, Newman Club. The committee consisted of Professors E.C. Helmreich (chairman), Eaton Leith, J.M. Moulton, and H.G. Russell, and Mr. Glenn R. McIntire. Under "Student Activity Groups," a photograph of the officers of the Newman Club appeared for the first time in the *Bugle* for 1959.
9. *Orient,* April 2, 1952.
10. Ibid., November 3, 10, 1954, December 15, 1954. President Coles had been consulted about the change of names, but he had not suggested it. For the constitutions of the B.I.F. adopted in May 1955 and amended in May 1961, see Sp. Col., Interfaith Forum, Folder, B.I.F. History; Folder, B.I.F. 1960s.
11. *Orient,* May 16, 1956.
12. *Portland Press Herald,* March 31, 1958, Sp. Col., Documentary History, October 22, 1957-May 22, 1958, p. 67, clipping.
13. Sp. Col., Documentary History, October 22, 1957-May 22, 1958, p. 67.
14. Question 12 of the questionnaire. See Appendix C of *The Conservative Tradition of Education at Bowdoin College.*

15. Ibid., pp. 84-85.
16. Ibid., p. 59. The three professors were: Alban Gregory Widgery, 1928-1929; Robert Henry Lightfoot, 1937-1938; Ronald Perkins Bridges, Spring 1954.
17. Ibid., pp. 78-80, app., p. 19.
18. That there was still need for action on discrimination by fraternities is substantiated by a "Census of Bowdoin Students with Reference to Religious Preference, October, 1953" made by Professor Orren C. Hormell. He found that there were five fraternities without any Jewish members, four with one member, two with three members. There was one fraternity which had forty-seven Jewish members, while there were no Jews among the Independents (Sp. Col., Interfaith Forum, bound typescript, no folder).
19. Coles Papers, Folder, Chapel, 1961-1962, Registrar's Archives; *Bowdoin College Catalogue,* 1961-1962, p. 67; 1962-1963, p. 83.
20. Coles Papers, Folder, Chapel, 1961-1962, Registrar's Archives.
21. Ibid., January 13, 1962.
22. *Orient,* January 11, 18, 1962; March 1, 8, 1962.
23. See his statement in *Orient,* March 1, 1963.
24. Ibid., January 11, 1963; letter to President Coles, Coles Papers, Folder, Chapel, 1962-1963, Registrar's Archives; *Bowdoin Alumnus* 40 (July 1966): 4.
25. *Orient,* January 11, 18, 1963.
26. Ibid., May 3, 1963; see also May 10, 17, 24, 1963.
27. Ibid., May 17, 24, 1963.
28. Ibid., May 24, 1963; See also letter by Robert S. Frank, Jr. '64, May 17, 1963.
29. Coles to Peter R. Seaver '64, president of the Student Council, June 20, 1963; Coles to Robert S. Frank '64, June 20, 1963; Frank to Coles, July 1, 1963, Coles Papers, Folder, Chapel, 1963-1964, Registrar's Archives.
30. Faculty Records, 1956-1968, October 14, 1963, p. 233.
31. Coles to the committee, October 23, 1963, Coles Papers, Folder, Chapel, 1963-1964, Registrar's Archives.
32. Nevertheless, Robert S. Frank, Jr. '64 wrote a long letter to the *Orient,* November 15, 1963, criticizing the administration for stalling on the policy of attendance at chapel.
33. Faculty Records, 1956-1968, February 4, 1964, March 9, 1964, pp. 257-260; *Orient,* March 13, 1964.
34. *Orient,* September 25, 1964.
35. Trustee Records, 1964-1965, June 11, 1964, p. 54.
36. Since 1974 the opening convocation, although it is held, has not been listed on the weekly college calendar.
37. *Bowdoin College Catalogue,* 1964-1965, p. 21.
38. *Orient,* March 11, 1966.
39. Faculty Records, 1956-1968, April 18, 1966, p. 338.
40. Ibid., June 6, 1966, p. 348.
41. Trustee Records, 1966-1968, June 1966, p. 85; Sp. Col., Charter and By-Laws of Bowdoin College, Effective July 1, 1966, ch. 8. The last phrase of this by-law about teaching "distinctly denominational tenets or doctrines" was dropped from the by-laws in January 1978 (Trustee Records, 1977-1978, p. 195).
42. Faculty Records, 1956-1968, December 12, 1966, p. 365.
43. *Orient,* March 3, 1967.
44. Faculty Records, 1956-1958, p. 388; *Orient,* May 5, 12, 1967.
45. Trustee Records, 1956-1968, June 1961, p. 370; Coles Papers, Folder, Chapel, 1961-1962, Registrar's Archives.
46. *Orient,* October 26, 1973.

47. Ibid., February 28, 1963, March 19, 1963. The B.I.F. is dropped and the B.C.A. reappears in the 1963 *Bugle*, p. 70.
48. *Orient*, March 19, 1963.
49. Ibid., February 28, 1963.
50. Ibid., March 19, 1963.
51. Ibid., May 10, 1963; *Bugle*, 1966, p. 44. The voting members of the council were to be the president, one delegate, and the faculty adviser of each member organization (By-Laws of the Interfaith Council, Sp. Col., Interfaith Forum, Folder, B.I.F. 1960s).
52. "This year the Newman Club has benefited from the formation of the Bowdoin Interfaith Council, which controls the budget of its three members. Under the impetus of this financial stability the Club has presented speakers of interest to Catholics and Non-Catholics" (*Bugle*, 1964, p. 117). The three organizations referred to were the Newman Club, the B.C.A., and the Bowdoin Student Religious Liberals Club.
53. Faculty Records, 1956-1968, June 10, 1963, pp. 224-225; Trustee Records, 1964-1965, February 1964, p. 27.
54. Faculty Records, 1956-1968, p. 224.
55. *Orient*, November 11, 1966; tape 9 of General Ledger for 1964-1965, Business Office.
56. *Orient*, February 7, 1975, p. 8; conversation with Father John Davis, who inaugurated the project.
57. Faculty Records, 1969-1971, p. 158; *Orient*, October 15, 22, 1971.
58. The folk mass was first celebrated at 9:00 P.M. in Conference Room A of the Moulton Union. On January 18, 1968, it was shifted to Terrace Under of the Moulton Union; on December 13, 1973, to the Chapel; on September 13, 1975, the time was shifted to 6:00 P.M., a week later to 6:15 P.M. on Saturdays; on February 21, 1976, it was shifted to the Main Lounge of the Moulton Union, on September 24, 1977, to the Lancaster Lounge; and on September 22, 1979, the time was shifted to 4:30 P.M. on Saturdays *(Bowdoin College Calendar)*.
59. Faculty Records, 1969-1971, p. 158; similar motions had been defeated in 1969 and 1970, ibid., pp. 46, 116.
60. In 1971-1972, 1972-1973, 1973-1974, 1975-1976, 1976-1977, 1977-1978. 1979-1980 funds were voted directly to the Newman Apostolate; in 1974-1975 and 1978-1979 they were voted to the Interfaith Council (Faculty Records). There is a file of the reports of the Faculty Committee on Student Activities Fee in the President's Office and some can be found in Special Collections. The minutes of the faculty no longer disclose what funds each activity receives.
61. The constitution of the Bowdoin Jewish Association is dated February 1968 (Sp. Col., Interfaith Forum, Folder, Religious Organizations other than Newman Club).
62. Faculty Records, 1956-1968, April 18, 1966, p. 336; *Orient*, September 30, 1966.
63. Faculty Records, 1956-1968, p. 437.
64. *Bowdoin College Catalogue*, 1979-1980, pp. 186-190.
65. It appeared last in *Bowdoin College Catalogue*, 1967-1968, p. 7.
66. R.K. Beckwith to A.P. Daggett, August 10, 1967, Coles Papers, Chapel, Folder, 1964-1968. Registrar's Archives.
67. Coles Papers, Chapel, Folder, 1964-1968. Registrar's Archives; *Orient*, September 29, 1967.
68. *Bowdoin College Calendar*, 1967-1968, 1968-1969.

69. The B.C.A. appeared for the last time in the *Bugle* for 1968. The *Bowdoin College Calendar*s carry no notice of the B.C.A. in this period; nor is there any mention of granting it student activities fees in the faculty committee report for 1970-1971 when, for once, the appropriation to the Interfaith Council is broken down. In that year only the Bowdoin Jewish Association, the Newman Apostolate, and the Student Religious Liberals received student activities money.
70. *Orient,* March 7, 1969; April 11, 1969.
71. Sp. Col., *Bowdoin College Calendar* for the period.
72. *Orient,* October 26, 1973; Sp. Col., *Bowdoin College Calendar* for the period.
73. *Bowdoin Alumnus,* 52 (Fall, 1978): 7-11.
74. *Bowdoin: An Introduction to the College, 1979-80,* pp. 38-39.
75. Smyth, *Three Discourses,* p. 70; Little, *Historical Sketch,* p. li.

Bibliography

Documentary Sources

The sources for the history of religion at Bowdoin are found in various places at the College. Most of the unpublished material is to be found in Special Collections (Sp. Col.) at the library. There is no comprehensive catalogue or guide to what is available here, and so one must rely heavily on the knowledge of the person in charge of the collection. Folders on graduates, containing miscellaneous clippings, letters, and other pertinent documents, are transferred to this collection from the Alumni Office when the last surviving member of a class has died. The manuscript material is largely in folders stored in archival boxes, and so I have cited the title of the box and the folder. Also in Special Collections are to be found files of the college paper, the *Orient;* the class yearbook, the *Bugle;* the college catalogues; the college calendars; and a most useful collection of clippings and other memorabilia called the Documentary History.

The Trustee and Overseer records are kept in the safe in the Business Office, as are the important reports of the Visiting Committee. For the early years a number of these yearly reports are gathered together in bound volumes; later ones are filed in separate folders, and the more recent are bound in with the Trustee records. At times these reports have the pages numbered, at other times not, and so precise citation is not always possible. Appended to the committee reports are unpaged reports which for many years each member of the faculty made to the committee. In the file cabinets of the Business Office there is also much valuable manuscript material, for example, files on the funds establishing named professorships or scholarships. There are also records of the appropriations and expenditures of student activities fees for various student organizations.

Faculty records are in Special Collections, except for the most recent ones, which are kept in the safe in the storage room of the Registrar's Office, here called Registrar's Archives. The student record cards for the more recent classes are also kept here. File cabinets in this storage room have an assortment of papers of the more recent college administrations. There are also numerous files in the President's Office.

In my footnotes, when it seemed necessary, I have indicated in which depository the particular material is to be found. Except for a few special studies this documentary material is not listed in the bibliography. To facilitate finding the complete bibliographical reference for the abbreviated titles used in the footnotes, books, pamphlets, and magazine articles have all been listed together in this bibliography.

Books and Special Studies

Addresses at the Inauguration of Kenneth Charles Morton Sills as President of Bowdoin College, June 20, 1918. Brunswick, 1918.

Addresses at the Inauguration of the Rev. William DeWitt Hyde as President of Bowdoin College, Wednesday, June 23, 1886. Brunswick, 1886.

Addresses of Rev. Jesse Appleton, D.D., Late President of Bowdoin College: Delivered at the Annual Commencements, from 1808 to 1818; with a Sketch of his Character. Brunswick, 1820.

Appleton, Rev. Jesse. *The Works of Rev. Jesse Appleton, D.D., Late President of Bowdoin College, embracing his Course of Theological Lectures, and his Academic Addresses and a Selection from his Sermons with a Memoir of his Life and Character.* Edited by Alpheus S. Packard. 2 vols. Andover, 1837.

Ashby, Thompson Eldridge. *A History of the First Parish Church in Brunswick, Maine.* Edited by Louise R. Helmreich. Brunswick, 1969.

Atkins, Gaius Glenn and Fagley, Frederick L. *History of American Congregationalism.* Boston, 1942.

Axtell, John L. *The Educational Writings of John Locke: A Critical Edition with Introduction and Notes.* Cambridge, 1968.

Bowdoin Alumnus. Brunswick, 1927-.

Bowdoin: An Introduction to the College, 1979-80. Brunswick, 1979.

Bowdoin College Calendar. Brunswick, 1937-. Published weekly.

Bowdoin College Catalogue. Brunswick, 1807-. Published annually.
   First issued as broadsides and after 1822 as bound volumes.

The Bowdoin Orient, Brunswick, 1871-.
   Now heralded as "The Oldest Continuously-Published College Weekly in the United States."

Brauer, Jerald C. *Protestantism in America: A Narrative History.* Philadelphia, 1953.

Brault, Gerard J. "A Checklist of Portraits of the Campus of Bowdoin College Before the Civil War." Typescript. 1960. Special Collections, Bowdoin College.

Brown, Herbert Ross. *Sills of Bowdoin: The Life of Kenneth Charles Morton Sills, 1879-1954.* New York, 1964.

Buck, Charles Rinker. "Thomas Cogswell Upham. A Study of the Moral Philosopher in New England with a Commentary on the Elements of Mental Philosophy: The Outline of Disordered Mental Action, and the Philosophical and Practical Treatise on the Will." Honors thesis, Bowdoin College, 1973.

Bugle. Brunswick, 1858-.
   The class yearbook.

Burnett, Charles T. *Hyde of Bowdoin: A Biography of William DeWitt Hyde.* Boston, 1931.

Chadbourne, Ava Harriet. *A History of Education in Maine: A Study of a Section of American Educational History.* Orono, Me., 1936.

Chamberlain, Joshua Lawrence. *The New Education: President Chamberlain's Inaugural Address, July 19, 1872.* Brunswick, 1879.
   The Bowdoin library does not have a copy of the published address but has a typescript in Special Collections.

"The Charter of Bowdoin College (Effective January 25, 1974)." Mimeographed.
   Has amendments to the charter.

Charter of Bowdoin College Together with Various Acts of the Legislature and the Decision of the Circuit Court and the By-Laws of the Overseers. Brunswick, 1850.

Chenault, Kenneth. "The Blackman at Bowdoin." Honors thesis, Bowdoin College, 1973.

Clark, Calvin Montague. *History of Bangor Theological Seminary*. Boston, 1916.

──. *History of the Congregational Churches in Maine: History of the Maine Missionary Society, 1807-1925*. Vol. 1. Portland, 1926.

Cleaveland, Nehemiah and Packard, Alpheus Spring. *History of Bowdoin College with Biographical Sketches of its Graduates from 1806 to 1879, Inclusive*. Boston, 1882.

Cohen, Sol, ed. *Education in the United States: A Documentary History*. 5 vols. Westport, 1973-1974.

"Complete Progress Report of Study, What is a Christian College?" *Christian Education* 34 (December 1951): 257-320.

"The Conservative Tradition in Education at Bowdoin College: Report of the Committee on Self Study." Typescript. Brunswick, 1955.

A printed report was published by the College in 1956 but does not contain the valuable appendices of the original.

"Contributors to Bowdoin College from 1846 to 1852, including the subscriptions of 1842." Bound volume. Special Collections, Bowdoin College.

Cook, Walter L. *Bangor Theological Seminary: A Sesquicentennial History*. Orono, Me., 1971.

Cross, Robert M. "Joshua Lawrence Chamberlain." Honors thesis, Bowdoin College, 1945.

Deems, Mervin M. *Maine—First of Conferences: A History of the Maine Conference—United Church of Christ*. Bangor, 1974.

Descriptive Catalogue of the Art Collections of Bowdoin College. Brunswick, 1930.

Eckert, Christian. *Peter Cornelius*. Leipzig, 1906.

Ellis, Rev. M. "The Legal Situation of the Congregational Colleges with Reference to the Denomination." *The Pacific; San Francisco, Cal.* Special Collections, Bowdoin College. Documentary History, 1888-1891, p. 121.

Everett, Charles Carroll. *Leonard Woods: A Discourse*. Brunswick, 1879.

First Annual Reunion of the Bowdoin Alumni Association of New York at Delmonico's, January 19, 1871. New York, 1871.

Foster, Benjamin Browne. *Down East Diary*. Edited by Charles H. Foster. Orono, Me., 1975.

Fuller, Melville Weston. "Anniversary Address, Thursday, June 28, 1894." In *Memorial of the One Hundredth Anniversary of the Incorporation of Bowdoin College*. Brunswick, 1894.

General Catalogue of Bowdoin College and the Medical School of Maine, 1794-1894. Brunswick, 1894.

Contains the "Historical Sketch" by George Thomas Little. There is also a memorial edition of this catalogue which contains addresses delivered at the centennial observances.

General Catalogue of Bowdoin College and the Medical School of Maine: A Biographical Record of Alumni and Officers, 1794-1950. Edited by Philip S. Wilder. Brunswick, 1950.

General Catalogue of Bowdoin College and the Medical School of Maine: A Biographical Record of Alumni and Officers, 1900-75. Edited by Edward Born. Brunswick, 1978.

Hall, B.H. *A Collection of College Words and Customs*. Rev. and enl. Cambridge, Mass., 1856.

Hamlin, Cyrus. *My Life and Times*. Boston, 1893.

Handy, Robert T. *A Christian America: Protestant Hopes and Historical Realities*. New York, 1971.

Harris, Samuel. *Inaugural Address, August 6, 1867.* Brunswick, 1867.
Hatch, Louis C. *The History of Bowdoin College.* Portland, 1927.
Hawthorne, Nathaniel. *Fanshawe and Other Pieces.* Boston, 1876.
Helmreich, Louise R., ed. *Our Town: Reminiscences and Historical Studies of Brunswick, Maine, from the Collections of the Pejepscot Historical Society.* Brunswick, 1967.
Herring, C.M. *Historical Discourse at the Semi-Centennial of the Berean Baptist Church of Brunswick at Brunswick, September 2, 1890.* Brunswick, 1890.
Hitchcock, Roswell D. *A Sermon Delivered at the Dedication of the New Chapel of Bowdoin College, Thursday, June 7, 1855.* Brunswick, 1855.
Hopkins, C. Howard. *History of the Y.M.C.A. in North America.* New York, 1951.
Howell, Roger, Jr. *A New Humanism: The Inaugural Address of Roger Howell, Jr., Tenth President of Bowdoin College, October 3, 1969.* Brunswick, n.d.
Hudson, Winthrop S. *Religion in America.* New York, 1965.
Hyde, William DeWitt. *The College Man and the College Woman.* Boston, 1906.
The Hymnal. Philadelphia: General Assembly of the Presbyterian Church in the United States, 1946.
Hymns for Worship. New York: Council of North American Student Christian Movements of the World's Student Christian Federation, 1939.
The Inaugural Address Delivered in Brunswick, September 2, 1802, by the Rev. Joseph McKeen, A.M. and A.A.S., at his Entrance on the Duties of President of Bowdoin College: With a Eulogy, Pronounced at his Funeral, by the Reverend William Jenks. Portland, 1807.
Inauguration of James Stacy Coles, October 13, 1952. Bowdoin College Bulletin, 308. Brunswick, 1953.
Jenks, William. *An Eulogy Pronounced in Brunswick, (Maine) July 18th, 1807, at the Funeral of the late Rev. Joseph McKeen, D.D., A.A.S., and President of Bowdoin College.* Bound with *The Inaugural Address Delivered in Brunswick, September 2, 1802 by the Rev. Joseph McKeen.* Portland, 1807.
King, Willard W. *Melville Weston Fuller: Chief Justice of the United States, 1888-1910.* New York, 1950.
Laws of Bowdoin College. Hallowell, 1817.
There are numerous subsequent revised editions of these laws published in Brunswick.
Lincoln, Charles S.F. *The Story of the first Hundred Years of St. Paul's Episcopal Church in Brunswick, Maine, 1844-1944.* Brunswick, 1944.
Little, George Thomas. "A Historical Sketch of Bowdoin College during its First Century." In *General Catalogue of Bowdoin College and the Medical School of Maine, 1794-1894,* pp. ix-cxii. Brunswick, 1894.
Memorial of the One Hundredth Anniversary of the Incorporation of Bowdoin College. Brunswick, Maine, 1894.
This is a special edition of *General Catalogue of Bowdoin College and the Medical School of Maine, 1794-1894* and contains addresses and poems given at the commemorative exercises.
Minot, John Clair and Snow, Donald Francis. *Tales of Bowdoin: Some Gathered Fragments and Fancies of Undergraduate Life in the Past and Present Told by Bowdoin Men.* Augusta, 1901.
Mitchell, Wilmot Brookings. *A Remarkable Bowdoin Decade, 1820-1830.* Brunswick, 1952.
Morison, Samuel Eliot. *The Founding of Harvard College.* Cambridge, 1935.
———, ed. *The Development of Harvard University Since the Inauguration of President Eliot, 1869-1929.* Cambridge, 1930.

Named Professorships at Bowdoin College. Bowdoin College Bulletin, 399. Brunswick, 1976.

Nason, Everett H.; Hall, Norma; Nason, Susan A; and Purinton, Edith. "History of the United Methodist Church of Brunswick, Maine, 1821-1973." Typescript. Brunswick, 1979.

Olmstead, Clifton E. *History of Religion in the United States.* Englewood Cliffs, N.J., 1960.

Orient. See *Bowdoin Orient.*

Packard, A.S. *Address on the Life and Character of Thomas C. Upham, D.D., Late Professor of Mental and Moral Philosophy in Bowdoin: Delivered at the Interment, Brunswick, Me., April 4, 1872.* Brunswick, 1873.

———. "Historical Sketch of Bowdoin College." *The Quarterly Register* 8 (Nov. 1835): 105-117.

———. *Our Alma Mater: An Address delivered before the Association of the Alumni of Bowdoin College, August 5, 1858.* Brunswick, 1858.

Paley, William. *Natural Theology or Evidences of the Existence and Attributes of the Deity Collected from the Appearances of Nature.* New ed. Boston, 1855.

———. *A View of the Evidences of Christianity in Three Parts: Part I Of the direct Historical Evidence of Christianity and wherein it is distinguished from the Evidence alleged for other Miracles. Part II Of the Auxiliary Evidences of Christianity. Part III A brief Consideration of some popular Objections.* 3 vols. in one. Boston, 1795.

Park, Edwards A. *The Life and Character of Leonard Woods, D.D., LL.D.* Andover, 1880.

Pierson, William H., Jr., *The Corporate and the Early Gothic Styles.* American Buildings and Their Architects. Garden City, N.Y., 1978.

Potter, Barrett. *Bowdoin College: Report to the Treasurer Describing Land of the College in Brunswick, Maine.* Brunswick, 1898.

———. "Bowdoin College: Titles and Donations of Funds, 1794-1898." Bound manuscript. Special Collections, Bowdoin College.

President's Report. Brunswick: Bowdoin College, 1892-. Published annually.

Report on the Needs of the College (Committee of the Alumni). Bowdoin College Bulletin, 158. Brunswick, 1926.

Report on the Needs of the College (Committee of the Faculty). Bowdoin College Bulletin, 152. Brunswick, 1926.

Report on the Needs of the College (Committee of the Students). Bowdoin College Bulletin, 153. Brunswick, 1926.

Robinson, Clement F. "Banner and Spire," *Bowdoin Alumnus* 4 (May 1930): 92-97.

Sills, Kenneth Charles Morton. *Baccalaureate Address, June 16, 1918.* Brunswick, 1918.

———. *Baccalaureate Address, June 19, 1921.* Brunswick, 1921.

———. *Joseph McKeen (1757-1807) and the Beginnings of Bowdoin College, 1802.* New York: Newcomen Society of England, American Branch, 1945.

Smith, Marion Jaques. *General William King: Merchant, Shipbuilder, and Maine's First Governor.* Camden, Me., 1980.

Smyth, Egbert C. "Address on the Religious History of the College, Wednesday, June 27, 1894." In *Memorial of the One Hundredth Anniversary of the Inauguration of Bowdoin College.* Brunswick, 1894.

———. *Three Discourses Upon the Religious History of Bowdoin College, During the Administrations of Presidents McKeen, Appleton, and Allen.* Brunswick, 1858.

Songs of Bowdoin. Compiled and edited by George A. Foster '05, Neal W. Allen '07, and James M. Chandler '08. New York, 1906.

Souvenir of the 50th Anniversary of St. John the Baptist Parish. Brunswick, Maine, 1877-1927. Brunswick, 1927.

"Student Religious Preference, Classes 1930-1948." Compiled by Clara Hayes. Bound manuscript. Special Collections, Bowdoin College.
    Includes religious preferences of students from 1920-1921 to 1936-1937. Members of the classes of 1930-1948 are listed by name under various denominations.

Van Dyke, Henry. *Responsive Readings Selected from the Bible and Arranged Under Subjects: For Use in the Chapel of Harvard University.* Boston, 1899.

Wallace, Willard M. *Soul of the Lion: A Biography of General Joshua L. Chamberlain.* New York, 1960.

Weston, Isaac. "History of the Association of Ministers of Cumberland County, Maine, from 1787 to 1867." *The Congregational Quarterly* 9 (1867): 334-347.

"What is a Christian College." *Christian Education* 34 (Dec. 1951): 257-320.

Wheeler, George Augustus and Wheeler, Henry Warren. *History of Brunswick, Topsham, and Harpswell, Maine, Including the Ancient Territory Known as Pejepscot.* Boston, 1878.

Whiteside, William B. *The Boston Y.M.C.A. and Community Need: A Century's Evolution, 1851-1951.* New York, 1951.

Williamson, Joseph. "Condition of the Religious Denominations of Maine, at the Close of the Revolution." *Collections of the Maine Historical Society* 7(1876): 217-229.

Woods, Leonard. *An Address Delivered on the Opening of the New Hall of the Medical School of Maine, February 21, 1862.* Brunswick, 1862.

Index

Adams, George Eliashib, 28, 59, 82, 103, 104-5, 109; called to First Parish Church, 32; his "Boot and Shoe Display," 114
Adams, Samuel, signs charter, 4
Abbot, John, 11, 13, 16, 23
Abbott, John S. C., 82-83
Allen, William (pres. 1820-32), 31, 38, 89, 173 n. 56; removed and restored to office, 61, 64; plans for new chapel, 63-65; resignation, 65
Alpha Rho Upsilon, 148-49; resolution on chapel attendance, 157-58
Amherst College, 52, 95, 108-9
Anderson, Alice, 10
Anderson, Rufus, 52
Andover Theological Seminary, 35-36, 92, 102, 109
Appleton, Jesse (pres. 1807-19), 30-31, 38-39, 49, 61; his lectures, 37-39, 59; proposal to name new chapel in his honor, 68
Appleton, John, 65-66
Apthorp, Harrison Otis, 86
Athenaean Literary Society, 51, 60, 73, 124
Ashby, Thompson Eldridge, 133

Bailey, Winthrop, 30
Bangor Theological Seminary, 35, 99-100, 107, 110, 174 n. 5; proposed move to Bowdoin, 102-3
Banister Hall, 79, 136
Banister, Wm. B., 79
Baptists, 1, 5, 52, 74; in Brunswick, 20-21, 175 n. 45
Barr, Richard D., 166
Beckwith, Robert K., 146
Bell, Mrs. Harriet, 93
Benevolent Society, 58-59
Bermuda North, 163
Blacks at Bowdoin, 128, 150
Blanket Tax, 135, 151, 162
Board of Commissioners for Foreign Missions, 52
Bond, Elias, 53
Bonfires, 54-55
Boody, Henry L., gifts to the College, 95-96, 186 n. 37
Booker, Alfred J., 116
Booker, Ira P., 93
Bowdoin Christian Association (B.C.A.), 133, 135, 151-52, 154, 168; and racial questions, 147, 149-50; changes name to Bowdoin Interfaith Forum, 155, 161, 197 n. 1; and self-study project, 156; resolution on chapel attendance, 158; demise, 162. See also Young Men's Christian Association
Bowdoin Christian Fellowship, 166
Bowdoin College, petitions for founding a college, 2-3; first members of the Boards, 5, 35; charter, 4-5, 169 n. 11; lands, 5, 9; location of, 3-4, 9; laws, 13-14, 38-46, 159, 170 n. 23; early admission requirements, 14, 36, 170 n. 24; early curriculum, 15-16, 35-38; relations to First Parish, 21-33, 92, 102, 103-5; students studying for the ministry, 5, 35-36, 52-53; and temperance, 39-41, 55-56, 59-60; a "Christian College," 5-7, 61-62, 102, 105, 118, 132-33, 136, 151-53, 165, 192 n. 6, 197 ns. 108, 110; Declaration on relations with Congregationalists, 75-77, 89, 181 n. 54; support of fund drives by Congregationalists, 74-78, 99-100; and Congregational Conference, 99-100; vesper services, 108-9, 159-61, 165-67; music at, 119-22; courses in religion, 15-16, 139-40, 144-45, 164-65; religious preference of students, 128-29, 135, 192 ns. 127, 128. See also Chapel entries; First Parish Church; Sunday services
Bowdoin, James (governor of Massachusetts), 3
Bowdoin, James (patron of the College), 3-4, 10, 70; letter to Overseers, 4, 169 n. 10; estate, 67-69, 89
Bowdoin Interfaith Forum (B.I.F.), 155-56, 161. See also Bowdoin Christian Assoc.

Boyd, George William, 42
Bradbury, James Ware, 78
Bridge, Horatio, 42
Briggs, John Abner, 46
Brown, Clark, 21, 24
Brown, Jerry W., 165
Brown University, 13, 51-52, 108
Browne, Tho., 2
Browne, William, 32
Brunswick, college to be located in, 4, 9; religious divisions among early settlers, 19-20; first meeting house, 19; separation of church and parish, 21; various churches organized, 175 n. 45. *See also* First Parish Church
Burnett, Charles Theodore, 122, 139
Byington, Ezra Hoyt, 114-15

Caluvian Society, 28
Cargill, James, 51
Carnegie Foundation, 94, 97-98, 102, 105, 127
Catholics, in early Maine, 1; at Bowdoin, 127-29; and campus religious associations, 127, 129, 155; services in chapel, 143, 194 n. 55; sponsors weekly folk mass, 163, 168, 199 n. 58. *See also* Newman Club
Chamberlain, Joshua Lawrence (pres. 1871-83), 35, 38, 114, 119; and fund drive, 93, 100; biographical note, 110; inaugural address, 110-11, 188 n. 14; proposes changes at Bowdoin, 111-13; donates window to First Parish Church, 115; supports military training at Bowdoin, 115; admits some women to classes, 128
Chandler, Peleg W., 46
Chapel choir, 119-22, 166
Chapel (old), built, 22-23, 171 n. 17; enlarged and moved, 23; bell installed and "stolen," 23, 44-45; library, 22, 63-66; belfry removed, 44-45; student depredations, 45; organ provided, 57; art gallery, 64-66; heating, 65, 171 n. 17; sold and removed, 78-79
Chapel (new), 29, 62, 66; plans in 1825, 63; location, 64-65; ladies help raise funds, 66-67; laying of cornerstone, 70-73; dedication, 82-83; final cost, 83; proposal to name it Appleton Chapel, 68; proposal to call it King Chapel, 68-71, 73, 80-82, 183 n. 17; library, 63-66, 79, 83-85, 184 n. 94; art gallery, 63-66, 83, 84-85; heating, 84-85, 115; panel pictures, 85-87, 184 n. 98; organ, 120-21, 136; chimes, 135-36, 161; flag pole incident, 140-42; problem of acoustics, 151, 154, 184 n. 103; front entrance lights, 161; memorial cross, 152, 154, 157; bell no longer used for classes, 161; climbing of spires, 182 n. 68. *See also* Upjohn
Chapel services, hours of, 16, 108-9, 111-12, 147, 151; student attendance, 16, 42-43, 62, 107, 112-13, 115-19, 137-38, 140-42, 147, 154, 157, 159-60; faculty attendance, 16, 118, 137, 189 n. 61; evening prayers except on Sunday ended, 109, 112, 188 n. 19; Sunday morning prayers ended, 115-16; rush, 118; forums as an alternative, 159-61; convocation and first chapel service, 159; college sponsored program ended, 160-61. *See also* Sunday services; Vespers
Chapman, Henry L., 87, 120, 125-26
Charter, 4-5, 169 n. 11
Chase, Stanley P., 149-50
Cheever, Ebenezer, 51
Chittim, Richard Leigh, 158
Christian Association, 126, 143. *See also* Bowdoin Christian Association
Christian Union, 57-58
Christian Science Association, 168
Christian Science, 99
Church on the Hill, 33, 114, 132, 187 n. 75. *See also* First Parish Church
Cilley, Jonathan, 43
Civil War, 56, 84, 107, 167
Clark, William, 42
Cleaveland, Nehemiah, 10, 119
Cleaveland, Parker, 15, 22, 24, 59
Coffin, Ebenezer, 20-21
Cogswell, Jonathan, 49
Colby (Waterville) College, 44, 52, 74
Coles, James Stacy (pres. 1952-67), 95, 152; inaugural address, 153; and chapel program, 153-54, 157-58; baccalaureate services, 155-56; resignation, 165
College Preachers, 123-24, 136, 191 n. 97
Collins, Mrs. Ebenr. (Susan), 77, 91, 93, 123, 185 n. 27
Collins Professorship, 37, 77, 82-83, 89, 97, 105, 108-9, 112, 120, 125, 185 n. 1; founding and holders of the chair, 91-93; present use of funds, 94-95
Committee on Religious Activities, 133, 135, 139, 143, 154-55
Congregationalists, number of ministers in Maine (1784), 1; ties with the College, 21-24, 74-77, 89-90, 94-103; and Bowdoin fund drives, 74-78, 93, 99. *See also* First Parish Church
Coons, Leroy W., 126
Cornelius, Peter, 86

Index

Crocker, George Oliver, 120
Crocker, Oliver, 120
Cronham, Charles R., 136
Cumberland Association of Ministers, 2
Cummings, Asa, 65
Cummings, Nathan, 86, 184 n. 99
Curtis, Cyrus Hermann Kotzschmar, 136

Daggett, Athern P., 167; acting president, 165
Dartmouth College, 52, 95, 109
Daveis, Clarke S., 29, 57, 65, 67, 70; address on laying the cornerstone of the new chapel, 73; address on dedication of the chapel, 82-83
Davis, John, 42
Day of Prayer for Colleges, 54, 123
Deane, Samuel, 2
Deems, Mervin M., 99
Delano, Benjamin, 93
Dennis, Rodney Gove, 51
Divinity schools, founded, 35-36
Dodge, Asa, 53
Dole, Daniel, 53
Dole of the Raxian, 60
Dreer, Samuel H., 128
Dunlap, Robert, first settled minister in Brunswick, 20
Dunlap, Robert P., 65, 71, 73
Dunning, Robert D., 26
Dwight, William Theodore, 72, 83

Edwards, Jonathan, 6
Ellingwood, John Wallace, 77, 80
Ellis, Samuel D., 42
Enigma Society, 60
Enteman, Willard Finley (pres. 1978-80), ix; inaugural address, 167; resignation, 168
Episcopal Students Association, 143, 163. *See also* St. Paul's Episcopal Church
Evans, George, 70, 75

Fast days, 54-55
Feeney, Daniel J., 155
Fessenden, William Pitt, 78
Field, Edward M., 119
Files, Prof. and Mrs. George T., 123
First Parish Church, covenant on basis of Congregationalism, 20; church and parish recognized as separate entities, 21; first meeting house burned down, 172 n. 19; erection of second meeting house, 23-26; obtains own bell, 27; dove as a weathervane, 28; relations with the College, 21-33,

92, 102-5; erection of third meeting house, 28-30; vestry on School Street, 28, 30, 173 n. 44; student galleries, 25-26, 28, 30, 32, 43, 103-4, 114-15; college pew, 25-26, 30; and commencements, 24-30; suspends afternoon services, 109; organ in meeting house, 119; and College Preachers, 123-24; students conduct services, 162. *See also* Church on the Hill
Flagpole incident, 140-42
Flandrin, Hippolyte, 87
Freshman handbook, 125-26, 135
Forums, as alternatives to chapel services, 159-61
Foster, Benjamin Browne, 54
Fraternities, 60, 90, 126, 135, 143; and racial discrimination, 147-50, 156, 196 n. 84
Fuller, Americus, 53
Fuller, Melville Weston, 35
Furber, Henry J., 87

Gardiner, Robert Hallowell, 65, 67-70, 75
Geoghegan, William Davidson, 158, 164-65
Gerrish, Frederick H., 87
Gerrish, William, 87
Gibbons Club, 127-28
Gillett, Gordon E., 143
Glee Club, 60, 119, 121, 162
Goodenow, Daniel, 65
Goodrich, Chauncey W., 143
Goodwin, Ichabod, 54
Greason, Arthur LeRoy (pres. 1981-), ix; appointed dean of students, 157; and chapel requirement, 157-58; appointed acting president, 168; elected president, 168
Greene, Joseph K., 53

Hale, Mrs. Sarah W., 79
Hamilton College, 109
Hamlin, Cyrus, 49, 53, 57
Hancock, John, 3-4
Hanley, Daniel Francis, 167
Harris, Samuel (pres. 1867-71), 38; inaugural address, 107-8, 187 n. 57; and denominational control, 100; ending of evening prayers, 109-10; resignation, 110
Harvard University, 2, 6-7, 10-11, 13, 52, 74, 85, 108-9, 126; Divinity School, 36, 167
Hatch, Louis C., 58
Hawthorne, Nathaniel, 43, 179 n. 72
Hillel Foundation, 164
Hitchcock, Roswell Dwight, 82-83, 92-93
Hiwale, Anand Sidola, 52-53, 126

Howell, Roger, Jr. (pres. 1969-78), biographical note, 165; inaugural address, 165; resignation, 167
Hutchins, Charles C., 120
Hyde, William DeWitt (pres. 1885-1917), 36-39, 116-21, 128, 136, 152; inaugural address, 36, 100-2; his "Offer of the College," 33, 151, 153, 165; comments on President Woods, 89-90; Carnegie pension plan, 94, 98; support of the Y.M.C.A., 93-94, 125-26; and denominational control, 100-2; as a speaker, 116, 122; and College Preachers, 123-24; death, 131

Interfaith Council, 162-64

Jaegers, 54
Jenks, William, 14
Jews, 128-29, 147-50, 196 n. 84, 197 n. 18; and the Y.M.C.A., 129; and the B.C.A., 129, 164; Jewish Association, 164, 168. *See also* Fraternities
Johnson, Alfred, 3, 65
Johnson, E.D., 125
Jump, Herbert A., 117, 124, 126

Kahill, J. B., 87
Keep, John, 31
Kendrick, Nathaniel C., 151, 157-58
King, James G., 80
King, General William, 65; gift to the College, 68-73, 80-81; chapel no longer to be known as King Chapel, 82; death, 81
King, Mrs. William (Anna N.), 68-69, 81-82
Kisman, John D., 65
Kotzschmar, Hermann, 121

Lane Seminary, 92
Langley, Miles Erskine, 126
Lathrop, Francis, 87
Lawrence, Amos, 68
Lawrence, Mrs. Amos, 77
Lee, Shepard, 164
Leith, Eaton, 158
Library, in chapel, 22, 63-65, 79, 83, 85, 184 n. 94
Lightfoot, Robert H., 145
Lincoln, Charles S. F., 53
Lincoln, Isaac, 71
Lincoln, John D., 87
Little, George Thomas, 88, 110, 116
Locke, John, 6
Lockhart Society, 57, 119
Longfellow, Henry Wadsworth, 43; religious affiliation, 57, 173 n. 65

Longfellow, Stephen, 43
Longley, James B., 148
Lutherans, at Waldoboro, 1

McArthur, Arthur, 42
McConaughy, James Lukens, 126-27, 139
MacCormick, Austin H., 133, 139
McIntire, Glenn Ronello, 95
McKeen, Joseph (pres. 1802-07), 61; elected president, 9; biographical sketch, 9-11; inaugural address, 11-13; and college laws, 13-14; subjects taught, 15; chapel services, 16; and erection of the first chapel, 22; and First Parish, 21, 23-24, 30
McKeen, Joseph (treasurer), 61, 67
McLean, D. D., 133
Madison, Arthur A., 128
Maine Hall, 23, 49, 65
Maine Historical Society, 83
Maine Missionary Society, 121
Marrett, Miss Edna T., 87
Masonic lodge, laying of chapel cornerstone, 71-73
Massachusetts General Court, and Bowdoin charter, 1-4
Massachusetts Hall, 22, 24, 63-64; first known as College House, 9; named, 11; bell moved, 27, 172 n. 34
Mead, Asa, 31-32
Means, Robert, 42
Medical school, 59, 78-79, 87, 108
Melcher, Samuel, and first chapel, 22-23, 171 n. 17; builds second meeting house, 24; and second chapel, 64, 79
Methodists, in early Maine, 1; church in Brunswick, 175 n. 45
Middlebury College, 51-52
Miller, John, 30
Millet, Samuel, 42
Ministerial scholarships, 98-99
Missionary Society of Inquiry, 57
Morison, Samuel Eliot, 6
Mueller, Mr. (artist), 86
Munson, Samuel, 53

Nelson, Mrs. Elizabeth M., 93
Newell, William Stark, 161
Newman Club, 154-55, 162-64; sponsors Bermuda North project, 163-64, 168; Project Babe, 168; folk mass, 163, 168, 199 n. 58
Newman, Samuel Phillips, 61
Newport, Sir Francis, 49
Nixon, Paul, appointed dean, 131-32; and chapel attendance, 142-43; comment on

Index

religious forums, 194 n. 59
Noyes, Daniel J., 91

Otto, Charles, 86

Pacific Congregational Seminary, 102
Packard, Alpheus Spring, 11, 54, 56, 68, 120, 125; appointed Collins Professor, 93; memorial window in First Parish Church, 105; on acoustics in chapel, 184 n. 103
Packard, C., 28
Palmer, Warren, 143
Parker, Isaac, 35
Payson, Edward Payson, 135-36
Payson, William Martin, 135-36
Pejepscot Proprietors, 19-20
Perry, Mrs. William, 87
Peucinian Society, 27, 51, 60, 73, 124
Phillips Andover Academy, 10, 97
Phillips, James S., 53
Phrenology Society, 60
Pierce, Franklin, 43
Pierce, Josiah, 78
Poor, Henry V., 101-2
Porter, Benjamin J., 24
Porter, Mrs. Benjamin J., 80
Porter, David R., 126
Pratt, Phineas, 51
Praying Society (Circle), 50-57, 59, 112, 115, 162; society becomes Praying Circle, 55; Circle becomes Y.M.C.A., 124
Prentiss, George Lewis, 91
Presbyterians, 9-10, 52, 97; in early Maine, 1; in early Brunswick, 19-20
Princeton University, 52

Quakers, 1, 43

Religion courses in the curriculum, 15-16, 139-40, 143-45, 164-65
Religious Forum, 143-44, 155-56, 195 n. 59
Religious preference of students, 128-29, 135, 192 ns. 127, 128
Richardson, William, 65
Robert College, 53
Roberts, Charles P., 43-44, 58, 60, 72
Roberts, Gary R., 165-66
Rothlisberger, Rodney J., 166
Russell, Henry G., 145
Ruffin, Bernard C., III, 166
Russwurm, John Brown, 128

St. Paul's Episcopal Church, 95, 113, 132, 143, 166, 175 n. 45
Savage, William T., 98

Scholarships with religious preferences, 98-99
Schroeder, John Charles, 145
Scott, Roderick, 126
Self-study project, 156
Seniors' Last Chapel, 122-23, 167
Sewall, Jotham B., 114
Sheats, John E., 166
Shepley, Ether, 37, 91
Sills, Kenneth Charles Morton (pres. 1918-52), 5, 38, 58, 153, 163; and religious preferences of students, 129, 135; appointed dean, 131; elected president, 131; a leading Episcopalian, 132; inaugural address, 132; opposition to denominational clubs on campus, 135, 154, 193 n. 13; as a chapel speaker, 136, 138; appoints committee to study needs of the College, 137-38; on chapel services, 138-39; and courses in religion, 139-40, 143-44; and chapel attendance, 140-42, 147, 151; on church hymns, 146; and Armistice Day observances, 167; Bowdoin as a "Christian College," 132-33, 136, 151-52, 193 n. 6
Sills, Mrs. Kenneth (Edith Lansing), 153
Smith, Charles Henry (Cosine Smith), 41, 113-14
Smyth, Egbert C., 49, 51, 56, 59; appointed Collins Professor, 92; and attendance at Sunday afternoon services, 108; reports on attendance at Sunday services, 113
Smyth, William, 44, 46, 54, 82; memorial window in First Parish Church, 105
Snell, Charles, 43
Snow, Benjamin Galen, 53
Social Gospel, 122
Southgate, Frederic, 42, 51
Southgate, Horatio, 53
Sparks, Jared, 86
Staley, Ronald, 166
Stanwood, David, 42
Stanwood, William, 26
State of Maine scholarships, 58
Stendahl, Kristen, 167
Stevens, Oliver Crocker, 120
Stockbridge, Wm. H., 121
Stone Professorship, 94, 97
Stone, Mrs. Valeria L., 97
Stone, William, 43
Storer, Bellamy, 85
Storer, Seth, 42
Story, Joseph, 61
Stowe, Calvin Ellis, 54, 56, 61-62; appointed Collins Professor, 92
Stowe, Mrs. Calvin E. (Harriet Beecher), 92

Student activities fees, 162-63. *See also* Blanket Tax
Student Religious Liberals, 163-64
Sunday services, student attendance, 17, 32-33, 42-43, 62, 107-9, 111-16; end of compulsory attendance, 117; vespers, 109, 112, 146, 151, 154, 159, 165-67. *See also* First Parish Church, student galleries

Tallman Professors, 139, 156, 195 n. 72
Tappan, Benjamin, 91
Taylor, Burton Wakeman, 158
Taylor, Charles C., 119
Temperance Society of the Maine Medical School, 59
Thacher, Josiah, 2
Theological Society, 49-51, 57, 59
Thompson, Abner B., 71
Thorndike Club, 147-48, 196 n. 83
Thorndike, George, 16
Thorndike Oak, 16
Tiemer, Mrs. Paul, 161
Tillotson, Frederic E. T., 146-47
Titian's *Danae*, 85-86, 184 n. 99
Trinity College, 74
True, I. R., 70

Unitarian-Universalist Association, 163
Unitarians, 1, 35, 74, 78, 113; Unitarian Society, 57, 175 n. 45
Universalist Church, 126, 175 n. 45
Union College, 52, 109
Union Theological Seminary, 92, 102, 109
Upjohn, Richard, 28, 67-70, 74, 79-80; payments to, 182 n. 73. *See also* Chapel (new)
Upham, Thomas C., 32, 44, 82; and the Declaration on relations to Congregationalism, 73-74; gifts to the College, 77, 91, 183 n. 77; resignation, 108

Vinton, Frederic, 87
Vesper services, 108-9, 146, 151, 159-60, 165-67. *See also* College Preachers
"Virtue and Piety," 76, 132, 153, 165; as mentioned in charter, 5; Jonathan Edwards on, 6; John Locke on, 6

Walker gallery, 79, 84; Walker Art Building, 79
Walker, Theophilus W., 79
Wass, Edward Haines, 122, 136
Wesleyan University, 12, 140
Wheeler, Crosby H., 53
Wheeler, Gervase, 79, 182 n. 69

Widgery, Alban Gregory, 139
Wilde, William Cobb, 42
Wilder, Philip Sawyer, 158, 162, 195 n. 62
Willard, Joseph, 10
William and Mary College, 52
Williams College, 13, 52, 140
Williams, Samuel, 10
Williams, Simon, 10
Wilson, Jeffrey, 167
Winkley, Henry, 96-97, 186 n. 39
Winkley Professorship, 94, 96-97, 131
Winthrop, proposed college, 2
Wise, John, 42
Wood, Henry, 42
Woodruff, Frank Edward, 93
Woods, Leonard (pres. 1839-66), 28, 38, 59, 61, 91; elected president, 65, 89; and new chapel, 65-73, 77, 80-82, 85-86; as a disciplinarian, 43, 89-90; and denominationalism, 100
Works, David A., 148
World War I, 126, 132-33
World War II, 129, 147-48

Yale University, 13, 52, 74, 95, 108-9, 145
Young Men's Christian Association (Y.M.C.A.), 94, 119, 129, 168; founded at Bowdoin, 57, 124; period of greatest activity, 124-27, 133-34; Bowdoin Y.M.C.A. song, 134; becomes known as Bowdoin Christian Association, 134. *See also* Bowdoin Christian Association